New Casebooks

TWELFTH NIGHT

New Casebooks

New Casebooks

TWELFTH NIGHT

gender role reversal.
female independence — mens
fear of it.

EDITED BY R. S. WHITE

Introduction, selection and editorial matter
© R. S. White 1996

First published 1996 by
MACMILLAN PRESS LTD
Houndmills, Basingstoke, Hampshire RG21 6XS
and London
Companies and representatives
throughout the world

ISBN 0–333–60676–0 hardcover
ISBN 0–333–60677–9 paperback

A catalogue record for this book is available
from the British Library.

10   9   8   7   6   5   4   3   2   1
05   04   03   02   01   00   99   98   97   96

Printed in Hong Kong

Contents

Acknowledgements

The editor and publishers wish to thank the following for permission to use copyright material:

Michael D. Bristol, for 'The Festive Agon: The Politics of Carnival' from *Carnival and Theater: Plebian Culture and the Structure of Authority in Renaissance England* (1985) Methuen & Co, by permission of Routledge; Dymphna Callaghan, for '"And all is semblative a woman's part": Body Politics and *Twelfth Night*', *Textual Practice*, 7 (1993), by permission of Routledge; Barbara Everett, for 'Or What You Will', *Essays in Criticism*, 35 (1985), by permission of Essays in Criticism; Stephen Greenblatt, for 'Fiction and Friction' from *Shakespearean Negotiations: The Circulation of Social Energy in Renaissance England* (1988). Copyright © 1988 The Regents of the University of California, by permission of Oxford University Press and University of California Press; Geoffrey Hartman, for 'Shakespeare's Poetical Character in *Twelfth Night*' from *Shakespeare and the Question of Theory*, ed. Patricia Parker and Geoffrey Hartman (1985) Methuen & Co., by permission of Routledge; Elliot Krieger, for '*Twelfth Night*: "The morality of indulgence"', from *A Marxist Study of Shakespeare's Comedies* (1979), by permission of Macmillan Ltd; Cristina Malcolmson, for '"What You Will": Social Mobility and Gender in *Twelfth Night*' from *The Matter of Difference: Materialist Feminist Criticism of Shakespeare* (1991). Copyright © Cristina Malcolmson 1991, by permission of Harvester Wheatsheaf and Cornell University Press; Leonard Tennenhouse, for 'Power on Display' from *Power on Display: The Politics of Shakespeare's Genres* (1986), Methuen & Co, by permission of Routledge.

Every effort has been made to trace all the copyright holders but if any have been inadvertently overlooked the publishers will be pleased to make the necessary arrangement at the first opportunity.

General Editors' Preface

The purpose of this series of New Casebooks is to reveal some of the ways in which contemporary criticism has changed our understanding of commonly studied texts and writers and, indeed, of the nature of criticism itself. Central to the series is a concern with modern critical theory and its effect on current approaches to the study of literature. Each New Casebook editor has been asked to select a sequence of essays which will introduce the reader to the new critical approaches to the text or texts being discussed in the volume and also illuminate the rich interchange between critical theory and critical practice that characterises so much current writing about literature.

In this focus on modern critical thinking and practice New Casebooks aim not only to inform but also to stimulate, with volumes seeking to reflect both the controversy and the excitement of current criticism. Because much of this criticism is difficult and often employs an unfamiliar critical language, editors have been asked to give the reader as much help as they feel is appropriate, but without simplifying the essays or the issues they raise. Again, editors have been asked to supply a list of further reading which will enable readers to follow up issues raised by the essays in the volume.

The project of New Casebooks, then, is to bring together in an illuminating way those critics who best illustrate the ways in which contemporary criticism has established new methods of analysing texts and who have reinvigorated the important debate about how we 'read' literature. The hope is, of course, that New Casebooks will not only open up this debate to a wider audience, but will also encourage students to extend their own ideas, and think afresh about their responses to the texts they are studying.

John Peck and Martin Coyle
University of Wales, Cardiff

Introduction

R. S. WHITE

It is significant that an important, recent book, Hugh Grady's *The Modernist Shakespeare*,[1] at no time analyses or interprets a single play by Shakespeare. The subtitle, *Critical texts in a material world*, indicates that its subject is criticism itself, theoretical assumptions underlying criticism, and the shifts in critical fashions and approaches from the early twentieth century up to the 1990s. This is not uncommon in recent criticism, since, even when dealing with single texts, theorists are not primarily engaged in 'illuminating the play' but in understanding different reading and textual practices. As a consequence, although the present book is ostensibly on *Twelfth Night*, its real subject is to a large extent the nature of criticism itself. The essays exemplify a range of recent and developing critical approaches which are not uniquely applicable to one play but can be used to analyse others.

Grady's book itself is a good starting point. His argument is that the 1990s are witnessing a paradigm shift in criticism, away from assumptions that are 'modernist' towards ones that are postmodernist. Criticism, for example, is less concerned with concepts like unity and character, and more with fragmentation and disruption. It is just as interested in contexts (historical, political, linguistic, social, gender) as texts, and is thus 'materialist' in its conception of a play as reflecting social practices and processes rather than 'universal truth'. Talk of 'timelessness' has been replaced by 'historical difference'. Unity is under onslaught from a variety of directions: language itself is seen by some as self-sufficient and arbitrary in its signifying practices and thus far too playfully unstable to carry identifiable, unified 'themes', while to other critics it is apparent that what is left unsaid, and what is deferred, is just as much a part of the text as what is said, undermining and disintegrating anything that might appear to be a conscious, unified 'statement'. Most centrally, postmodernist movements (at least as Grady uses the term, which may not command universal agreement among practitioners) posit that all works of culture, whether 'high' art or 'popular', are constructions, rather than transparent mediums allowing us to see 'truth'. Marxists, feminists, and new historicists, alongside reader response and reception theorists, argue that inevitably, and perhaps rather depressingly, the constructions reflect the attitudes of dominant institutions which are usually built upon the vested interests of male, bourgeois, western and white agencies. They exclude or marginalise views other than their own, while at the same time bearing traces of inner resistance or opposition to dominant orthodoxies. It is possible to disagree with Grady's arguments, but at least his brief 'map' of the thorny area of recent theory is helpful in allowing us to get our bearings.

I

The pieces reproduced in this book are chosen as representing a range of critical approaches available today, not only to *Twelfth Night* but to all plays by Shakespeare. They are diverse enough to resist being grouped under a corporate name, such as 'postmodern', and in fact some approaches are engaged in gentle warfare and certainly dialogue with the others, as we shall see. In the final analysis the labelling of an approach is no more than a crude shorthand, for we may find that a feminist or a Marxist approach (although there are honest differences between the two) may be equally helpful in giving us new and detailed illumination of *Twelfth Night*. On the other hand, the significance of writers wishing to call themselves something (deconstructionist, new historicist or something else) is quite typical of the recent trend to be explicit about critical method, rather than obscuring assumptions and ideologies under the old banners of 'objectivity' and 'universal truth'. At the same time, to allow for opportunities of new growth, there must be room for approaches that cannot be labelled, and that rely on curiosity-driven engagement with the material.

I should enter a word of reassurance before a student embarks on these critical essays and extracts. While some of them, such as those by Hartman, Krieger, Everett and Greenblatt, are written in a very clear and entertaining way, others will initially intimidate some readers with their style. In some cases we are made to feel that a new approach requires a new language of explication. I suggest that a first reading might be used to pick up an impression of the diversity of methodological approaches on offer. After this stage, wrestling with the detail of individual essays will lead to rapidly enhanced understanding of them and of *Twelfth Night*, since the underlying issues will have been grasped, and will open up some new and exciting ways of reading Shakespeare.

Geoffrey Hartman's essay (1) is a good one to start with, since it provides some links between the older criticism and the new. If we were to label Hartman's approach, we should find two terms which immediately pitch us into literary theory. First, he practises reader response theory, and secondly he provides a deconstructionist account of *Twelfth Night*. Reader response means, quite simply, that the focus is shifted away from the text and towards the reader, or readers, of the text. Before those who recall that Shakespeare wrote plays for the theatre, and not for readers, complain, I should mention that there is also available an audience response theory, but it is true that at the heart of Hartman's own method lies a belief in an infinity of diverse and individual 'readings' rather than group responses in the theatre. Hartman begins his essay with a rapid survey of older critics' accounts of 'the poetical character of Shakespeare', such as A. C. Bradley's and John Middleton Murry's. His point, however, is not to explain how these writers were right or wrong, but to stress that in *all* criticism, of whatever persuasion, choices have been made, convictions are assumed, and chosen interests are maintained, all of which tell us more about the critic as reader than about some mythical but sacred thing called the Shakespearian text. (For example, Hartman is known as a Romantics specialist, he refers many times to Keats in this essay, and his whole reading betrays certain 'Keatsian' attitudes.) Readers construct writings, largely to reflect their own preoccupations, and in doing so they can enlighten other readers, opening up fresh perspectives. Hartman's own preferred choice is to examine in detail not large, thematic issues, but language in its moment-by-moment elusiveness. He looks back to William Empson as a critic who allows us to 'fracture' texts, to avoid building up 'totalising structures' and instead to work on the basis that 'Rigour consists in having the local reading undo an established symmetry'.[2] Obviously the search for 'unity' goes out the window. This is one way of understanding that otherwise frightening term 'deconstruction'. Once we look at the extraordinary feats of language in *Twelfth Night*, apparently turning itself inside out in puns, witty rhetoric and 'devices', then we may find ourselves both delighted by the sheer play of it all, and our grasp of, and even interest in, larger issues which are used to find unity (theme, character, 'seeing the play as a whole', etc.), diminished, undermined and hopelessly destabilised. Here is how Hartman puts it:

> It seems to me there is no mystery, no *Abgrund* (abyss), except language itself, whose revelatory revels are being staged, as if character were a function of language, rather than vice versa.
>
> To the question, what filling (fulfilling) is in this fooling, the best reply might be that, in literature, everything aspires to the condition of language, to the gift of tongues; that the spirit – wanton as it may be – of language overrides such questions, including those of character and identity.[3]

He then revels enthusiastically in the sheer pleasure of language's slipperiness and vitality in *Twelfth Night*, inviting us to do the same.

One assumption that supports reader response theory is another destabilising fact. As Laurie E. Osborne demonstrates (in an article not reprinted here because its detail is of interest mainly to specialists),[4] even the brigade formerly feared by all, editors, who insist on the sacred 'authority' of '*the* text', are coming to the realisation that there is never just one text. This is true even for the very straightforward case of *Twelfth Night*, where only one contemporary version exists, that in the First Folio volume which was the first 'collected works of Shakespeare' put together by friends in 1623, some seven years after his death. Pointing to some insoluble, linguistic problems in *Twelfth Night* as printed in the Folio, Osborne finds signs of loose ends and flaws which cannot have been 'intended' by Shakespeare and which simply cannot be resolved. The text itself becomes as unstable as is language in Hartman's account, and it is to some extent reconstructed by editors on the page and directors in the theatre, all making creative choices. Osborne goes on, using a kind of audience response approach, to argue that performance texts over the centuries have shown very significant differences from each other. The logic of the argument is that we can neither recover an 'original' text nor hope to establish an 'authentic' *Twelfth Night*, either on the page or stage. Instead, we are given freedom to make our own choices and enjoy the sheer range of possibilities, a conclusion completely at one with Hartman's.

Despite his celebration of plural readings, Hartman does make a passing sideswipe at other groups of critics who call themselves variously cultural materialists or new historicists, Marxists or feminists – those who search texts for underlying 'ideologies':

> Bradley integrates Shakespeare by the deft pathos of an imaginary portrait. Today's ideological critics would probably purge this portrait of everything but Shakespeare's representation of power-relations and hierarchy.[5]

This sounds like a very major disagreement with many of the critics represented in this anthology – the Marxist Krieger, the new historicists Greenblatt and Tennenhouse, the feminists Malcolmson and Callaghan. Hartman would argue that these critics work by reducing *Twelfth Night* to a set of ideological structures available in Shakespeare's social and political contexts which he unknowingly perpetuates and never changes. This attack seems unnecessary and a lapse from Hartman's own philosophy that *Twelfth Night* 'requires a certain tolerance or liberality of interpretation'.[6] Given the diversity of ideological approaches which are represented, I think a careful reading of the essays reveals that no critic of any sensitivity is locked into such a simple-minded conception of ideology, and that on the other hand, highly focused and selective readings can genuinely enlighten us about an aspect of the play which we had not noticed. But it is undeniable that many, perhaps most, recent critics do follow a line that emphasises some notion of ideology in power relations. A broad term to describe the practices of such commentators is cultural materialism – the attempt to see a play like *Twelfth Night* as a complex reflection of social and political processes which cannot be avoided by the artist (or the reader) in any historical period.

Michael Bristol (essay 3), for example, states that theatre is not only an art form but a 'social institution', and that we may legitimately examine the material circumstances of Elizabethan theatre as a public gathering place, 'a privileged site for the celebration and critique of the needs and concerns of the *polis* [political state]'.[7] His own approach is a modified form of the argument proposed by earlier critics such as C. L. Barber and Mikhail Bakhtin, that theatre is an enactment of Carnival, the spirit of collective misrule. He explicitly addresses Hartman's point by insisting that theatre as Carnival is *not* 'an ideological finished product' of Elizabethan political assumptions, but rather 'a negative critique that demystifies or "uncrowns" power, its justificatory ideology ...'[8] He adds that there is also a 'positive critique' reaffirming collective traditions of ordinary folk who firmly 'resist penetration and control by the power structure'. In discussing *Twelfth Night*, Bristol exemplifies his theory by suggesting that the play represents the very struggle between the 'festive agon [misrule]' of Carnival battling against 'Lenten tendencies' towards seriousness. The battle is over the issue of 'political succession'.[9]

Leonard Tennenhouse (essay 4) is another who takes seriously the historical and ideological contexts of *Twelfth Night*, by looking not at folk traditions but at high politics. He reminds us of the obvious but often neglected fact that the play, like all of Shakespeare's romantic comedies which give us representations of vital women such as Viola, was written and performed when a queen was on the throne:

> during this period it became possible to imagine patriarchal power embodied in a female, which obviously opened a whole new set of possibilities for representing power on the stage ... Shakespearian comedy foregrounds the instrumentality of female desire.[10]

Tennenhouse does find in *Twelfth Night*, as in the earlier romantic comedies by Shakespeare, a recurring ideological pattern, that 'happy endings' are achieved by, and even depend upon, 'the transfer of patriarchal power to a woman'.[11] This in itself, he argues, could happen so consistently only under a female monarch, but the sombre coda is that marriage relocates power, a more gentle and humane version of power perhaps, back to the male. Elizabeth, we remember, never married, which was, according to this theory, politically adroit.

Elliot Krieger's book (from which essay 2 is taken) announces in its title that it is *A Marxist Study of Shakespeare's Comedies* and so, as we would expect, ideology is understood in the particular terms of a class war, where one class grows fat at the expense of another. Taking issue with the earlier critic John Hollander, who described the prevailing tone of the play as 'the morality of indulgence', Krieger argues that the material in *Twelfth Night* dramatises 'aristocratic protection':

Only a privileged social class has access to the morality of indulgence: if the members of the ruling class find their identities through excessive indulgence in appetite, the other characters in the play either work to make indulgence possible for their superiors or else, indulging themselves, sicken and so die.[12]

To adapt the last line of Shakespeare's Sonnet 94, 'Lilies that fester smell far worse than weeds'. Krieger argues that Barber's seminal approach did not place the notion of festive release in its context of social class relations, and he thus anticipates the more politicised, carnivalesque approach by Bristol. It is worth pointing out that Krieger was using the word ideology in Shakespearian criticism in 1979, some time before the others represented here, a reminder that the whole mode of analysis, arguably, derives from Marxist principles even when a critic is not individually Marxist.

Stephen Greenblatt acknowledged himself at least to be influenced by Marxism, but he has forged an individual approach which he dubbed new historicism. It has proved immensely influential, and still raises the ire of deconstructionist followers of Hartman, such as Howard Felperin.[13] It is hard to see why new historicism has been so controversial, since it chimes agreeably with most of the approaches represented in this collection. Greenblatt's characteristic technique is to begin, rather like a preacher beginning a sermon, with some historically based anecdote which seems to have little or nothing to do with the play he will be addressing. He then obliquely opens up the play by finding that it mirrors something of an underlying ideology enacted in the anecdote. In the entertaining essay (5) in this book, he sets up a story of reported transvestism in a small French town in 1580 as 'one of those shadow stories that haunt the plays', which 'Shakespeare almost, but not quite, retells ...'.[14] He then freewheels into Elizabethan medical accounts of sexuality, glancing at androgyny, homoeroticism, female desire, clitoral size and hypothesised ejaculation, and the bodily processes of coupling. (Dympna Callaghan in her essay (6) speaks also about what is known today as 'body politics', but in a less playful, more feminist way than Greenblatt.) In a feint which Hartman ought to appreciate, Greenblatt then sees the 'friction' of sex as energising and as metaphorically standing behind the witty language of *Twelfth Night*, as characters verbally spar, metaphorically board and generally excite each other with language as a substitute for gratification of their bodily parts. 'Dallying with words is the principal Shakespearean representation of erotic heat.'[15] Although Greenblatt has insisted upon the necessity to 'historicise Shakespearean sexual nature, restoring it to its relation of negotiation and exchange with other social discourses of the body', he has, like the consciously ahistorical Hartman (who would probably deny the possibility of ever effectively historicising from the present vantage point), found the 'enactment of verbal friction'[16] to be the play's centre of attention.

At this point it may even be worth suggesting that if readers were not made aware of labels such as deconstructionist, new historicist and Marxist, the essays collected here would more easily be seen to contribute to larger and far more important changes that came during the 1980s. Critics of various persuasions began to refuse to claim for their accounts 'universal' applicability, even to deny such a notion altogether, and to shift away from taking for granted 'character' (which was an eighteenth-century invention) and 'unity'. Instead, high priority is placed on local details of language and oblique contemporary reference as points of entry into illumination of *Twelfth Night* and all Shakespearian texts, while context becomes a word even more important than text.

Feminists, like Marxists, have a distinctive ideological stance which they make explicit: overt challenge to male authority and to patriarchal structures, whether they locate these in the text (producing 'resistant readings' of hallowed 'classics') or in critics (producing deconstructive readings of older criticism). In many ways their contribution has challenged and changed more sacred cows of Shakespearian criticism than any of the other recent, theory-driven approaches. Feminists feel free to use any other approaches that are available, but with a special focus that makes them, virtually by definition, practising reader response critics. Christina Malcolmson (essay 7) links up the Marxist focus on social mobility and class issues with *Twelfth Night*'s questioning of gender stereotypes, by suggesting that the rigid structures of the traditional order are destabilised, deconstructed even, by the wilful confusion of gender stereotypes. For example, a female servant can rise to match her male master, and, generally speaking, female triumphs come at the expense of male inadequacies. Lisa Jardine, in an essay published in 1992 which is not included here, suggests other ways of interpreting the Viola figure, by presenting historical evidence about the sexual availability of young servants (and vagrants) of both sexes.[17]

Where Malcolmson's account is sympathetic to Shakespeare's presentation of gender struggle, Dympna Callaghan (essay 6) provides a much more resistant reading, arguing that in the 'politics of the body' dramatised in *Twelfth Night* the casualties are women, as the play re-enacts the oppression, marginalising and sexual humiliation of women in many ways, including the use of the apparently playful, but in reality demeaning, vehicle of male actors playing females.

Once again, it might be superficially concluded that there are violent quarrels between critics who are even ostensibly of the same persuasion, but I would argue that each approach, in a sense, could not exist without the other, since the fundamental concentration on underlying ideologies, and the rejection of traditional habits, such as seeking unity and claiming the existence of universals, are swept away. There is constant debate, dialogue and creative disagreement between our band of critics, but they would in turn group themselves together in rejection of conventional and conservative criticism which, they would say, is ideologically grounded while claiming not to be; covertly partisan while claiming 'objectivity'.

I end my selection with an essay chosen deliberately to reopen debates which literary theorists may have thought closed forever. Barbara Everett's 'Or What You Will' (essay 8) in no identifiable way can be classified or grouped amongst deconstructionists, new historicists, Marxists or self-proclaimed feminists. On the other hand, the essay cannot be safely parcelled off as old-fashioned formalism, impressionism, or discredited bourgeois humanism of a patriarchal kind, since it is open, tentative and personal. Furthermore, Everett's sense of the niceties of social class behaviour, while not paraded with any fanfare, is more subtle and incisive than many a Marxist's, her alertness to playful verbal subtleties is at least no less keen than Hartman's, her pervading reference to music is as powerfully deployed as other critics' emphases on words and language, and her descriptions of sexual politics in action are as gender-based as those of feminists. This article might even be seen to have a disconcerting effect of making all the ideologically grounded approaches seem over-solemn, and sometimes just as monolithic and dogmatic as those they opposed and rejected.

Fortunately, there is a point of resolution that is as neat as Shakespeare's own happy ending achieved through the visual revelation of twins. I would argue that the real drift of criticism over the last decades has been inexorably in the direction of reader response theories, and the blossoming of a plurality of individual readings all of which can lead to refreshed understandings of *Twelfth Night* as of any play. Everett, like all the other writers in this collection, is at heart a reader response critic, as equally opposed to the older universalists as her postmodern companions, but unlike some of them, she practises an 'open-endedness' and the 'tolerance' that Hartman calls for.

II

Let us try a little playfulness of our own. Somehow none of the readings which claim ambitious, postmodern newness, has the capacity to surprise us as much as the play itself. Terry Eagleton, tongue in cheek and provocatively, writes,

> Though conclusive evidence is hard to come by, it is difficult to read Shakespeare without feeling that he was almost certainly familiar with the writings of Hegel, Marx, Nietzsche, Freud, Wittgenstein and Derrida.[18]

And, we might add, Lacan, Foucault, Lyotard; Irigaray, Cixous and Kristeva, if only because the text can be *read* in a Lacanian, Kristevan, etc., way. To state another set of paradoxes in a different way: if Elizabethan plays are historically embedded in a context of political, social and cultural 'negotiations' (Greenblatt's word) or ideologies that can be confidently deconstructed, how odd it is that on the one hand the Marxist playwright Brecht could appropriate *Coriolanus* to socialism, and on the other a former British Chancellor of the Exchequer[19] could say that this play proves Shakespeare was a Tory. How odd it is that *King Lear* can be directed by Kotsintsev as a soviet communist satire on a decadent aristocracy living fatly in a land of lean beggars, while equally plausibly it is performed by Olivier as the final rage against mortality of a bourgeois man who is concerned about the fate of his wealth and property after his death. Krieger implicitly assumes that much the same could be said of *Twelfth Night*. The answer to these paradoxes lies again in a recognition that texts do not construct themselves, but it is readers, critics, performers and audiences – none of whom has a monopoly on 'the truth' – who construct the writings of Shakespeare in whatever image they choose, whether modernist or postmodernist, socialist or capitalist.

In this sense, *Twelfth Night* can be as postmodern about itself as can any modern critic. It is unlikely that a deconstructionist would use the following words, except in a spirit of conscious inter-textuality, but such a one would surely find the spirit of a deconstructive impulse behind Feste's radical scepticism about language:

> **Clown** ... To see this age! A sentence is but a chev'ril glove to a good wit – how quickly the wrong side may be turned outward!
> **Viola** Nay, that's certain: they that dally nicely with words may quickly make them wanton.
> **Clown** I would therefore my sister had had no name, sir.
> **Viola** Why, man?
> **Clown** Why, sir, her name's a word, and to dally with that word might make my sister wanton. But indeed, words are very rascals, since bonds disgraced them.
> **Viola** Thy reason, man?
> **Clown** Troth, sir, I can yield you none without words, and words are grown so false, I am loath to prove reason with them.
> **Viola** I warrant thou art a merry fellow, and car'st for nothing.
>
> (III.i.11–27)

Words may be intended as no more and no less than signifiers, and yet they can be made to signify anything, including exactly the opposite of the intended meaning, by a creative and/or un-sympathetic listener. Right from the beginning of the play we see in operation Shakespeare's notorious habit of turning anything into a pun, like playing wantonly with words. Even in this passage of apparently lighthearted banter there are the kinds of shoals and slippages that attract the attention of modern theorists: Viola, the figure addressed by Feste as 'sir', is designated female and yet played by a boy, while Feste's sister without a name – like Viola/Cesario's non-existent sister who never told her love – is not mentioned elsewhere, and is of dubious textual existence let alone relevance within the play. Marginalities, liminalities like these are the very stuff of the postmodernist aesthetic. In this play the instability of language can be seen as analogous to the 'unstaid and skittish' (II.iv.18) fickleness and arbitrariness of sexual attraction which drives the narrative plot. Moreover, the play proclaims that meaning is not found or even decoded, but by effort *made*, as is clear to the stage witnesses of Malvolio's 'construction' of the enigmatic and, on the face of it, meaningless letter he receives. 'Observe his construction of it' (II.ii.181) advises Maria, with the sageness of a late twentieth-century semiotician, and we do, with amusing and entertaining results. It is interesting that learned articles are still being written today about what M,O,I,A and 'her Cs, her Us and her Ts' signify, in an effort to construct (or deconstruct) them. Metatheatrical critics such as J. L. Calderwood,[20] who are at least halfway to the postmodern belief in textual relativity, of course leap on Fabian's shift of perspective in 'If this were played upon a stage now, I could condemn it as an improbable fiction' (III.iv.135): in answer to this, we may say it is, he doesn't, do we? The denouement of the play itself depends on such illusionary tricks. Even the magical realism of South American and Spanish novels and their derivatives, often a test-case and model for new, theoretically inclined critics and novelists, can be used as a reader's strategy in dealing with the 'natural perspective that is and is not' (V.i.219) to describe the strange and destabilising simultaneous appearance of identical twins. It may be an Illyrian optical illusion apparently the work of nature, but more directly it is the construction of a dramatist, asking for the cooperation of an audience in 'making something' of the experience enacted before them. These examples are not isolated, they characterise *Twelfth Night*. They give a new meaning to the play's alternative title, *What You Will*.

Obviously critics acute to the construction of gender stereotypes will busily construct and deconstruct and reconstruct a play whose centre is, as postmodernists may say, an ambivalent simulacrum – identical twins, one female and one male (but both originally played by males) – who may *look* the same but act in opposite ways. The 'woman' is disguised as a man, but is fainthearted and pacifist, and has a voice which is as the maiden's organ and in whom all is 'semblative a woman's part' (I.iv.35). And why stop at these relatively conventional observations? Surely *Twelfth Night* can be read and performed not only as a romantic comedy but also as its opposite: as a scathing, satirical critique of western conventions of romantic love: Orsino's 'love' for Olivia is possessive, unrequitable and self-indulgent, Toby's for Maria is a matter of casual, drunken conveniency ('Come by and by to my chamber'), Malvolio's desire to marry Olivia is not love but self-aggrandisement and class revenge of servant over mistress. Orsino's eventual 'love' for Viola is suspiciously sudden, and seems little more than a matter of sexual availability (significantly, he insists that s/he will be his fancy's queen only when s/he wears a woman's clothes). And Viola's 'love' for the gormless and fickle Orsino is at best a helplessly biological compulsion, unworthy, as she herself knows, of an intelligent, independent woman, something to be pitied rather than celebrated. Ironies are compounded when, again, we recall that a boy would have played the part. Close examination of virtually all Feste's statements reveals him trenchantly criticising these golden lovers for simply wasting time. It is not difficult, then, and not against the grain, to see *Twelfth Night* as the ultimate deconstruction of courtly love and more broadly of the whole stable of western love traditions. And yet, it must be insisted, it is *also* a romantic comedy affirming love, showing that 'what you will' (what you want *or* what you decide) is the only humanly possible way through the labyrinth of passion.

There are other directions that new criticism could explore. Malvolio, a hero for critics from Charles Lamb's time until about 1980, is now very little talked about, but a new historicist, interested in the origins of the English Civil War, would find material to work on in the equivocal references to him as 'a kind of puritan', as well as in the overall representation of a decadent, aristocratic society challenged by youthful, bourgeois *arrivistes* like Viola and Sebastian. Disjunctions of time and perspective, which would make Italo Calvino and Umberto Eco envious, pervade *Twelfth Night* and are at their most problematically intense in the epilogue. After a play full of romantic sentiment, music, nostalgia and so on, the last words by Feste – who seems to occupy the role of a postmodern critic within the fiction – evoke the wind and the rain, knaves and thieves, tosspots with drunken heads (Sir Toby without the sentiment), marriage regretted, and generally the cold concerns of daylight, the hangover after the Bakhtinian mardi gras. It is all bundled away with a spectacular shift from a golden fiction to a group of bedraggled actors trying to scrape a living in a world which has grown old, windy and wet:

> A great while ago the world begun,
> With hey, ho, the wind and the rain,
> But that's all one, our play is done,
> And we'll strive to please you every day.
>   (V.i.404–7)

The peculiarity of this play, as indeed of all Shakespeare's writings, is that, while plays undoubtedly exist only in others' readings, whether on stage or in the study, yet they subvert, parody, escape and mock the terms of all such readings. The words will not lie down tamely like a mouldy old lion in an old-fashioned circus subdued by a lion-tamer, accepting acquiescently a particular reading. There are always other words to bite the critic in the leg, or in theoretical ways to fractionalise, factionalise, marginalise and explode all that seems to one critic central, to centralise all that seems aberrant, wayward and oblique. While authorising readers and directors to construct it, renew it, again and again, yet *Twelfth Night* refuses to be constrained by critical or directorial authority of any kind, and in this sense is always postmodern, if not beyond. In a world of words it is appropriate to give the last, teasing ones, to the play: 'But that's all one ...'.

NOTES

[All quotations from *Twelfth Night* in this Introduction are taken from The Arden Shakespeare edition of the play, ed. J. M. Lothian and T. W. Craik (London, 1975).]

1. Hugh Grady, *The Modernist Shakespeare: Critical texts in a material world* (Oxford, 1991).

2. See p. 18 below.

3. See pp. 23, 29 below.

4. Laurie E. Osborne, 'The Texts of Twelfth Night', *English Literary History*, 57 (1990), 39–61.

5. See p. 17 below.

6. See p. 28 below.

7. See p. 72 below.

8. See p. 73 below.

9. See pp. 73, 78 below.

10. See pp. 82, 84 below.

11. See p. 90 below.

12. See pp. 39–40 below.

13. Howard Felperin, *The Uses of the Canon: Elizabethan Literature and Contemporary Theory* (Oxford, 1990).

14. See p. 92 below.

15. See p. 115 below.

16. See pp. 98, 115 below.
17. Lisa Jardine, *Still Harping on Daughters* (Brighton, 1983, 2nd edn 1989).
18. Terry Eagleton, *William Shakespeare* (Oxford, 1986), Introduction.
19. Nigel Lawson, interviewed in the *Guardian*, 5 September 1983.
20. James L. Calderwood, *Shakespearean Metadrama* (Minneapolis, MN, 1971).

1

Shakespeare's Poetical Character in *Twelfth Night*

GEOFFREY H. HARTMAN

I

Writing about Shakespeare promotes a sympathy with extremes. One such extreme is the impressionism of a critic like A. C. Bradley, when he tries to hold together, synoptically, Feste the fool and Shakespeare himself, both as actor and magical author. Bradley notes that the Fool in *Lear* has a song not dissimilar to the one that concludes *Twelfth Night* and leaves Feste at the finish-line. 'But that's all one, our play is done ...'[1] After everything has been sorted out, and the proper pairings are arranged, verbal and structural rhythms converge to frame a sort of closure – though playing is never done, as the next and final verse suggests: 'And we'll strive to please you every day.' Bradley, having come to the end of an essay on Feste, extends *Twelfth Night* speculatively beyond the fool's song, and imagines Shakespeare leaving the theatre:

> the same Shakespeare who perhaps had hummed the old song, half-ruefully and half-cheerfully, to its accordant air, as he walked home alone to his lodging from the theatre or even from some noble's mansion; he who, looking down from an immeasurable height on the mind of the public and the noble, had yet to be their servant and jester, and to depend upon their favour; not wholly uncorrupted by this dependence, but yet superior to it and, also determined, like Feste, to lay by the sixpences it brought him, until at least he could say the word, 'Our revels now are ended,' and could break – was it a magician's staff or a Fool's bauble?[2]

The rhetoric of this has its own decorum. It aims to convey a general, unified impression of a myriad-minded artist. Shakespearian interpreters have a problem with *summing up*. Leaning on a repeated verse ('For the rain it raineth every day'), and more quietly on the iteration of the word 'one' (**Lear**: 'Poor Fool and knave, I have one part in my heart /That's sorry yet for thee'; **Feste**: 'I was one, sir, in this interlude; one Sir Topas, sir, but that's all one'), Bradley integrates Shakespeare by the deft pathos of an imaginary portrait. Today's ideological critics would probably purge this portrait of everything but Shakespeare's representation of power-relations and hierarchy. Such critics might note that the portrait's final question serves only to emphasise the artist's marginality, his loneliness or apartness, as if by a secret law of fate being an artist excluded Shakespeare from social power in the very world he addresses.

The relation of 'character' in the world (domestic or political) to 'poetical character' (the imaginary relations to that same world which make up our image of a particular artist) is always elusive. Especially so in the case of Shakespeare, of whose life we know so little. A myth evolves, given classic expression by Keats, that the mystery or obscurity enveloping Shakespeare's life is due to the fact that a great poet has no 'identity', that he is 'everything and nothing' – as Bradley's evocation also suggests. John Middleton Murry's book on Shakespeare begins with a chapter entitled 'Everything and Nothing' in which Murry explores his reluctant conclusion that 'In the end there is nothing to do but to surrender to Shakespeare'. 'The moment comes in our experience of Shakespeare when we are dimly conscious of a choice to be made: either we must turn away (whether by leaving him in silence, or by substituting for his reality some comfortable intellectual fiction of our own), or we must suffer ourselves to be drawn into the vortex.'[3]

The focus moves, in short, to the character of the critic, determined by this choice. Can *we* abide Shakespeare's question? Does the critic have a 'character' of his own, or is he simply a bundle of responses accommodated to a special institution or audience: university students and dons, or other drama buffs, or the general public? Unlike Eliot, say, or Tolstoy, Murry has no body of creative writing to back up the importance of his interpretive engagements. There is, nevertheless, a sense that the critic's identity is formed by his selfless encounters with artists of Shakespeare's stature.

The 'vortex' that threatens readers, according to Murry, includes the fact that Shakespeare delights as much in Iago as Imogen (Keats's words); and to shuffle off our ordinary conceptions of character – in Murry's phrase, the 'mortal coil of moral judgement' – is both painful and necessary. Always, Murry claims, 'when Shakespeare has been allowed to make *his* impression, we find the critic groping after the paradox of the poetical character itself as described by Keats'. In an earlier essay, closer to Bradley's era, Murry had already put the problem of Shakespeare criticism in terms that showed how aware he was of reactions to the 'vortex'. He rejects the ' "idea"-bacillus' that reduces Shakespeare to universal themes or the creation of character-types, yet he refuses to relinquish his rigorous quest for 'the centre of comprehension from which he [Shakespeare] worked'. Programmatic as it is, Murry's statement of 1920 remains relevant:

> Let us away then with 'logic' and away with 'ideas' from the art of literary criticism; but not, in a foolish and impercipient reaction, to revive the impressionistic criticism which has sapped the English brain for a generation past. The art of criticism is rigorous; impressions are merely its raw material; the life-blood of its activity is in the process of ordonnance of aesthetic impressions.[4]

The rejection of impressionism leads, if we think of Eliot, and of Murry himself, simply to a more rigorous formulation of the paradox of the impersonal artist. For Murry it meant comparing Christian and post-Shakespearian (especially romantic) ways of annihilating selfhood. Blake becomes even more crucial for such a formulation than Keats. G. W. Knight also joins this quest. Other rigorous escape routes, that lead through impressionism beyond it, make Shakespeare's language the main character of his plays, the everything and nothing. Empson's colloquial fracturing of Shakespeare's text, from *Seven Types* through *Complex Words*, as well as Leavis's emphasis on the 'heuristico-creative quality of the diction' avoid, on the whole, totalising structures. Rigour consists in having the local reading undo an established symmetry.

Another form of rigour, historical scholarship, can be outrageously speculative. (The trend was always there in the work of editors who unscrambled perplexing expressions or normalised daring ones.) One might escape the Shakespearian vortex by discovering a firm historical emplacement for the plays, by clarifying their occasion as well as the characters in them. The work of referring the plays back to sources mysteriously transformed by Shakespeare (minor Italian novellas, or poetics derived from Donatus and Terence, such as the 'forward progress of the turmoils'5) gives way to an ambitious reconstruction of a particular, sponsoring event. The quest for the identity of W. H. or the Dark Lady or the exact festive occasion of *Twelfth Night* exerts a prosecutory charm that attests to the presence of character in the critic-investigator (that stubborn, scholarly sleuth) as well as in Shakespeare the historical personage. Consider what the ingenious Leslie Hotson does with the 'jest nominal', or play on names. It is as intriguing as anything ventured by newfangled intertextualists.

Hotson claims in *The First Night of Twelfth Night* that the figure of Malvolio is a daring take-off of a high official in Elizabeth's court: Sir William Knollys, Earl of Banbury and Controller of her Majesty's household. This ageing dignitary, we are told, had become infatuated with a young Maid of Honour at Court, Mall (Mary) Fitton. In the 'allowed fooling' of Twelfth Night festivities, 'old Beard Knollys', suggests Hotson, 'is slaughtered in gross and detail'. Here is his description of how it was done:

> while exposing both the Controller's *ill-will* – towards hilarity and misrule – and his *amorousness* in the name *Mala-voglia* (Ill Will or Evil concupiscence) Shakespeare also deftly fetches up Knollys' ridiculous love-chase of Mistress Mall by a sly modulation of *Mala-Voglia* into '*Mal'-voglio* – which means 'I want Mall', 'I wish for Mall', 'I will have Mall'. It is a masterpiece of mockery heightened by merciless repetition, with the players ringing the changes of expression on '*Mal'-voglio* ... it will bring down the house.6

The play becomes a *roman à clef*, and so delivers us from a verbal vertigo it exposes. Shakespeare's improvisational genius, moreover, his extreme wit and opportunism, may recall the methodical *bricolage* by which earlier mythmakers, according to Lévi-Strauss, sustained their tale. Here it explicitly pleases or shames the ears of a court-centred audience. Yet this shaming or delighting is not necessarily in the service of good sense or the *status quo*, for it can subvert as well as mock and purge. The one thing it does, as in the case of the Controller, is to acknowledge the law of gender – of generation and succession – which, as Erasmus saw, compels us to play the fool. Such allowed slander, whether or not reinforced by Elizabethan festivities, by periods of compulsory licence, also penetrates Shakespearian tragedy:

Even he, the father of gods and king of men, who shakes all heaven by a nod, is obliged to lay aside his three-pronged thunder and that Titanic aspect by which, when he pleases, he scares all the gods, and assume another character in the slavish manner of an actor, if he wishes to do what he never refrains from doing, that is to say, to beget children.... He will certainly lay by his gravity, smooth his brow, renounce his rock-bound principles, and for a few minutes toy and talk nonsense.... Venus herself would not deny that without the addition of my presence her strength would be enfeebled and ineffectual. So it is that from this brisk and silly little game of mine come forth the haughty philosophers.[7]

II

Generation and Succession are so fundamental to almost all classes and types of humanity that to reduce them to their verbal effects might seem trivialising. Yet, as Erasmus's Folly hints, the very category of the trivial is overturned by these forces. The 'striving to please every day', which is the fate of the player, is equally that of lover and courtier. It quickens even as it exhausts our wit. It points to a relentless need for devices – words, stratagems. More is required than a 'tiny little wit' to sustain what every day demands.[8]

There exist eloquent characterisations of Shakespeare's understanding of the common nature of mankind. As Bakhtin remarks of another great writer, Rabelais, there are crownings and uncrownings at every level.[9] No one is exempt, at any time, from that rise and fall, whether it is brought on by actual political events or social and sexual rivalry, or internalised pressures leading to self-destructive illusions and acts. The vicissitudes of Folly and Fortuna go hand in hand. Yet no conclusions are drawn; and it does not matter what class of person is involved – a Falstaff, a Harry, a King Henry; a clown, a count, a lady; a usurper, a porter. What happens happens across the board, and can therefore settle expressively in a language with a character of its own – apart from the decorum that fits it to the character of the person represented. The pun or quibble, Shakespeare's 'fatal Cleopatra', is a quaint and powerful sign of that deceiving variety of life. Hazlitt, following Charles Lamb, remarks that Elizabethan 'distinctions of dress, the badges of different professions, the very signs of the shops' were a sort of visible language for the imagination. 'The surface of society was embossed with hieroglyphs.'[10] Yet the showiest and most self-betraying thing in Shakespeare is the flow of language itself, which carries traces of an eruption from some incandescent and molten core, even when hard as basalt, that is, patently rhetorical.

Structurally too, the repetitions by which we discover an intent – a purposiveness – do not resolve themselves into a unity, a 'one' free of sexual, hierarchical or personal differentiation. Feste's 'one' is an Empsonian complex word, which seeks to distract us, by its very iteration, into a sense of closure. Yet there is never an objective correlative that sops up the action or organises all the excrescent motives and verbal implications. Feste's phrase is found, for example, in the mouth of another clown figure, Fluellen, in a scene one could characterise as 'Porn at Monmouth' (*Henry V*, IV.vii). The scene, through the solecisms and mispronunciations of Fluellen, his butchery of English, makes us aware of what is involved in the larger world of combat, to which he is marginal. The catachresis of 'Kill the Poyes and the luggage!' expresses the cut-throat speed with which matters are moving toward indiscriminate slaughter. An end penetrates the middle of the drama; the grimace (if only linguistic) of death begins to show through.

Yet even here, as the action hits a dangerous juncture, as decisions become hasty and bloody, this verbally excessive interlude slows things down to a moment of humorous discrimination. Fluellen draws a comparison between Harry of Monmouth and 'Alexander the Pig' of Macedon (*Henry V*, IV.vii). That 'big' should issue as 'pig' is a fertile and levelling pun, which the macabre turn of this near-graveyard scene could have exploited even more; but the uncrowning of Alexander in Fluellen's mouth leads to a series of images (mouth, fingers, figures) that suggest a 'body' less mortal than its parts. Harry's transformation into King Henry, and Fluellen's comparison in his favour – that Harry's bloodthirsty anger is more justified than Alexander's – appear like a jesting in the throat of death, a vain distinction already undone by the battlefield context that levels all things, as by an earthy vernacular, or quasi-vernacular, that can slander all things in perfect good humour.

It seems impossible, then, to describe the poetical character of Shakespeare without raising certain questions. One concerns the character of the critic (choices to be made in reading so strong and productive a writer); another what happens to language as it nurtures a vernacular ideal that still dominates English literature. A third, related question is whether what that language does to character and to us can be summed up or unified by methodical inquiry. Does an 'intellectual tradition' exist, as Richards thought, to guide us in reading that plentiful 'Elizabethan' mixture? 'The hierarchy of these modes is elaborate and variable', he writes about sixteenth- and seventeenth-century literature. To 'read aright', Richards continues, 'we need to shift with an at present indescribable adroitness and celerity from one mode to another.'[11]

By 'modes' Richards means different types of indirect statement, which he also characterises as 'metaphorical, allegorical, symbolical', yet does not define further. In some way they are all non-literal; at least not directly literal. Like Coleridge, whom he quotes, Richards is impressed by the role that 'wit' plays in Shakespeare's time, although he does not discuss the complicit or antagonistic and always showy relation between wit and will. He simply accepts Coleridge's thesis on wit and Shakespeare's time:

> when the English Court was still foster-mother of the State and the Muses; and when, in consequence, the courtiers and men of rank and fashion affected a display of wit, point, and sententious observation, that would be deemed intolerable at present – but in which a hundred years of controversy, involving every great political, and every dear domestic interest, had trained all but the lowest classes to participate. Add to this the very style of the sermons of the time, and the eagerness of the Protestants to distinguish themselves by long and frequent preaching, and it will be found that, from the reign of Henry VIII to the abdication of James II, no country ever received such a national education as England.[12]

Yet Coleridge's notion of 'national education' may be too idealistic – Arnoldian before the letter. It downplays the subverting character of Shakespeare's wit, one that is not put so easily in the service of the nation-state and its movement toward a common language. The 'prosperity of a pun', as M. M. Mahood calls it, in what is still the most sensitive exploration of the subject,[13] offended rather than pleased most refiners of English up to modern times. 'Prosperity' may itself covertly play on 'propriety', which is precisely what a pun questions. The speed and stenography, in any case, of Shakespeare's wordplay in the comic scenes undoes the hegemony of any single order of discourse, and compels us to realise the radically social and mobile nature of the language exchange. And, unlike the novel (which allows Bakhtin his most persuasive theorising), these scenes display less a narrative or a pseudo-narrative than *oral graffiti*. Verbally Shakespeare is a graffiti artist, using bold, often licentious strokes, that make sense because of the living context of stereotypes, the *commedia dell'arte*, and other vernacular or popular traditions.

Is it possible, then, to see Shakespeare *sub specie unitatis*, as the younger Murry thought? 'There never has been and never will be a human mind which can resist such an inquiry if it is pursued with sufficient perseverance and understanding.'[14] Yet in this very sentence 'human mind' is fleetingly equivocal: does it refer only to the object of inquiry, Shakespeare's mind, or also to the interpreter's intellect, tempted by the riddle of Shakespeare? The later Murry too does not give up; but now the unity, the 'all that's one', is frightening as well, and associated with *omnia abeunt in mysterium*: all things exit into mystery.[15]

It seems to me there is no mystery, no *Abgrund*, except language itself, whose revelatory revels are being staged, as if character were a function of language, rather than vice versa. More precisely, as if the locus of the dramatic action were the effect of language on character. *Twelfth Night* will allow us to examine how this language test is applied. If we admire, however ambivalently, the way Iago works on Othello by 'damnable iteration' (cf. **Falstaff**: 'O, thou hast damnable iteration, and art indeed able to corrupt a saint' [I *Henry IV*, I.ii.90]), or the way Falstaff shamelessly converts abuse into flattery, we are already caught up in a rhetoric whose subversive motility, moment to moment, can bless or curse, praise or blame, corrupt words or (like Aristotle's eulogist) substitute collateral terms that 'lean toward the best'.[16] It is this instant possibility of moving either way, or simultaneously both ways, which defines the Shakespearian dramatic and poetical character. In *Twelfth Night*, with Feste a self-pronounced 'corrupter of words' (III.i.37), and Malvolio's censorious presence, the verbal action challenges all parties to find 'comic remedies', or to extract sweets from weeds and poisons.[17]

III

'Excellent,' says Sir Toby Belch, 'I smell a device.' 'I have't in my nose too', Sir Andrew Aguecheek echoes him (II.iii.162). Toby is referring to the plan concocted by Maria, Olivia's maid, of how to get even with the strutting and carping Malvolio, steward of the household. The device is a letter to be written by Maria in her lady's hand, which will entice Malvolio into believing Olivia is consumed with a secret passion for him, his yellow stockings, cross-garters and smile. The device (not the only one in the play – Bertrand Evans has counted seven persons who are active practisers operating six devices)[18] succeeds; and Malvolio, smiling hard, and wearing the colours he thinks are the sign commanded by his lady, but which she happens to detest, is taken for mad and put away.

The very words 'I smell a device' contain a device. Toby, mostly drunk, knows how to choose his metaphors; and Andrew, not much of a wit ('I am a great eater of beef, and I believe that does harm to my wit'), merely echoes him, which makes the metaphor more literal and so more absurd. A device is also a figure, or flower of speech; both meanings may be present here, since the content of the device is literary, that is, a deceivingly flowery letter. Flowers smell, good or bad as the occasion may be. 'Lilies that fester smell far worse than weeds' (Sonnet 94). Sometimes figures or metaphors fly by so thick and fast that we all are as perplexed as Sir Andrew:

> **Andrew**   Bless you, fair shrew.
> **Maria**   And you too, sir.
> **Toby**   Accost, Sir Andrew, accost. (...)
> **Andrew**   Good Mistress Accost, I desire better acquaintance.
> **Maria**   My name is Mary, sir.
> **Andrew**   Good Mistress Mary Accost –
> **Toby**   You mistake, knight. 'Accost' is front her, board her, woo her, assail her.
> **Andrew**   By my troth, I would not undertake her in this company. Is that the meaning of 'accost'?
> **Maria**   Fare you well, gentlemen.
> **Toby**   And thou let part so, Sir Andrew, would thou might'st never draw sword again!
> **Andrew**   And you part so, mistress, I would I might never draw sword again. Fair lady, do you think you have fools in hand?
> **Maria**   Sir, I have not you by th' hand.
> **Andrew**   Marry, but you shall have, and here's my hand.
> **Maria**   Now, sir, thought is free. I pray you bring your hand to th' buttery bar and let it drink.
> **Andrew**   Wherefore, sweetheart? What's your metaphor?
> **Maria**   It's dry, sir.
>
> (I.iii.46–72)

Awkward Andrew starts with a mild oxymoron and compounds the error of his address to Mary by a further innocent mistake – the transposition of a common verb into a proper noun, which not only unsettles parts of speech but creates a parallel euphemism to 'fair shrew' through the idea of 'good Accost'. The entire scene is constructed out of such pleasant errors – failed connections or directions that hint at larger, decisive acts (accosting, undertaking, marrying). At line 62 the verbal plot becomes even more intricate, as Andrew strives to 'address' Mary a second time. 'Marry' (l.66) is an oath, a corruption of the Virgin's name; but here, in addition to echoing 'Mary', it may be the common verb, as Andrew tries to be witty or gallant by saying in a slurred way (hey, I too can fling metaphors around!), 'If you marry you'll have me by the hand, and here it is.' (He forgets that that would make him a fool, like all married men.) Maria bests him, though, suggesting a freer kind of handling, with a new metaphor that – I think – may be licentious. What is that 'buttery bar'? Probably, in function, a bar as today, for serving drinks; but could it be her breasts or ... butt? That same 'bar', by a further twist or trope, echoes in Maria's 'marry, now I let go your hand, I am barren' (l.77). No wonder Andrew, out of his range, stutters, 'Wherefore, sweetheart? What's your metaphor?'

Somewhere there is always a device, or a 'hand' that could fool just about anyone. Nobody is spared, nobody escapes witting. Yet it remains harmless because all, except Malvolio, play along. There is rhetoric and repartee, puns and paranomasia, metaphor upon metaphor, as if these characters were signifying monkeys: the play expects every person to pass the test of wit, to stand at that bar of language. Yet 'wherefore?' we ask, like simple Andrew.

That question returns us to the poetical character. It 'is not itself', Keats wrote, 'it has no self – it is every thing and nothing – It has no character.' He says other things, too, which make it clear he is thinking mainly of Shakespeare. 'It lives in gusto, be it foul or fair, high or low, rich or poor, mean or elevated – It has as much delight in conceiving an Iago as an Imogen. What shocks the virtuous philosopher (a Malvolio in this respect) delights the chameleon Poet. It does no harm from its relish of the dark side of things any more than for its taste for the bright one; because they both end in speculation' (letter to Richard Woodhouse, 27 October 1818).

Much depends on that word 'speculation' in Keats; a 'widening speculation', he also writes, eases the burden of life's mystery, takes away the heat and fever (letter to J. H. Reynolds, 3 May 1818). You have to have something to speculate with or on; some luxury, like a delicious voice, whose first impact you remember. Speculation is making the thing count again, as with money, yet *without fearing its loss.*[19] The Shakespearian language of wit is like that. Though penetrated by knowledge of loss, aware that the most loved or fancied thing can fall 'into abatement and low price, / Even in a minute!' (I.i.13–14), it still spends itself in an incredibly generous manner, as if the treasury of words were always full. However strange it may seem, while everything in this play is, emotionally, up or down – each twin, for example, thinks the other dead; Olivia, in constant mourning and rejecting Orsino, is smitten by Viola / Cesario in the space of one interview – while everything vacillates, the language itself coins its metaphors and fertile exchanges beyond any calculus of loss and gain. When I hear the word 'fool' repeated so many times, I also hear the word 'full' emptied out or into it; so 'Marry' and 'Mary' and 'madam' ('mad-dame') and 'madman' collapse distinctions of character (personality) in favour of some prodigious receptacle that 'receiveth as the sea' (I.i.II). No wonder modern critics have felt a Dionysian drift in the play, a doubling and effacing of persons as well as a riot of metaphors working against distinctions, until, to quote the ballad at the end, 'that's all one'.

IV

I think, therefore I am. What does one do about 'I act' or 'I write'? What identity for that 'I'? For the poet who shows himself in the inventive wit of all these personae? *Twelfth Night* gives an extraordinary amount of theatrical time to Sir Toby Belch and Sir Andrew Aguecheek, and to clowning generally. These scenes threaten to erupt into the main plot, which is absurd enough, where love is sudden and gratuitous, as in Orsino's infatuation for Olivia (two O's) or Viola's for Orsino, or Olivia's for Cesario. Everything goes o – a in this play, as if a character's destiny depended on vowelling. 'M.O.A.I. doth sway my life' (II.v.109). Whose *hand* directs this comic tumult of mistaken identities, disguises, devices, and names, that even when they are not Rabelaisian or musical scrabble (Olivia: Viola) or transparent like Malvolio (the evil eye, or evil wish) are silly attempts at self-assertion? So it doesn't really help when Sebastian in II.i.14–18 identifies himself. 'You must know of me then, Antonio, my name is Sebastian, which I called Roderigo; my father was that Sebastian of Messaline whom I know you have heard of.' We have two Sebastians, and one Sebastian is Roderigo. In addition, as we know by this point in the drama, Sebastian and Viola (that is, Cesario) are identical twins, born in the same hour, both saved from the 'breach' a second time when they escape shipwreck and find themselves in a land with the suggestive name of Illyria – compounded, to the sensitive ear, out of Ill and liar/lyre. So also Viola enters the play punning, or off-rhyming. 'And what should I do in Illyria? / My brother he is in Elysium' (I.ii.3–4).

The question, then, relates to identity and destiny, or who has what in hand; it is also related to the question of questioning itself, that kind of speech-act, so close to trial and testing, and the legalese or academic lingo in a play perhaps performed at an inn-of-court. In late medieval times, from the twelfth century on, there was a shift in 'pedagogical technique (and corresponding literary forms) from the *lectio* to the *disputatio* and *questio* ... from primary concern for the exegesis of authoritative texts and the laying of doctrinal foundations toward the resolution of particular (and sometimes minor) difficulties and even the questioning of matters no longer seriously doubted, for the sake of exploring the implications of a doctrine, revealing the limits of necessity and contingency, or demonstrating one's dialectical skills.'[20] Another authority writes that 'Even the points accepted by everybody and set forth in the most certain of terms were brought under scrutiny and subjected, by deliberate artifice, to the now usual processes of research. In brief, they were, literally speaking, "called into question", no longer because there was any real doubt about their truth, but because a deeper understanding of them was sought after.'[21] From contemporary reports of the 'Acts' at Oxford when Elizabeth visited, we know that these questions and *quodlibets* maintained themselves at least ceremonially.[22] Is *Twelfth Night's* subtitle, 'What You Will,' a jocular translation of *quodlibet*? What significance may there be in the fact that in I.iii.86–96 Toby passes from 'No question' to '*Pourquoi*' to 'Past question?' My own question is: *Pourquoi* these 'kikshawses' ('quelques choses')? Wherefore, Shakespeare? What's your metaphor for?

Testing and questing seem connected immemorially: it is hard to think of the one without the other, especially in the realm of 'Acts' which assert authority or identity by playful display. Even the Academy participates that much in the realm of romance. But my comments are meant to lead somewhat deeper into a drama that relishes the night-side of things with such good humour. If there are

low-class mistakes, as when Andrew thinks Toby's 'Accost' refers
to Mary's name, there are also the high-class mistakes, Orsino's
love, principally, that starts the play with a fine call for music in
verses intimating that nothing can fill desire, fancy, love. Its appetite
is like the sea, so capacious, so swallowing and changeable. 'If
music be the food of love, play on.' *Play on* is what we do, as
'Misprision in the highest degree' (I.v.53) extends itself. Everything
changes place or is mis-taken, so that Orsino believes himself in
love with Olivia but settles 'dexteriously', as the Clown might say,
for Viola; while poor Malvolio is taken for mad and confined in a
place as gloomy as his temperament. We tumble through the
doubling, reversing, mistaking, clowning, even cloning; we never
get away from the tumult of the words themselves, from the 'gratil-
lity' (another clown-word, that is, gratuitousness or greed for tips,
tipsiness) of Feste's 'gracious fooling', as when Andrew, probably
tipsy himself, and stupidly good at mixing metaphors, mentions
some of the clown's other coinages: 'Pigrogromitus' and the
'Vapians passing the equinoctial of Queubus' (II.iii.23–4).

It is not that these funny, made-up words don't make sense: they
make a kind of instant sense, as Shakespeare always does. Yet a
sense that can't be proved, that remains to be guessed at and
demands something from us. Does 'equinoctial' hint at solstice or
equinox festivals, if *Twelfth Night* was performed on the day the
title suggests;[23] is 'Queubus' mock Latin for the tail or male, or a
corruption of 'quibus', 'a word of frequent occurrence in legal doc-
uments and so associated with verbal niceties or subtle distinctions'
(C. T. Onions)? Did the audience know it was slang for fool in
Dutch ('Kwibus')?

The text requires a certain tolerance or liberality of interpretation: yellow cross-garters in the realm of construing, 'motley in
the brain' (I.v.55). To quote Andrew – and it should be inscribed on
the doors of all literature departments: 'I would I had bestowed
that time in the tongues that I have in fencing, dancing, and
bear-baiting. O, had I but followed the arts!' (I.iii.90–3).

There exists a modern version of another 'antic' song about the
twelve days of Christmas (cf.II.iii.85). If Twelfth Night, the climax
of Christmastide rejoicing, asks that we fill up the daystar's ebb,
then the emphasis falls on giving, on true-love giving. Twelfth
Night, formally the feast of Epiphany, is when divinity appeared,
when Christ was manifested to the Gentiles (the Magi or three
kings). Presence rather than absence is the theme. *Twelfth Night* is

not a religious play, and yet its 'gracious fooling' may be full of grace. The great O of Shakespeare's stage draws into it the gift of tongues; and in addition to the legal or academic metaphors, the food and sexual metaphors, and other heterogeneous language strains, occasionally a religious pathos, impatient of all these indirections, maskings, devices, makes itself heard. 'Wherefore are these things hid? Wherefore have these gifts a curtain before 'em?' (I.iii.122–3) To the question, what filling (fulfilling) is in this fooling, the best reply might be that, in literature, everything aspires to the condition of language, to the gift of tongues; that the spirit – wanton as it may be – of language overrides such questions, including those of character and identity.

Does Orsino, the Duke, have an identity, or is he not a plaything of fancy; and is love not represented by him as both arbitrary in what it fixes on and as 'full of shapes' and 'fantastical' as the entire play? These people seem in love with words rather than with each other. More exactly, the embassy of words and the play of rhetoric are essential tests for both lover and object of love. When Curio tries to distract the Duke from his musical and effete reflections by 'Will you go hunt, my lord?' (I.i.16), Orsino answers, startled, 'What, Curio?' meaning 'What d'you say?', which is misunderstood when Curio replies, 'The hart', after which the Duke can't restrain himself from an old quibble equating hart, the animal, and heart, the seat of love:

> Why, so I do [hunt], the noblest that I have.
> O, when mine eyes did see Olivia first,
> Methought she purg'd the air of pestilence;
> That instant was I turn'd into a hart,
> And my desires, like fell and cruel hounds,
> E'er since pursue me.
>
> (I.i.18–23)

The hunter becomes the hunted; but it is also suggested (though we may not be convinced) that the Duke finds a heart in himself – a sensitivity where previously there was nothing but a sense of privilege.

We see how thorough this full fooling is. In Shakespeare the poetry – the prose too – is larger than the characters, enlarging them but also making their identities or egos devices in an overwhelming revel. The revels of language are never ended. This does not mean that language is discontinuous with the search for identity or a 'heart'. Orsino's first speech already introduces the gracious theme of giving and receiving, of feeding, surfeiting, dying, reviving, playing on. Love and music are identified through the metaphor of the 'dying fall' (I.i.4), also alluding, possibly, to the end of the year; and, ironically enough, the Duke's moody speech suggests *a desire to get beyond desire* – to have done with such perturbations, with wooing and risking rejection, and trying to win through by gifts and manoeuvres. 'Give me excess of it, that, surfeiting,/The appetite [for love, not just for music] may sicken, and so die' (I.i.2–3). At the very end of the play, with the Clown's final song, this melancholy desire to be beyond desire returns in the refrain 'The rain it raineth every day', and the internal chiming of 'that's all one, our play is done'. Even in this generous and least cynical of Shakespeare's comedies, love is an appetite that wants to be routinised or exhausted, and so borders on tragic sentiments.

In drama, giving and receiving take the form of dialogic repartee. Shakespeare makes of dialogue a charged occasion, two masked affections testing each other, always on guard. Usually, then, there is a healthy fear or respect for the other; or there is a subversive sense that what goes on in human relations is not dialogue at all but seduction and domination. To have real giving and receiving – in terms of speech and understanding – may be so strenuous that the mind seeks other ways to achieve a simulacrum of harmony: maybe an 'equinoctial of Queubus' brings us into equilibrium, or maybe festivals, like Christmas, when there is at-one-ment, through licensed licence, through the principle of 'what you will', of freely doing or not doing. (Twelve, after all, is the sign of the temporal clock turning over into One.) But the turn is felt primarily at the level of 'gracious fooling' in this Christmas play. Hazlitt goes so far as to say 'It is perhaps too good-natured for comedy. It has little satire and no spleen.' And he continues with an even more significant remark, which I now want to explore: 'In a word, the best turn is given to everything, instead of the worst.'

V

The poetical genius of Shakespeare is inseparable from an ability to trope anything and turn dialogue, like a fluctuating battle, to the worst or best surmise. I see the dramatic and linguistic action of *Twelfth Night* as a turning away of the evil eye. It averts a malevolent interpretation of life, basically Malvolio's. Though Malvolio is unjustly – by a mere 'device' – put into a dark place, this too is for the good, for he must learn how to plead. That is, by a quasi-legal, heartfelt rhetoric, he must now turn the evidence, from bad to good. In IV.ii.12ff. a masquerade is acted out which not only compels us to sympathise with Malvolio, making him a figure of pathos, but which repeats, as a play within the play, the action of the whole. Malvolio is gulled once more, baited like a bear – the sport he objected to. Yet the spirit of this comedy is not that of revenge, malice or ritual expulsion. All these motives may participate, yet what rouses our pity and fear is the way language enters and preordains the outcome. Shakespeare brings out the schizoid nature of discourse by juxtaposing soft or good words, ordinary euphemisms ('Jove bless thee, Master Parson', '*Bonos dies*, Sir Toby', 'Peace in this prison') with abusive imprecations ('Out, hyperbolical fiend', 'Fie, thou dishonest Satan', 'Madman, thou errest'). Malvolio is subjected to a ridiculous legal or religious quizzing: a 'trial' by 'constant question'. As in so many infamous state proceedings, he can get nowhere. He has to cast himself, against his temperament, on the mercy of the clown he condemned, though never actually harmed: 'Fool, I say', 'Good fool, as ever thou wilt deserve well at my hand', 'Ay, good fool', 'Fool, fool, fool, I say!', 'Good fool, help me to some light and some paper: I tell thee I am as well in my wits as any man in Illyria' (**Feste**: 'Well-a-day that you were, sir!'), 'By this hand, I am! Good fool, some ink, paper, and light.'

Every word suddenly receives its full value. A man's life or freedom depends on it. It is not quibbled away. Yet words remain words; they have to be received; the imploration is all. 'By this hand' is more than a tender of good faith, the visible sign of imploration. It is the handwriting that could save Malvolio, as that other 'hand', Maria's letter-device, fooled and trapped him. Ink, paper, and light, as for Shakespeare himself perhaps, are the necessities. They must dispel or counter-fool whatever plot has been, is being, woven.

The spectator sits safely, like a judge, on the bench; yet the reversal which obliges Malvolio to plead with the fool reminds us what it means to be dependent on what we say and how (generously or meanly) it is received. To please every day, like a courtier, lover or actor, leads us into improvisations beyond the ordinary scope of wit. It puts us all in the fool's place. It is everyone, not Feste alone, who is involved, when after a sally of nonsense Maria challenges him with 'Make that good' (I.v.7). That is, give it meaning, in a world where 'hanging' and 'colours' (collars, cholers, flags, figures of speech, I.v.1–6) are realities. But also, to return to Hazlitt's insight, give what you've said the best turn, justify the metaphor at whatever bar (legal) or buttery (the milk of mercy) is the least 'dry' (I.iii.72). 'The rain it raineth every day.'

Bakhtin's view, inspired by the development of literary vernaculars in the Renaissance, that each national language is composed of many kinds of discourse, dialogic even when not formally so, and polyphonic in effect, can be extended to the question of Shakespeare's poetical character. There is no one heart or one will ('Will'). Andrew's querulous 'What's your metaphor?' or Maria's testing 'Make it good' or the Clown's patter ('"That that is, is"; so I, being Master Parson, am Master Parson; for what is "that" but "that"? and "is" but "is"?' [IV.ii.15–17]) impinge also on the spectator/reader. Yet in this world of figures, catches, errors, reversals, songs, devices, plays within plays, where motley distinguishes more than the jester, and even Malvolio is gulled into a species of it, moments arise that suggest a more than formal resolution – more than the fatigue or resignation of 'that's all one' or the proverbial 'all's well that ends well'. So when Viola, as the Duke's go-between, asks Olivia, 'Good madam, let me see your face' (where the 'good', as in all such appeals, is more than an adjective, approaching the status of an absolute construction: 'Good, madam', similar in force to Maria's 'Make it good'), there is the hint of a possible revelatory moment, of *clarification*. The challenge, moreover, is met by a facing up to it. Yet the metaphor of expositing a text, which had preceded, is continued, so that we remain in the text even when we are out of it.

Olivia   Now, sir, what is your text?
Viola   Most sweet lady –
Olivia   A comfortable doctrine, and much may be said of it. Where lies your text?
Viola   In Orsino's bosom.
Olivia   In his bosom? In what chapter of his bosom?
Viola   To answer by the method, in the first of his heart.
Olivia   O, I have read it: it is heresy. Have you no more to say?
Viola   Good madam, let me see your face.
Olivia   Have you any commission from your lord to negotiate with my face? You are now out of your text: but we will draw the

curtain and show you the picture. (*Unveiling*) Look you, sir, such
a one I was this present. Is't not well done?
Viola   Excellently done, if God did all.

(I.v.223–39)

I was, not I am; by pretending she is a painting, just unveiled, the
original I is no longer there, or only as this picture which points to
a present in the way names or texts point to a meaning. The text,
however, keeps turning. There is no 'present': no absolute gift, or
moment of pure being. Yet a sense of epiphany, however fleeting, is
felt; a sense of mortality too and of artifice, as the text is sustained
by the force of Olivia's wit. 'Is't not well done?' Olivia, like Feste,
must 'make it good'. The mocking elaboration of her own
metaphor allows speech rather than embarrassed or astonished
silence at this point. The play (including Olivia's 'interlude')
continues. There is always more to say.

From *Shakespeare and the Question of Theory*, ed. Patricia Parker
and Geoffrey Hartman (New York and London, 1985), pp. 37–51.

NOTES

[Geoffrey Hartman begins his essay not, as might be expected, by looking
at 'the text' but instead at 'the character of the critic', in order to show that
no matter how 'rigorous' a critic seems to be, s/he is revealing a degree of
speculation. This is a fundamental tenet of recent criticism, and Hartman
shows its implications when applied to older criticism. Moving on to his
own preference, deconstructive criticism, he argues, using *Twelfth Night*
as the example, that the arbitrariness of language is not only a major theme
of the play but is also the reason for critical differences. Ed.]

1. All quotations from *Twelfth Night* are taken from the Arden
    Shakespeare edition, ed. J. M. Lothian and T. W. Craik (London and
    New York, 1975).

2. 'Feste the Jester', in *A Miscellany* (London, 1929), p. 217.

3. John Middleton Murry, *Shakespeare* (London, 1936), pp. 17–19. At
    the end of his book Murry appends a short imaginary dialogue with
    Shakespeare, more fanciful than Bradley's surmise.

4. 'Shakespeare Criticism', in *Aspects of Literature* (New York, 1920),
    p. 200. Eliot's epigraph to *The Sacred Wood* (1921) from Rémy de
    Gourmont ('Eriger ses impressions en lois ...') discloses the common

problem of going beyond impressionism without becoming unduly scientific (i.e. following the Taine–Brunetière tradition).

5. Consult, for example, J. V. Cunningham, *Woe or Wonder: The Emotional Effect of Shakespearean Tragedy* (1951), especially 'The Donatan Tradition'; and Ruth Nevo, *Comic Transformations in Shakespeare* (London and New York, 1980).

6. Leslie Hotson, *The First Night of Twelfth Night* (New York, 1955), ch. 5, 'Malvolio'.

7. Desiderius Erasmus, *The Praise of Folly*, trs. from the Latin, with an essay and commentary, by Hoyt Hopewell Hudson (Princeton, NJ, 1941), pp. 14–15.

8. Consider, in this light, the vogue of courtesy books in the sixteenth century, of which the most famous, Baldassare Castiglione's *The Book of the Courtier*, was done into English by Sir Thomas Hoby in 1561, and reprinted 1577, 1588 and 1603. Book 2 of *The Courtier* treats exhaustively the decorum of jesting.

9. Mikhail Bakhtin, *Rabelais and His World*, trs. Helene Iswolsky (Cambridge, MA, 1968). See especially ch. 3, 'Popular-festive Forms'. Bakhtin mentions the feast of Epiphany, and claims that the common element of both official and unofficial carnivals was that 'they are all related to time, which is the true hero of every feast, uncrowning the old and crowning the new'. A significant footnote adds that, actually, 'every feast day crowns and uncrowns'. See also Bakhtin's second chapter on 'The Language of the Marketplace in Rabelais'. (For some amusing remarks on Shakespeare and Rabelais, cf. Hotson, *The First Night*, pp. 155ff.) C. L. Barber in *Shakespeare's Festive Comedy: A Study of Dramatic Form and its Relation to Social Custom* (1959) explores the same area.

10. William Hazlitt, *Lectures on the Literature of the Age of Elizabeth* (1820), ch. 1.

11. I. A. Richards, *Coleridge on Imagination* (London, 1968), p. 193.

12. As quoted by Richards, ibid., p. 193.

13. M. M. Mahood, *Shakespeare's Wordplay* (London, 1957).

14. Murry, *Aspects*, p. 199.

15. Murry, *Shakespeare*, pp. 17–18.

16. See Hudson, *The Praise of Folly*, p. xxiii. Also, on the related matter of 'praise-abuse', Bakhtin, *Rabelais*, p. 458: 'The virginal words of the oral vernacular which entered literary language for the first time are close, in a certain sense, to proper nouns. They are individualised and still contain a strong element of praise-abuse, which makes them suitable to nicknames.' On word-formation in Rabelais (often suggestive

for Feste's 'gracious fooling'), see Leo Spitzer, *Linguistics and Literary History* (Princeton, NJ, 1948).

17. William Hazlitt, '*Twelfth Night*', in *Characters of Shakespeare's Plays* (1817).

18. Bertrand Evans, *Shakespeare's Comedies* (Oxford, 1960), p. 118.

19. Just as in comedy, according to Donatan principles, turns of fortune should not include the danger of death (*sine periculo vitae*, cf. Cunningham, *Woe or Wonder*). Since Leibniz defined music as a species of unconscious counting or arithmetic, and music enters so prominently into *Twelfth Night* (as *musica speculativa* as well as *musica practica* – see John Hollander, 'Musica mundana and *Twelfth Night*', *English Institute Essays: Sound and Poetry*, ed. Northrop Frye [New York, 1957]), an interesting analogy begins to form between comedy, music, and the Shakespearian language of wit. In this respect, the issues of gender difference and succession return, for the action of *Twelfth Night* is simply the release of Orsino and Olivia from their single state, which cannot occur without the separating out of Viola/Cesario and Viola/Sebastian ('One face, one voice, one habit, and two persons!? A natural perspective, that is, and is not!' [V.i.214–15]). That 'one' is redeeemed from both singleness and duplicity: the confounding in singleness, as Sonnet 8, with its explicit music metaphor, suggests, should turn into a harmony of 'parts that thou shouldst bear', a concord of 'all in one'. Cf. however Marilyn French's surprising conclusion in *Shakespeare's Division of Experience* (New York, 1981) that the one not in harmony, Malvolio, wins out in the end as the embodiment of society's repressive stewardship. 'Constancy is required; love must lead to marriage; and marriage must lead to procreation' (p. 123).

20. David C. Lindberg, *Theories of Vision from Al-Kindi to Kepler* (Chicago and London, 1976), p. 145.

21. M.-D. Chenu, OP, *Understanding St Thomas*, as quoted by Lindberg, ibid., p. 145.

22. See 'The Grand Reception and Entertainment of Queen Elizabeth at Oxford in 1592', from a MS Account by Philip Stringer, printed in *Elizabethan Oxford*, ed. Charles Plummer (Oxford, 1877). Cf., on the quodlibets, the same collection of tracts, 18, and the unflattering description of such exercises as they still prevailed into the later eighteenth century, by Vicesimus Knox: *Reminiscences by Oxford Men, 1559–1850*, ed. Lilian M. Quiller Couch (Oxford, 1892), pp. 160–7. According to J. Huizinga, *Homo Ludens* (1944), ch. 9, the 'whole functioning of the medieval university was profoundly agonistic and ludic'. The word 'Act' was formally applied to the degree exercises which conferred the Bachelor and Master of Arts. The use of 'act' in Shakespeare (as in *Hamlet* V.ii.346 and *Winter's Tale* V.ii.86ff.) includes that sense of the presence of a conferring authority.

23. Cf. T. H. Gaster, *Thespis: Ritual, Myth and Drama in the Ancient Near East* (New York, 1950). Chapter 2, especially, discerns in ritual dramas a uniform pattern of *kenosis*, or emptying, and *plerosis*, or filling. The twelve nights after which Shakespeare's play is named could reflect the *agon* or combat of those two tendencies: a combat to determine the character of such days, whether they are fasts or feasts, lenten (under the aegis of Malvolio) or copious. The twelve days between December 25 and January 6 have, moreover, a special relation to calendar time: they may be epagomenal or intercalary (Gaster, p. 10, and cf. p. 369) and as such linked to an 'occlusion of personality'. Yet is not all fictional time intercalary? 'Twelfth Night' in Shakespeare may stand for every such day or night which requires a *release* of that 'lease' on life which has to be annually renewed, yet which here is a human and ever-present rather than ritually determined necessity.

2

Twelfth Night: 'The morality of indulgence'

ELLIOT KRIEGER

In 1959 C. L. Barber's book *Shakespeare's Festive Comedy*[1] and John Hollander's article '*Twelfth Night* and the Morality of Indulgence'[2] challenged, with similar arguments, Morris P. Tilley's long-accepted thesis that *Twelfth Night* advocates a mean between extremes. Tilley saw *Twelfth Night* as 'a philosophical defence of a moderate indulgence in pleasure, in opposition on the one hand to an extreme hostility to pleasure and on the other hand to an extreme self-indulgence'.[3] Hollander reacted against the entire tendency to place *Twelfth Night*, to find a moral 'position' for the play. Hollander argued that in *Twelfth Night* Shakespeare substituted 'what one might call a moral process for a moral system' (p. 229), that the 'essential action' of this moral process is:

> to so surfeit the Appetite upon excess that it 'may sicken and so die'. It is the Appetite, not the whole Self, however, which is surfeited: the Self will emerge at the conclusion of the action from where it has been hidden. The movement of the play is toward this emergence of humanity from behind a mask of comic type.
>
> (p. 230)

This 'action', according to Hollander, ensures that Orsino, 'embodying the overpowering appetite for romantic love' (p. 231), Olivia, 'despite herself, a private glutton' (p. 231), and Sir Toby, with his 'huge stomach for food and drink' (p. 237) all '[kill] off' an 'excessive appetite through indulgence of it' (p. 238) and supply the 'liver, brain, and heart', with 'one self king' (I.i.37–9; pp. 231, 239).

Each protagonist surfeits his or her 'misdirected voracity' and thereby achieves 'rebirth of the unencumbered self' (pp. 238–9). Hollander argued that 'everybody' achieves this rebirth: Orsino is supplied with Viola, 'his fancy's queen', Olivia with 'Cesario or king' (p. 239), 'Toby and Maria are married, Aguecheek chastened, etc.' (p. 239).

The supposed inclusiveness of Hollander's process – note how his 'etc.' hedges – depends on his assumption that Feste and Malvolio remain 'outside the action' or are 'left unaccounted for' (pp. 232, 239), that neither 'has doffed his mask of feasting' (p. 233). Hollander asserted that Feste, who 'represents' the 'very nature' of the action is 'unmotivated by any appetite, and is never sated of his fooling' (pp. 232–3), and that Malvolio, who 'alone is not possessed of a craving directed outward' is the only character who 'cannot morally benefit from a period of self-indulgence' (p. 233).

Barber's argument was a little more abstract, and its thesis, that *Twelfth Night* 'moves ... through release to clarification' (p. 242), depended on the context that his book established. Yet Barber, like Hollander, presupposed that *Twelfth Night* does not demonstrate a static mean between extremes but enacts a movement toward excess that, reaching an extreme point, restores the social order of the play to its healthy norm. Barber's analysis of *Twelfth Night* derives from his assumption that:

> just as a saturnalian reversal of social roles need not threaten the social structure, but can serve instead to consolidate it, so a temporary, playful reversal of sexual roles can renew the meaning of the normal relation. One can add that with sexual or with other relations, it is when the normal is secure that playful aberration is benign.
>
> (p. 245)

The 'security' out of which the festive release emerges is essential to Barber's analysis of *Twelfth Night*. Barber argued that *Twelfth Night* exhibits 'the use and abuse of social liberty' (p. 248); but he qualified 'liberty' by a subtle reference to social class: 'the play exhibits the liberties which gentlemen take with decorum in the pursuit of pleasure and love' (p. 248).

The word *gentlemen* opens a whole realm of thought that Hollander excludes and that Barber overlooks. By loosely applying the moral process he has abstracted from the play to the play as a whole, instead of to selected characters within the play, Hollander managed to ignore completely the social distinctions that *Twelfth Night* so obviously delineates. He can argue that because Orsino and Olivia have external objects for their appetites, whereas Malvolio loves only himself, Malvolio's indulgence is 'perverted' rather than 'excessive' (p. 234), and consequently that Malvolio does not deserve 'rebirth of the unencumbered self', 'fulfilment' in 'one self king': 'His story effectively and ironically underlines the progress towards this fulfilment in everybody else, and helps to delineate the limitations of the moral domain of the whole play' (p. 235). Hollander gives little attention either to Viola's indulgence or to her fulfilment. He asserts, unconvincingly, that to indulge 'she commits' herself to the love-game with Olivia 'with redoubled force' (p. 236) and he assumes that to be 'Orsino's mistress' will fulfil her 'liver, brain, and heart'. He supposes that Sebastian has 'no real identity apart from Viola' (p. 237). Hollander has little or nothing to say regarding the fulfilment any of the other characters find at the conclusion. In fact, the particular moral process that Hollander has so eloquently described in the abstract does not, when applied to the characters and action of *Twelfth Night*, seem 'to encompass everybody' (p. 239): Orsino, Olivia, and perhaps Sir Toby indulge, surfeit, and emerge; but Viola and Sebastian emerge without having indulged, Malvolio indulges and is, according to Hollander, justifiably submerged. The other characters are left out of the process and out of account.

When we apply the abstractions of Hollander's analysis to the characters within the play, we can see that the 'morality of indulgence' applies to and protectively circumscribes the ruling class of *Twelfth Night*. According to Hollander, the excessive behaviour that is moral when enacted by Orsino, Olivia, and Sir Toby is 'perverted' when enacted by Malvolio. In fact, however, Malvolio's self-love differs from the obviously narcissistic preoccupations of Orsino and Olivia and the egoistic revelry of Sir Toby *only* because decorum forbids one of his rank to 'surfeit on himself' (p. 234). Hollander correctly notes that the play does not praise Malvolio 'as an example of righteous bourgeois opposition to medieval hierarchies' (p. 234), for Malvolio accepts degree – he opposes only his subordinate position within an hierarchical society. The play, however, does not dramatise strategies of bourgeois opposition so much as of aristocratic protection. Only a privileged social class has access to the morality of indulgence: if the members of the ruling class find their identities through excessive indulgence in appetite, the other characters in the play either work to make indulgence possible for their superiors or else, indulging themselves, sicken and so die.

Barber, like Hollander, deftly sidesteps the issue of social class in his discussion of festive release in *Twelfth Night*, although his descriptions of liberty and festivity seem continually to point toward acknowledgement of social privilege:

> What enables Viola to bring off her role in disguise is her perfect courtesy, ... Her mastery of courtesy goes with her being the daughter of 'that Sebastian of Messalina whom I know you have heard of': gentility shows through her disguise ...;
>
> (p. 248)

or:

> Sir Toby is gentlemanly liberty incarnate, a specialist in it .... Because Sir Toby has 'faith' – the faith that goes with belonging – he does not need to worry when Maria teases him about confining himself 'within the modest limits of order'.
>
> (p. 250)

Barber, however, does not pursue the social aspects of his observations, and the principle of festive release remains, as throughout Barber's book, abstracted from the class relations that constitute its context. Because he abstracts festivity from the class relations in the drama, Barber ignores the effect that social class has on the definitions and applications of such key terms as *courtesy* (in regard to Viola), *liberty* (in regard to Feste), and *decorum* (in regard to Malvolio). For Feste, Barber writes, to 'sing and beg' – that is, to work and be dependent – constitutes a 'liberty based on accepting disillusion' (p. 253). Barber distinguishes Malvolio's desire 'to violate decorum', to rise in stature, from true 'liberty' because Malvolio wants to enjoy the authority that accompanies stature, to 'relish to the full' the 'power' decorum has 'over others' (p. 255). The 'liberty' of saturnalia, therefore, contrary to Barber's premise, does not reverse social roles, in that the authority relinquished by the ruling class cannot be enjoyed by the subservients because that violation of decorum would contrast with the 'genuine, free impulse' (p. 255) with which the ruling class asserts its authority. The violation of decorum must, according to Barber, be treated 'as a kind of foreign body to be expelled by laughter' (p. 257).

We cannot really understand festive release or the morality of indulgence until we remove these categories from the realm of abstraction as pure movement or process, place them within social categories, and see that they emerge from the play so as to allow the aristocracy to achieve social consolidation. In other words, we must redefine the moral process as a ruling-class ideology. Each character in *Twelfth Night* embodies a particular individual action – retreat, disguise, aspiration – taken within an hierarchic society. These actions, separate strategies for achieving or asserting identity, when taken together dramatise the social conditions and consequences that circumscribe each individual action. *Twelfth Night*, as a unified action, distinguishes the strategies from one another, the luxury of aristocratic retreat from the catastrophe of a servant's aspirations. Those who talk about movement, process, strategy, sympathy, or essential action outside of the social distinctions that the play maintains censor the ideological aspect of the play. In fact, the social distinctions do not form incidental aspects of a fairy tale romance; they are essential to the plot and theme of *Twelfth Night*. One aristocratic protagonist, after all, becomes a servant, and the difference between her experiences and assumptions as aristocrat and those imposed upon her as servant exposes the problem of social stratification and demonstrates the interdependence of retreat and social station.

'ONE SELF KING' *The Aristocrats*

The second world in *Twelfth Night* does not correspond to a dimension in space; the protagonists retreat inward. While geographically remaining within the primary-world territory, the protagonists retreat from the everyday demands of time, from the restrictions that the primary world imposes on consciousness. The second world in *Twelfth Night* thus appears as less of a physical or spatial fact, more of a private enterprise, an accomplished attitude. In *Twelfth Night* the *self* becomes the second world, as the protagonists replace community with privacy, society with individuality.

In accordance with its emphasis on the privacy of retreat, *Twelfth Night* contains, in fact, three separate retreats from time, three separately created second worlds: Sir Toby's, Olivia's, and Orsino's. Sir Toby, in his retreat, enacts extreme opposition to decorum and to care: 'I am sure care's an enemy to life' are nearly his first words

(I.iii.2–3), and he maintains that attitude throughout the play – "I care not; give me faith say I" (I.v.128–9). Sir Toby's faith obviates the need for him to perform, in the secular sense, works. His faith – that goes with belonging (to Olivia's family and therefore household) as Barber says – obverts care, or social responsibility. Through care one relinquishes privacy, one acknowledges the presence of others in the world. Care, which holds together a community in a system of mutual attention and shared responsibility, is *not* an enemy to life. But Sir Toby's opposition to care in effect isolates him from others, frees him from order ('I'll confine myself no finer than I am', I.iii.10–11) and from time ('We did keep time, sir, in our catches', II.iii.93) but also from consequence and from activity:

> Sir Andrew   Shall we [set] about some revels?
> Sir Toby   What shall we do else? were we not born under Taurus?
> (I.iii.135–8)

Although Sir Toby 'belongs' within the social order, he has no permanent, everyday responsibility for the maintenance of that order. Through his freedom from time and responsibility Sir Toby attempts to extend his ego-boundaries so as to convert into a social norm his permanent condition of irresponsibility. Sir Toby, therefore, as part of the narcissistic process that creates the second world, replaces external objects with his own ego, or, inversely, incorporates and consumes all those in his presence: he forces everyone to care for him while using the enforced incompetence of drunkenness and the willed oblivion of time in order to protect himself from the possibility of caring for others. Sir Toby's freedom from time does not, in short, replace permanent everyday responsibility with the temporary holiday celebration of good fellowship; rather, Sir Toby's holiday depends on *his* permanent freedom from responsibility. He uses the mechanisms of revelry and celebration so as to create a private and fundamentally selfish holiday world.

Olivia retreats from community, from the everyday world, by enforcing a separation between time and society. She imprisons time inside her doors, behind which:

> ... like a cloistress she will veiled walk,
> And water once a day her chamber round
> With eye-offending brine.
> (I.i.27–9)

Olivia makes time meaningless to her life by converting time into pure measurement; she uses time so as to keep her ritual actions – once a day, for seven years – regularly and evenly separated. Olivia's time, therefore, creates stasis and, rather than marking change and transformation, as Feste's song indicates that it does –

> What's to come is still unsure.
> In delay there lies no plenty,
> Then come kiss me sweet and twenty;
> Youth's a stuff will not endure
>   (II.iii.49–52)

– time for Olivia measures similarity and repetition. Her ritual mourning does not acknowledge death, but, by making the future entirely predictable and controlled, her mourning protects against loss and decay, refuses to mourn. Olivia perverts rather than rejects the communality of care by directing it toward one no longer in the world, reserving care for her 'brother's dead love, which she would keep fresh /And lasting in her sad remembrance' (I.i.30–1). Olivia's private and solipsistic retreat, much more obviously than Sir Toby's, keeps her separate from the needs and desires of others, as her veiled face symbolises.

Perhaps, though, regarding Olivia's veil, the emphasis falls on *will* (she *will* veiled walk), on her intentions. Her love for Cesario breaks her out of the privacy of her retreat – she lifts her veil – and returns her abruptly, against her will, to a community, the world of love and of care, which everyday time controls and dominates. A unique stage direction in Shakespeare's works – '*clock strikes*' (III.i.129) – interrupts Olivia's courtship of Cesario. Hearing the clock, Olivia acknowledges the passage of time and the effect time has on her actions: 'The clock upbraids me with the waste of time' (l.130). When she marries Sebastian, she incorporates a consciousness of time into her pursuit of happiness: 'Blame not this haste of mine. If you mean well. /Now go with me, and with this holy man' (IV.iii.22–3). By the end of the drama Olivia's private second world has dissolved into a world of community, the world of time.

Orsino retreats from the community of the everyday world by imposing his will on his environment. He transforms environment into a series of non-autonomous objects and actions, things arranged for his contemplation and commentary. His familiar opening lines clearly indicate this:

If music be the food of love, play on,
Give me excess of it; that surfeiting,
The appetite may sicken, and so die.
That strain again, it had a dying fall;
O, it came o'er my ear like the sweet sound
That breathes upon a bank of violets,
Stealing and giving odour. Enough, no more,
'Tis not so sweet now as it was before.
(I.i.1–8)

His own contemplations and comments take precedence over the
independent, temporal flow of the music: *Twelfth Night* does not
open with music but with a precise, detailed analysis of Orsino's
subjective reaction to music, with the projection of Orsino's consciousness. In effect, the Duke converts the objective time that the
laws of aesthetic harmony and composition control into the
'shapes' of his own 'fancy' (l.14). With the same process of conversion through imposition of will Orsino forces the words and
actions of all those in his environment to serve his private, subjective needs. Everything in Orsino's environment – Curio's
straightforward language (l.16), Olivia's straightforward rejection,
the 'sweet beds of flow'rs' (l.39), Viola's devout attendance, Feste's
'old and antique song' (II.iv.3) – loses its autonomy and becomes an
adjunct of and accompaniment to the Duke's psychological condition, his emotions. Each time the Duke confronts the world he
deprives others of their autonomy, superimposes consciousness of
his subjective needs on the experiences and needs of others. As a
consequence, Orsino attends to his own feelings while he overlooks
the feelings others show toward him: Olivia rejects him, Feste
mocks him, his page loves him.

Orsino's ability to deprive others of their autonomy converts
people into objects and, as a phase within a narcissistic process, it
does more: it transforms the objects into aspects of Orsino's subjectivity. By making himself the only subject in the world, Orsino
has both withdrawn from and circumscribed the world: he has
withdrawn his ego from the world but, by depriving others of their
autonomy, he has then drawn the world *into* his ego. The
behaviour of others in the world thereby appears to be not
autonomous action taken by other people but manifestations of
Orsino's own subjective feelings. Withdrawing from the world, he
has increased his power to control, or to feel in control of, the
world.

Each of the three private, inward retreats of *Twelfth Night* extends and expands the protagonist's ego, not by projecting the self into nature but by making the world smaller than, or an aspect of, the self. In each of the second worlds in *Twelfth Night* the protagonist – Sir Toby, Olivia, Orsino – diminishes the time, conditions, and people in the primary world so that the desires and emotions of the self can predominate in, or over, the world. The second worlds of *Twelfth Night* – separate and distinct from one another – each replace the multiplicity of community with 'one self king'.

'TO HIS IMAGE ... DID I DEVOTION' *The Ideal Servants*

Viola's entry into Illyria suggests that she, too, will engage in some form of second-world retreat: her personality seems to depend on her ability to master adversity, to control her environment through language, gesture, and disguise. As Barber describes Viola's initial function in the plot:

> The shipwreck is made the occasion for Viola to exhibit an undaunted, aristocratic mastery of adversity – she settles what she will do next almost as though picking out a costume for a masquerade ... What matters is not the event, but what the language says as gesture, the aristocratic, free-and-easy way she settles what she will do next and what the captain will do to help her.
>
> (pp. 241–2)

Barber, as usual, is more accurate than he realises: emphasise the word *aristocratic*, and the class aspect of Viola's 'mastery' becomes immediately apparent. When she first appears, her relation to her environment parallels that of Orsino to his; she treats the world and the people in it as objects available for her to use. As she 'settles' what the captain will do to help her – 'I'll serve this duke;/Thou shalt present me as an eunuch to him' (I.ii.55–6) – she denies, in a subtle way, the captain's autonomy, the possibility of an opposition of wills, the possibility that the captain may be unwilling or unable to help her.

Of course more than just language and gesture allows Viola to decide the 'form' of her 'intent' (l.55). She accompanies her calm distribution imperatives by a distribution of money: 'For saying so, there's gold' (l.18); 'I prithee (and I'll pay thee bounteously)' (l.52). In this respect Viola acts much as did Rosalind when entering Arden: she uses the distribution of gold, or of the aristocratic mastery of language that bespeaks gold, to buy the good will of those whom she meets and to purchase stature within a pre-existent, functioning community. Viola, also like Rosalind, has an enthusiastic, playful regard for disguise. She has no particular motive for disguising herself either as a man or as a eunuch, but by adopting disguise she can transform the natural world, whose forces have deprived her of identity and nearly of life, into a playground. Through disguise she plans to transform the objective social conditions that she will find in Illyria into aspects of her consciousness, into subjective qualities, props for the game that she hopes to initiate and control.

In order to control and to treat the environment as an aspect of one's own consciousness, to make of the world a second world, one must maintain sufficient social stature within the primary world. Here we see one of the central distinctions between Rosalind's actions in Arden [in *As You Like It*] and Viola's in Illyria: the two protagonists assume different roles in their plays not because of their different temperaments and personalities (Viola's greater deference and timidity, for example), but their personalities appear to differ because of the different social roles that they adopt, or that their disguises force on them. Rosalind uses her disguise to increase her autonomy; she escapes from the tyrannous persecution by Duke Frederick as she becomes a master, a landowner who hires labour. Viola, however, in adopting her disguise, assumes a subservient position within a functioning society; without at first knowing it, she becomes part of the objectified landscape of Orsino's court. Viola, as a consequence, experiences a gradual and frightening loss of control; her language remains, as Orsino says, 'masterly' (II.iv.22), but never at any subsequent point in the play can she exert the same authority that she did initially over the captain. We can, in fact, chart a course to mark the disintegrating authority and the increasing subservience and dependence that Viola undergoes during the play as we observe her language change from the calm, assured imperatives of the first act:

> Conceal me what I am, and be my aid
> For such disguise as haply shall become
> The form of my intent. I'll serve this duke;
> ...

> What else may hap, to time I will commit,
> Only shape thou thy silence to my wit,
> (I.ii.53–5, 60–1)

to the apostrophes she can utter only in solioquy by Act II:

> Disguise, I see thou art a wickedness
> Wherein the pregnant enemy does much.
> ...
> O time, thou must untangle this, not I,
> It is too hard a knot for me t'untie,
> (II.ii.27–8, 40–1)

to the prayer that, no longer able either to command others or to control her own stage-space, she must utter as an aside:

> Pray God defend me! A little thing would make me tell them how
> much I lack of a man.
> (III.iv.302–3)

Viola's second-world strategy disintegrates as she becomes treated, with increasing humiliation and danger, as an object within the second worlds of Orsino, Olivia, and Sir Toby. Because she disguises herself as a servant, she assumes a 'barful' (I.iv.41) rather than a liberating role; like the other servants in the comedies, Viola – or, Cesario, rather – makes possible the continued liberty of the aristocrats while relinquishing her/his own autonomy.

Whereas Rosalind moves throughout *As You Like It* toward a point of complete, almost mystical control, Viola moves throughout *Twelfth Night* toward a point of complete danger, coincident with her increasing objectification in the role of servant. The final point in Viola's objectification as a servant occurs when Orsino threatens to kill her to 'spite' Olivia:

> But this your minion, whom I know you love,
> And whom, by heaven I swear, I tender dearly,
> Him will I tear out of that cruel eye,
> Where he sits crowned in his master's spite.
> Come, boy, with me, my thoughts are ripe in mischief.
> I'll sacrifice the lamb that I do love,
> To spite a raven's heart within a dove.
> (V.i.125–31)

Here Viola's initial, partially autonomous, role as mediator between Orsino and Olivia dissolves as Orsino incorporates her within his narcissistic fancy: the value of the servant's life has become incidental to the significance of Orsino's courtship and rejection. What's more, Viola responds to Orsino's whim with total acquiescence; she relinquishes her autonomy by placing her life at the absolute disposal of her master:

> And I most jocund, apt, and willingly,
> To do you rest, a thousand deaths would die.
>   (V.i.132–3)

Viola, who earlier had shown her aversion from physical combat – 'I am one that had rather go with sir priest than sir knight. I care not who knows so much of my mettle' (III.iv.270–2) – now most willingly participates in violent attack as the object or recipient of the violence. The passive attitude before Orsino's threatened violence that Viola adopts indicates several things about the position and the awareness Viola has achieved by this point in the play. Through her willingness to receive Orsino's violence in contrast with her fear of Sir Andrew's, Viola can of course declare aloud her love for Orsino, both through the sexual implications of 'die' and through her adorational response to Olivia's question:

> Where goes Cesario?
>   After him I love
> More than I love these eyes, more than my life,
> More by all mores than e'er I shall love wife.
>   (V.i.134–5)

But Viola's declaration of love, with the risk the declaration entails for her, raises several obvious problems. For one thing, what can she gain by such a declaration if in fact she is about to be sacrificed, to become an absolute object to be used and discarded by Orsino in his courtship of Olivia? Further, Viola gradually has realised the limitations her disguise and her subservient social role have imposed on her, has seen the authority with which she commanded the sea captain dissolve into her dependence on the good graces of such unreliable intermediaries as Sir Toby and the, to her, bewildering Antonio. Why should she be willing suddenly to give up all her former autonomy, to place herself completely at the mercy of people and forces beyond her control? One possible, but I think only partial, answer to these questions is that Viola knows that she only *appears* to be giving up her autonomy, that she acquiesces only as a rhetorical gesture, as her last act of submission in the role of servant before she has her aristocratic stature, in effect, thrust back upon her. Because she evidently has had a glimpse, through Antonio's mistakings, of the surprise ending of the play –

> Prove true, imagination, O, prove true,
> That I, dear brother, be now ta'en for you!
> (III.iv.375–6)

and:

> He nam'd Sebastian
> …
> O, if it prove,
> Tempests are kind and salt waves fresh in love,
> (III.iv.379–84)

– she knows that soon her brother will appear and that she will once again become Viola, an aristocratic woman. Consequently, at last aware that she soon will be freed from disguise, that the liberty of masking has not become a permanent state, hence no longer a liberty, she can transform her dependent condition into a freedom, she can declare as a page some of the amorous and erotic feelings that, as a woman and an aristocrat, it would be indecorous for her to utter.

Carried further, however, Viola's expression of her love for Orsino and of the complete objectification and, ultimately, annihilation that she appears or pretends to be willing to undergo to 'do' him 'rest' indicates what she and, more important, he assume to be the normative attitude of a servant toward his master. Viola knows that her submission to Orsino declares her love for a social equal, but, significantly, she makes her declaration while posing as a perfect servant, a complete subordinate. Viola's submission to Orsino's mischief is set against not the moral norm that one should not kill one person so as to spite another, but that one aristocrat has no proprietary right over the life of another. Olivia asks 'Cesario' to escape Orsino's objectification by announcing 'his' newly acquired stature:

> Alas, it is the baseness of thy fear
> That makes thee strangle thy propriety.
> Fear not, Cesario, take thy fortunes up,
> Be that thou know'st thou art, and then thou art
> As great as that thou fear'st.
> (V.i.146–50)

The accepted convention seems to be that one escapes from complete, sacrificial subservience only by elevation in stature, by declaring anew or revealing a true identity, not by asserting independence and autonomy from the master.

This brief exchange enacts the aristocratic fantasy of the condition of the ideal servant, as created from within the play by the characters: an aristocrat, albeit with ulterior motives, enacts the servant's willing submission. Viola uses the aristocratic fantasy of what an ideal servant would do for his master and would think of his master so as to demonstrate and declare the love she feels, as a social equal, for Orsino. Viola can use submission to declare her love in part because she knows that her page's disguise no longer imprisons her, but largely because she has never relinquished her class-bound perception of the servant's role and function. Viola fails to realise the vulnerability of the ideal servant: she acts in part out of the illusion that her perfect service to her master will make her more desirable, more a subject suitable for his love. She does not realise that the ideal servant in fact becomes more and more of an object, part of the environment or landscape, a natural resource there to be used, less and less of a person with his or her own autonomous feelings. The strategy of ideal service is the least likely way for Viola to win Orsino's love; if played out to the full, the strategy would have forced the master to murder the servant. Only because Viola can emerge from the assumed role of ideal servant does she escape the fatal consequences that her submission to Orsino would have brought down upon her, or, rather, upon 'Cesario'.

Antonio's relation to Sebastian parallels Viola/Cesario's to Orsino. Antonio alone in the play embodies the aristocratic fantasy of complete devotion to a master. Antonio gives up whatever stature he may have had – he at one time captained a ship, and, as Orsino admits, won 'fame and honour' doing so (V.i.59) – in order to serve Sebastian. Antonio speaks of his relation to Sebastian as something that has transcended his own will:

> I could not stay behind you. My desire
> (More sharp than filed steel) did spur me forth,
> (III.iii.4–5)

and as adoration, complete subjection before Sebastian's mastery:

> If you will not murther me for my love, let me be your servant;
> (II.i.35–6)

... to his image, which methought did promise
Most venerable worth, did I devotion;
(III.iv.362–3)

His life I gave him, and did thereto add
My love, without retention or restraint,
All his in dedication.
(V.i.80–2)

Further, Antonio, although aware of Sebastian's stature, loves
Sebastian without hope of financial gain or advancement:

My kind Antonio,
I can no other answer make but thanks,
And thanks; and ever oft good turns
Are shuffled off with such uncurrent pay.
(III.iii.13–16)

In fact, much like the *locus classicus* of the ideal servant, Adam in
As You Like It, Antonio gives his own money to his master
(ll.38–47). Unlike Viola, Antonio senses the ideal servant's vulnerability; his language continually refers to violence, enemies, and
danger:

I have many enemies in Orsino's court,
Else would I very shortly see you there.
But come what may, I do adore thee so
That danger shall seem sport, and I will go;
(II.i.45–8)

I do not without danger walk these streets.
(III.iii.25)

The danger that Antonio associates with his service to Sebastian,
however, comes from outside of the master–servant relationship,
from the danger contained within the environment into which his
service will lead him.

When Viola, whom he has mistaken for Sebastian, denies him,
his sense of the danger implicit in the master–servant relationship
suddenly shifts: Antonio comes to feel that the real danger to which
he is subject comes from *within* the master–servant relationship. He
confides to the two officers – 'Let me speak a little. This youth that
you see here /I snatch'd one half out of the jaws of death, ...'
(III.iv.359–60) thereby transforming the representatives of Orsino's
authority, his supposed opponents, into his associates, protectors

against the satanic evil with which he feels his master now opposes
him:

> But O, how vile an idol proves this god!
> Thou hast, Sebastian, done good feature shame.
> In nature there's no blemish but the mind;
> None can be call'd deform'd but the unkind.
> Virtue is beauty, but the beauteous evil
> Are empty trunks o'erflourished by the devil.
>
> (III.iv.365–70)

Antonio later confides similarly to Orsino himself – 'A witchcraft
drew me hither' (V.i.76) – completing the shift of his alliance from
his own master, his private deity, to the forces of social authority
outside the bond of his private, servile adoration.

Antonio, of course, suspects that his master has been incorporated into a position of relative authority within the same social
order that he had hoped they would both oppose. This becomes
even more apparent when Antonio is brought on stage to see Viola,
whom he still takes to be Sebastian, in the company of his enemy,
the Duke; as Jörg Hasler has pointed out, Viola's statement of
recognition – 'Here comes the man, sir, that did rescue me' (V.i.50)
– aggravates Antonio's feeling of rejection rather than creates a
feeling of puzzlement, in that Antonio must assume that 'rescue'
refers to his rescuing Sebastian from the sea, hardly to his intervention in a rather ridiculous street brawl.[4] Consequently, not until
Orsino says that Viola has 'tended upon' him for three months
(l.99) can Antonio begin to suspect an alternate interpretation of his
rejection; only then, for him, does mistaken identity begin to
replace the idea of outright rejection. When Sebastian enters,
Antonio realises, of course, that his master has not rejected him,
but, as many readers have noted, Antonio, like other outsiders in
Shakespeare's comedies, is left out of account in the reunions and
reconciliations that the final scene dramatises. When we think
about it, we sense that Sebastian could not conceivably allow his
faithful servant to be dragged off to prison by his brother-in-law;
Antonio's ending could not possibly be tragic. But the failure of the
last scene to emphasise, even to state, Antonio's restored faith in his
master's benevolence leaves the dramatic and emotional emphasis
that Antonio created stopped at the middle phase – the disillusion-
ment – of his adoration: Antonio's pained recognition of the
vulnerability and expendability of the ideal servant sticks with us.

Antonio's recognition of and response to his objectification reverses Viola's. Viola 'apt and willingly' allows herself to be treated as the object of Orsino's fancy because she knows that her restored aristocratic stature will also restore her subjectivity, hence her safety. Antonio had imagined for himself a microcosmic safety within the boundaries of his master–servant relationship: as Sebastian's servant he willingly braved the dangers of the world. He found, in the role of servant, a kind of second-world retreat, an imaginary replacement of the primary-world hardships with love and with sport:

> But come what may, I do adore thee so
> That danger shall seem sport, and I will go.
>   (II.i.47–8)

He realises, though, that he cannot achieve freedom or autonomy through ideal service to a master: he has a nearly tragic vision of the potential effects, the possibility of complete objectification, implicit in the role of servant. Subjective fulfilment through ideal service to a master is a fantasy imposed from above; when acted out by the servant, the dangerous consequences of ideal service become manifest. Antonio, like Viola, realises that creation of a second world requires either an initial or a maintained class status and autonomy. Viola can play out the complete objectification of the ideal servant just before she has her subjectivity restored, when danger has once more become, for her, a sport. Antonio rages against the sudden realisation that his subjective love for Sebastian has been objectified, that Sebastian 'grew a twenty year removed thing' (l.89) because, for him, the sport of ideal service has suddenly become a real danger.

'MEANS FOR THIS UNCIVIL RULE' *The Servants*

The ideal service exemplified by Viola and Antonio stands at an extreme within the play; the other servants are more concerned with self and occasionally with material reward for service. The other servants do not retreat into a second world bounded by the master–servant relationship, which, as Antonio and Viola's dangers show, obliterates one's self in pure devotion to a master. Rather, they each engage in service either to achieve some end, such as immediate reward or advancement in station, or else they serve without devotion either to self or other but simply to participate in the primary world of time. In fact, the minor characters, those who perform a specific and limited function in the play, refer explicitly to their consciousness of time. For example, the officer who arrests Antonio becomes impatient with Antonio's outburst against Viola/Sebastian:

> What's that to us? The time goes by; away!
>
> (III.iv.364)

Similarly, the priest, called upon to confirm Olivia and Viola/ Sebastian's marriage, adds that since the wedding ceremony:

>   my watch hath told me, toward my grave
> I have travell'd but two hours.
>
> (V.i.162–3)

By emphasising their consciousness of primary-world time, Shakespeare makes these functionaries serve the incidental purpose of emphasising the opposition between their own continued everyday existence and the timeless second worlds that the aristocratic protagonists have created. But another kind of normative service, that in which the servant retains consciousness of his or her own ego needs, more systematically opposes the ideal service of Viola and Antonio.

The most obvious example of this normative service is Feste's, quite obviously service for meed, not for duty. Feste demands and receives material reward from nearly all of the aristocrats in the play: Sir Toby and Sir Andrew (II.iii.31–4), Orsino (II.iv.67–9; V.i.27–49), Viola (III.i.43–53), and Sebastian (IV.i.19). Only Olivia is omitted, and I think that we must assume, despite Feste's claim to have his own house (III.i.5–7), that Feste is a regular dependent in Olivia's household: at least Maria's warning to Feste about Olivia's anger at his absence (I.v.1–30) and Viola's association of Feste with 'the Lady Olivia's father' (II.iv.11–12), as well as Feste's oblique admission that he 'belongs' to Olivia (V.i.8–9) suggest such a dependence. Feste's nearly obsessive concern with payment for services forms an obvious and absolute contrast with Viola's attitude toward material compensation; when Olivia offers to pay Viola for delivering Orsino's message, Viola responds abruptly:

> I am no fee'd post, lady; keep your purse;
> My master, not myself, lacks recompense.
>
> (I.v.284–5)

Olivia's reaction, in effect, inverts Viola's disregard for material reward and her subordination of herself within the boundaries of the ideal master–servant relationship; Olivia recognises an essentially aristocratic quality in Viola's contempt for material payment. After Viola departs, Olivia recalls in soliloquy her asking Viola about her parentage. Something that occurred between the original question (ll.277–9) and Viola's departure (l.288) – it can only be Viola's refusal of payment – has confirmed for Olivia the truth of Viola's response:

> Olivia 'What is your parentage?'
> 'Above my fortunes, yet my state is well:
> I am a gentleman.' I'll be sworn thou art.
> (I.v.289–91)

In fact, Viola's faith in the immutability of her class status and her residual belief that she can remain above material concerns allow her to adopt the aristocratic attitude toward service and toward payment; Olivia recognises that only an aristocratic personality could formulate an attitude of such subservience, and she responds to the aristocratic foundation of Viola's personality rather than to the subservient actions by which Viola's true class status, paradoxically, manifests itself.

Feste's dependence on material payment corresponds to his total indifference to the source of the payment. Feste roams from Olivia's household to Orsino's and shows no allegiance to any one master that could not, apparently, be bought by another, as, for example, Orsino pays Feste to defy Olivia's commands and bring Olivia out to speak with him (V.i.41–4). Because Feste performs for an audience as a professional, he does not depend on the master–servant bondage; as many have noted, and as Feste's concluding song emphasises, his role within the play recalls Shakespeare's role *vis-à-vis* the audience. But we should not make too much of Feste's independence. Although free of a patron, he depends on patronage, and he has hardly achieved anything like the independence of the journeyman wage labourer. In fact, rather than indicating the modern or bourgeois spirit, Feste's independence, his desire for continued material reward, for the purchase of his services, merely shows the other side of his faith both in the rigid social hierarchy and in his fixed place within the social system. His service occurs without flattery and hence without aspiration: although independent of a particular master, Feste cannot imagine himself as independent of his social role as fool, jester, clown, or buffoon. Feste exhibits self-effacement rather than personal vanity, *except* in so far as he identifies his self with his social role; he quickly comes to the defence of fools (I.v.97–8), and his grudge against Malvolio develops largely because of Malvolio's attack on the institution of 'these set kind of fools' (ll.83–9; cf. V.i.370–7).

Feste's version of independence, therefore, differs from bourgeois independence such as Shylock's [in *The Merchant of Venice*], in which one's stature depends only on one's wealth, as well as from what might be called renaissance independence in which, as Enid Welsford has written, 'self-expression rather than fulfilment of vocation' was the 'proper aim for the individual'.[5] Feste expresses his independence as the complete negation of self within the vocation, the social position; Feste is enclosed within the medieval hierarchies as much as Sir Toby, who, according to Barber, 'lives at his ease, enjoying heritage, the something-for-nothing which this play celebrates' (p. 250). Feste's attitude and Sir Toby's differ only in that Sir Toby's vocation – 'gentlemanly liberty incarnate' – guarantees him something for nothing, allows and encourages his absorption in self, whereas Feste's vocation guarantees nothing and requires his continued subordination of self to the needs and whims of others.

The other servants in the play – Maria, Valentine, and Curio (I do not quite know how or where to place Fabian) – also subordinate themselves to the needs of their social superiors, but through flattery and imitation rather than, as with Feste, through diversion. In the first scene of the play Valentine and Curio exist primarily in order to give the very echo to Orsino's extravagant use of language. Curio supplies the vehicle –

> Will you go hunt, my lord?
> What, Curio?
> The hart.
> Why, so I do, the noblest that I have
> (I.i.16–17)

– that Orsino's poetic licence operates; Valentine outdoes Orsino in his complex application of metaphoric language:

> ... like a cloistress she will veiled walk,
> And water once a day her chamber round
> With eye-offending brine; all this to season

A brother's dead love, which she would keep fresh
And lasting in her sad remembrance.
(I.i.27–31)

Valentine and Curio, like Duke Senior's courtiers in *As You Like It*, perform the function expected of subordinates in the second world by assuring the aristocratic protagonist that his version of retreat is not a solitary madness but is a way of reorganising life and thereby transforming society. They extend Orsino's private second-world retreat out into his environment; by imitating Orsino they dissolve his sense of a boundary between his narcissistic withdrawal and the resistance of the outside world.

Maria has a function similar to Valentine's and Curio's, although she has a more complex dramatic role in that she helps maintain the second-world retreats of two distinct, and in some ways opposed, social superiors: she helps to maintain the quiet and decorum of Olivia's house of mourning while encouraging Sir Toby in his continuous revelry. As the prime mover in the plot against Malvolio – she writes the letter, plants the bait, places the witnesses, prepares Olivia, goads Malvolio, even thinks up Feste's guise as Sir Topas – Maria alone gives shape and direction to Sir Toby's indulgence, which, as Fabian reports at the conclusion, has won her Sir Toby himself:

> Maria writ
> The letter at Sir Toby's great importance,
> In recompense whereof he hath married her.
> (V.i.362–4)

Significantly, despite her continuous encouragement of Sir Toby's revelry, she never, as it were, burns her bridges; not until Malvolio reveals the material evidence of the forged letter does Olivia have any suspicion that Maria has been working at cross-purposes, to dissolve as well as to maintain the ritual decorum of the household. For Maria has been serving Olivia's interests as well as Sir Toby's: Maria warns Sir Toby – twice (I.iii.4–6; II.iii.72–4) – and Feste (I.v.1–4) about offending Olivia. Perhaps aware of the importance Malvolio holds for Olivia (e.g. III.iv.62–3), Maria makes sure that word of her collaboration with Sir Toby does not get back to her mistress. Despite her ambitious role in the plot against Malvolio, Maria never challenges Malvolio to his face, although frequently she taunts him while he is leaving (II.iii.125) or after he has left the stage. Against Maria's involvement in the Malvolio-plot balances her serious concern for the maintenance of order – not, as may be the case with Malvolio, because of any personal predilection for decorum, but because her mistress wants the house to remain sad and civil. Because Maria does not care about the principle of decorum, she only wants Sir Toby to 'confine' himself (I.iii.8–9) and Feste to excuse his transgressions 'wisely' (I.v.30); she worries that the revelry she encourages might interfere with the illusion of decorum that she helps Olivia maintain. As a result, Maria encourages a particular *kind* of revelry: she transforms Sir Toby's drunken carousals and midnight catches into a sport that requires silent observation and, for the most part, non-interference. She manages to confine Sir Toby, to bring about the peace and quiet that she several times implores (e.g. II.iii.85, 103; III.iv.134) by diverting him to a game that must be played, as Fabian says, with 'peace, peace, peace' (II.v.51,57), 'no way but gentleness, gently, gently' (III.iv.110).

Maria facilitates both Sir Toby's and Olivia's second-world retreats, and in such a way as to encourage the coexistence of the two, despite their opposite natures. She supplies the echo to both of her masters, and assures both that others share their self-indulgent, timeless vision of the world, that the second world extends beyond the boundaries of their own egos. Her performance of this function, however, differs from Viola's and Antonio's ideal service and from Feste's professional service: she does not obliterate her own ego within her vocation or her servile capacity; rather, she uses service as a means of aspiration, for transcendence of service. Her service to Sir Toby proves the point, in that Sir Toby marries her with no other dowry but the jest against Malvolio (cf. II.v.182–5). Her service to Olivia may also be a strategy for social aspiration, which the undercurrent of competition for favour among all of the servants in *Twelfth Night* suggests exists within each household. We see elements of this competitive aspiration among servants, for example, when Valentine discusses Orsino's attitude toward Viola / Cesario:

> If the Duke continue these favors towards you, Cesario, you are like to be much advanc'd; he hath known you but three days, and already you are no stranger.
> **Viola**   You either fear his humour or my negligence, that you call in question the continuance of his love.
>
>   (I.iv.1–6)

Valentine expresses, clearly if subtly, the awareness of stature, the importance of remaining in favour, and the uncertainty introduced to the household by the arrival of a new servant.[6] Viola's statement seems to respond to some threatening or foreboding element contained within the tone of Valentine's seemingly off-handed statement; or else, perhaps, Viola herself introduces the topic of inconstancy, indicating the natural concern a new servant would have with the constancy of the master's favours. Maria may well know of a similar potential inconstancy in Olivia's favours; in fact, Malvolio warns her of such:

> Mistress Mary, if you priz'd my lady's favour at any thing more than contempt, you would not give means for this uncivil rule. She shall know of it, by this hand.
>
> (II.iii.121–4)

This acknowledgement of inconstant favour, and Malvolio's scolding and threatened report, combine to motivate Maria's action against Malvolio: her plot, among other things, humiliates a favoured fellow-servant.

Throughout *Twelfth Night* aspiration inevitably involves displacement. Viola's sudden rise to favour has displaced Valentine and Curio, both in that she assumes Valentine's function as Orsino's ambassador and in that Orsino literally removes Valentine and Curio from his environment to place Viola there alone:

> Orsino Who saw Cesario, ho?
> Viola On your attendance, my lord, here.
> Orsino Stand you awhile aloof. Cesario,
>   Thou know'st no less but all;
>
>   (I.iv.10–13)
>
> Orsino Let all the rest give place. [*Curio and Attendants retire.*]
>   Once more, Cesario ...
>
>   (II.iv.79)

Viola accomplishes this displacement involuntarily: her aristocratic nature draws her to the Duke's aristocratic bias. Because of her innate gentility, her imitation and extension of Orsino's language and mood is natural rather than acquired; she achieves her privileged position within Orsino's household because he recognises elements of himself in Viola: 'thou dost speak masterly' (II.iv.22), that is, like a master, he remarks. Maria, too, imitates her mistress, right down to their handwriting, which no one – but Olivia herself (V.i.345–7) – can tell apart. She achieves the temporary displacement of her rival Malvolio by encouraging him to imitate a false Olivia, the love-sick Olivia created by the forged letter. By the time Malvolio is restored to his place in Olivia's favour, Maria has been freed from the consequences of duplicity toward her mistress, having married into Olivia's family.

The sense of aspiration, either to greater favour or to a higher rank, manifested by Valentine and by Maria, contradicts Feste's medieval immersion in his vocation. Maria, especially, suggests the rudiments of the bourgeois belief in reward for individual merit and accomplishment. Through her service to Sir Toby she transcends service, rises to a higher social position. Her vocation allows her to express and to fulfil herself; this sense of self as an entity apart from service and apart from the bondage of service to one particular master suggests the initial phase of the development of the bourgeois consciousness, of the ideology of individual reward and opportunity. Maria is hardly a proto-bourgeoise, in that her aspiration supports and confirms rather than challenges the continued validity of aristocratic privilege, but with her abilities to separate self from vocation, to express self apart from imposed duty, and to earn by her actions advancement in social degree, only Maria in *Twelfth Night* indicates the bourgeois and Puritan emphasis on independence, competition, and the association of stature with merit.[7]

'TO BE COUNT MALVOLIO'

My use of the word *only* in the preceding sentence must have brought many readers up short. Surely, according to most readers of *Twelfth Night* Malvolio represents the spirit of bourgeois independence. Although few would argue that through Malvolio Shakespeare satirically portrays a Puritan, most accept that Malvolio embodies the modern emphasis on economy, that, as Oscar James Campbell has written, Malvolio is 'an enemy to the time-honoured English hospitality and liberality because of the strain it puts upon his lady's purse'.[8] To an extent, Malvolio seems a representative 'modern', partially because he resists the traditional hospitality of the English great house that supports such aristocratic ne'er-do-wells as Sir Toby and Sir Andrew, more so because, in direct contrast with Feste, Malvolio finds his vocation to be a humiliation and, he hopes, a temporary restriction. 'Art any more than a steward?' (II.iii.114), Sir Toby taunts him; and I suppose that Malvolio probably thinks to himself – 'Yes; I am Malvolio'. His sense that he is not bound to his vocation or to his degree, but that he has some form of personal autonomy that can be recognised and rewarded by society anticipates the modern separation of self from vocation.

But Malvolio expresses aspiration quite differently from Maria. Maria works so as to maintain the two second-world environments, the willed freedoms from time, established separately by Sir Toby and by Olivia. Maria's aspiration grows out of and depends upon the quality of the work that she performs; she rises in class as a reward for her service. Malvolio's aspiration – 'To be Count Malvolio!' (II.v.35) – does not depend on the work that he performs; he thinks of aspiration as a sudden elevation, a jump in class status that will occur because of the intervention of fortune (l.23) or of 'Jove and my stars' (l.172). Malvolio, that is, has the fantasy that he will jump class not as a result of the actions within the everyday world of time that he is ordered to perform but through the transformation of the everyday world into a world of wish-fulfilment, of projected desire. The yellow stockings that he is asked to wear will not, he feels, win Olivia; they will merely seal the contract that Fortune has drawn up. His sense of aspiration, and concomitantly of his own self-worth, is a second-world fantasy, an attempt to transform the world of time and space into a leisured world structured around a personal whim, to replace environment with ego. In this regard, Malvolio absolutely opposes the ideal service embodied by Viola and Antonio: the ideal servant is vulnerable because treated like an object by the master; the aspiring servant – what might be called the subjective or the self-conscious servant – is vulnerable because he adopts aristocratic methods, the aristocratic attitude toward the material world, without the implicit protection from the hardships of the world guaranteed by aristocratic status.

Ultimately, there is no fundamental difference between Malvolio's fantasy of narcissistic withdrawal into a world in which he can be Count Malvolio, sitting in state, 'having come from a day-bed' (ll.45, 48) and Orsino's narcissistic withdrawal into the Petrarchan conventions and the beds of flowers. The two second-world fantasies differ only in the social reaction and response that they elicit. Those near Orsino confirm his withdrawal from time:

they echo his language and thereby subordinate the world and their autonomy in the world to the Duke's ego, they assure Orsino that he is neither solitary nor mad. The social reaction to Malvolio's second world is just the opposite: others cut Malvolio off from the world, imprison him in darkness; they disconfirm his sense perceptions and accuse him of being mad. Certainly, madness pervades the play, but whereas Sir Toby and Orsino use madness as an indulgence, and Sebastian and Olivia find their wishes fulfilled in their madness, only Malvolio confronts madness as a restriction and a limitation.

Malvolio's imprisonment marks the limit that class status imposes on the 'morality of indulgence'. The fantasy that leads to Malvolio's imprisonment – his love for Olivia and his vision of himself as a Count – is not in the abstract ridiculous or perverse. Only when we apply the ruling-class assumptions about degree and decorum does it seem that Malvolio is sick of self-love, whereas Orsino and Olivia seem to engage in healthy, therapeutic folly and deceit. Nothing in the play supports Hollander's statement that Malvolio 'alone is not possessed of a craving directed outward, towards some object on which it can surfeit and die; he alone cannot morally benefit from a period of self-indulgence' (p. 233). Such a statement merely represents the critic's wholehearted adoption of the aristocratic attitude toward an indulgence manifested by someone of inferior stature. Orsino, Olivia, and Sir Toby behave just as egocentrically as does Malvolio, and Malvolio, like them, directs his indulgence outward in order to gratify his ego and to expand his ego-centred world. But, Hollander argues, aristocratic indulgence is moral or, as others have said, an 'education in matters of love',[9] whereas Malvolio's indulgence is perverse (Hollander), a parody (Jenkins), an extreme (Phialas), a violation of decorum and of the social order (Barber).

A ruling-class ideology operates within the play and prevents Malvolio from creating his own antithetic second world. The second world that Malvolio tries to create, however, is not antithetic to that ideology, for Malvolio accepts and supports the aristocratic assumptions about the need for respect, decorum, and propriety. The charge against Sir Toby – 'Is there no respect of place, persons, nor time in you?' (II.iii.91–2) – is retained, emphatically, in Malvolio's fantasy: 'telling them I know my place as I would they should do theirs' (II.v.53–4). It is quite wrong to see Malvolio's fantasy as egalitarian or as a bourgeois opposition to aristocratic norms. Malvolio attends scrupulously to each aspect of aristocratic behaviour, and in fact part of what he would hope to accomplish as Count Malvolio would be the 'amendment' of Sir Toby's behaviour, the restoration of Olivia's family to normality and decorum. Barber wrongly says that Malvolio has a 'secret wish ... to violate decorum himself' (p. 255). Rather, hoping to achieve the stature into which he was not born, Malvolio (perhaps, surprisingly, like Othello) profoundly respects the superficial accoutrements of rank, the display of decorum. Before he discovers Maria's forged letter Malvolio violates decorum only in that, while still a steward, he indulges aloud in his fantasies of aspiration. The enactment of fantasy must remain the aristocratic prerogative.

There is nothing tragic about Malvolio. The way his aspiration develops and is placed within the drama makes him, in fact, comic in the most elementary – the Bergsonian – sense of the word: he is a complex, dignified man who suddenly is reduced to a mechanism, an object. This reduction occurs when and because his private, second-world fantasy is drawn from him, brought from the world of ideas and mental abstractions out into the material world of time, actions, and community. The letter that Malvolio stoops to pick up marks, from his point of view, the boundary between these two worlds; his private (if overheard) fantasies take on objective status in the forged letter. The letter seems to Malvolio a licence for an exclusively aristocratic privilege: to transform a private, narcissistic fantasy into public behaviour. His narcissism does become public, enacted in the world, but the letter actually binds rather than licenses him: the letter prescribes Malvolio's actions to a set of imposed restrictions, rather than permits his behaviour to be, in true second-world fashion, modulated only by his changeable, subjective humour. The restrictions – the cross-garters, the enforced smiling, which so obviously go *against* his humour ('Sad, lady? I could be sad. This does make some obstruction in the blood, this cross-gartering, but what of that?' III.iv.20–2) – make him comic, largely because at the very moment at which he feels that he is at last enacting his subjective fantasies, we are aware that, more than ever, he is being manipulated, treated like an object.

When being treated like an object, Malvolio is in effect restored to his place within the social hierarchy. Malvolio's reduction moves in the exact opposite way from Viola's restoration of stature and thereby of autonomy. Viola helps to maintain and to confirm the whims and fantasies of her master, and she does so in part as a

mediated expression of her love for him. Malvolio enacts his own
fantasies, as an *immediate* expression of his love for Olivia.
Temporarily, Viola's willed subordination and Malvolio's willed
aspiration have the same effect: both Viola and Malvolio become
objectified, imprisoned within the role of servant. When her
aristocratic identity is discovered or revealed, however, Viola's
objectification reverses, and Orsino acknowledges her as an equal,
her 'master's mistress' (V.i.326); Viola becomes a subjective par-
ticipant in the social ceremonies of and beyond the conclusion.
Malvolio, however, has his sanity discovered or revealed only to be
confirmed as an object of laughter – 'the most notorious geck and
gull/That e'er invention play'd on' (ll.343–4) – and, for Feste, of
revenge (ll.376–7). The conclusion of *Twelfth Night* contains an
element of the Patient Griselda myth – complete subservience leads
to unexpected elevation – as qualified by the aristocratic face
behind Viola's subordinate mask; essentially, however, the conclusion confirms the aristocratic fantasy (Maria is, discreetly, kept
off-stage) that clarification is achieved when people are released
from indulgence and restored to the degree of greatness with which
they were born.

'ALL IS FORTUNE' *Ideology*

Twelfth Night develops a fundamental distinction between
Malvolio's trust in fortune and Viola's. Both characters, pretty
clearly, attribute their success or their chances for success in love to
a force outside of their own motives and actions. Viola calls this
external, controlling force 'time', but she imagines the abstraction
as something personal, to which or to whom she can speak and
commit herself:

> What else may hap, to time I will commit;
> (I.ii.60)

> O time, thou must untangle this, not I,
> It is too hard a knot for me t' untie.
> (II.ii.40–1)

Malvolio speaks more explicitly theistically in his references and
addresses to the external force to which he commits himself. He
assigns all power over earthly success or failure to 'fortune':

'Tis but fortune, all is fortune;
(II.v.23)

Saying, 'Cousin Toby, my fortunes, having cast me on your niece';
(ll.69–70)

but he associates the relatively abstract force of fortune with quasi-religious mechanisms:

I thank my stars, I am happy ... Jove and my stars be praised!
(ll.170–2)

I have lim'd her, but it is Jove's doing, and Jove make me
thankful! ...
... Well, Jove, not I, is the doer of this, and he is to be thank'd.
(III.iv.74–83)

Among recent critics of *Twelfth Night* there has been more dis-cussion, disagreement, and confusion about the issue of time and fortune and their different effects on Viola and Malvolio than about any other issue in the play. I think that some of the confusion, at least, derives from Julian Markels's article 'Shakespeare's Confluence of Tragedy and Comedy: *Twelfth Night* and *King Lear*'.[10] Markels set up an opposition between fortune and custom, and he argued that the theme of both *Twelfth Night* and *King Lear* is that 'man must stand fast by custom even in the face of Fortune' (p. 88), that the 'central villainy' in both plays is the belief in 'capri-cious fortune' instead of 'stable customs' (p. 81). In order to get to this thesis about villainy and fortune, Markels asserted that Malvolio, like Oswald, Goneril, and Edmund, has faith in 'the rule of capricious fortune instead of stable customs with cosmic sanc-tions' (p. 81), and, further, that Shakespeare everywhere opposes fortune to degree, that when degree is left out of the social order, 'fortune's devotees' (e.g. Richard III, Edmund) can 'get in the door' (p. 81).

In fact, however, neither in *Twelfth Night* nor anywhere else does Shakespeare oppose fortune itself to degree or custom. *As You Like It* initially opposes Fortune to Nature, and the ruling-class ideology within the play works to reconcile and identify the opposing terms so that the extant class structure can appear to be determined and justified by Nature. *Twelfth Night*, however, opposes fortune (as in chance) to human action and accomplishments, and the ruling-class ideology, which Malvolio *supports*, works to keep these opposing terms separated and distinct. By attributing degree and custom, the determinants of class status, to fortune rather than to action, the ideology fixes the social structure: it encourages a passive acceptance of one's social station and attributes the possibility for a rise in station to a force beyond human motive and control.

Some critics realise Markels's error and acknowledge that belief in fortune supports the customary social hierarchy; because most of these critics believe that Malvolio tries to upset the customary social hierarchy, however, each argues that Malvolio either does not believe in fortune or that he does so in the 'wrong' way. Carl Dennis, for example, argues – Malvolio's protestations notwithstanding – that, in contrast with Viola and Sebastian who 'regard fate as a power outside their control', Malvolio believes that merit, not fortune, causes his ascension.[11] B. S. Field, Jr, argues that Malvolio submits himself to fortune in the wrong way: whereas Viola submits to fortune and 'makes no attempt to alter that which is inalterable' and Sebastian has the ' "right" attitude toward the gifts and blows of Fortune' in that he does not consider whether or not he deserves what he has received, Malvolio assumes that fate is on his side, and therefore he misses the essential point of Viola's and Sebastian's stoicism – he thinks he *deserves* the advantages of fortune.[12] Yet Field's assumption that Malvolio believes in his deserts any more than do Viola and Sebastian is pure assertion, based on a backward interpretation of the play and on some tortured syllogisms: because stoicism is good and in *Twelfth Night* all good characters are rewarded, Malvolio, who is not rewarded, is not stoical. Free Field's analysis from his assumption that the conclusion marks a fair distribution of reward and punishment, and it will become clear that Malvolio's actions do not, after all, differ greatly from Viola's; he is more active and more optimistic in pursuit of his fate because he has been given good reason to be so, not because he has the 'wrong' attitude toward fortune.

Viola's, and Sebastian's, faith in fortune is not misplaced, for fortune, more than human action, dominates the conclusion. It is perchance that Viola herself was saved (I.ii.6) and it is more than chance – more like destiny – that she and Sebastian are reunited and that she becomes Orsino's mistress. But the conclusion not only enforces the benevolence of fortune, it also emphasises the restrictions on that benevolence: the conclusion applies fortune as a class-bound concept. Rather than seek fine discriminations between Malvolio's trust in fortune and Viola's, we should note that fortune rewards Viola for her faith and punishes Malvolio for his. In fact, the play concludes not with a sense of harmony and inclusion – the inclusion comprises only the two, perhaps the three, aristocratic couples – but of opposition, with, as Alexander Leggatt notes, the happiness of the lovers and the 'miracle' of Cesario alternating with the 'battered condition' of the clowns and 'played off against the uncontrollable world of time'.[13] Leggatt notices everything about this opposition but its class contents: the rewards of fortune, and of freedom from time, are circumscribed by the ruling class, but fortune is *separated* from Malvolio. Contrary to everything Markels's article asserted about it, fortune in *Twelfth Night* restores degree and decorum to the world of the play.

Several critics have tried to purge fortune of the class-bound qualities that the conclusion enforces. L. G. Salingar, for example, believes that the second half of *Twelfth Night* 'stresses the benevolent irony of fate'. Aware, perhaps, that this irony is benevolent only for some of the characters, that it is malevolent for or indifferent to others, Salingar relies on the familiar critical abstractions – balance and complement – so as to keep the 'design' of the play intact and free of all class-conflict and ideology: Antonio, according to Salingar, is 'outside the main sphere of the comedy', he 'helps keep the comic balance'; the Malvolio sub-plot is 'complementary to the problem of "time" in the main plot'.[14] More recently, F. B. Tromly [14] has argued that *Twelfth Night* shows that 'one can come to terms with life only by accepting the nature of things – delusion, vulnerability, and mortality'. Orsino, Olivia, Viola, and Sebastian do so, he says, and therefore nature draws them to happiness whereas Malvolio is excluded from happiness because of his 'secret desire ... to violate the social order'.[15]

Salingar and Tromly probably consider their interpretations of *Twelfth Night* to be 'neutral'; they certainly acknowledge no ideological basis for their generalisations about benevolence and happiness. But the ideological implications of what they say about *Twelfth Night* are grossly apparent. Fate, or the nature of things, they suggest, is a force outside of and beyond human control; one should respond to fate with passive acceptance. Further, happiness and benevolence consist of a restored social order, which excludes all those who seek to violate decorum (that is, to rise in class), or else of a 'triumph of natural love' for the ruling class, which balances against the defeat and exclusion of those 'outside the main sphere of the comedy' – that is, in the subplot;[16] that is, the servants and subservients. In short, some obvious social implications must accompany the advice to accept fortune, the benevolent irony of fate, or the nature of things; *Twelfth Night* shows that the ruling class benefits by such counsel and that others do not. The ideology is included as a theme *within* the play. *Twelfth Night* does not encourage its audience to accept the vicissitudes of fortune stoically; rather, the play shows that such moral advice serves the interests and fills the needs of a particular social class. Critics who abstract the aristocratic attitude toward fortune from the class contents of *Twelfth Night* and designate the aristocratic attitude as the theme of the whole play avoid recognising an ideology within *Twelfth Night* by adopting the ruling-class ideology as their own.

Which is exactly what Malvolio does *in* the play: he actually threatens the social order much less than he seems to. Just as he has the greatest respect for all of the accoutrements of aristocratic rank, just as he imitates the aristocracy in attempting to devise a second-world fantasy, he also adopts the ruling-class ideology in attributing his success, or his chances for success, to fortune, to Jove and his stars. Joan Hartwig has noted that Malvolio wants to attribute the control of events to Jove because 'as long as events are in the hands of a non-human control, man cannot destroy or divert the pre-determined order'. Hartwig observes that Sebastian is 'manipulated by Fate or by Fortune; Malvolio, by Maria and Feste', but she reduces the importance of her observation by concluding only that 'human manipulators parody supra-human control'.[17] Yet much more than parody operates here. Maria and Feste, acting upon Malvolio, represent the antithesis of chance – human will. By manipulating Malvolio, creating his destiny, they demonstrate the implicit limitation of the ruling-class attitude that 'all is fortune'.

'All is fortune' implies that people relate to nature as passive recipients who accept the 'nature of things', that fortune, primarily but not exclusively through birth, will determine one's place in the social hierarchy. The fantasy assumes that fortune certifies nature, that ultimately fortune and nature are identical. By accepting this fantasy, Malvolio refuses to act except when instructed from above, by what he assumes to be his 'stars', and he thus becomes vulnerable to the actions of those who do act within nature. Just as Malvolio cannot see the manipulations of Maria and, later, Feste, the ruling-class ideology that 'all is fortune', that fortune creates and determines nature, is meant to keep people, especially servants, blind to the opposite proposition: that people create nature as they act within time, as they bring about changes in the social order. The ruling-class ideology in *Twelfth Night* unifies the several aristocratic separate and private retreats into a single second-world strategy; the assertion that 'all is fortune' and that one should submit to the nature of things attempts to fashion an escape from the responsibilities of the world of time. In *Twelfth Night* Shakespeare acknowledges the existence of the impulse toward retreat from time and from nature, but he does not make the impulse a universal 'theme'; rather, he identifies the impulse with the class interests that it serves and he sets the attempt to equate nature with fortune against the everyday world in which people create their own nature and their own fortune, the world of history.

From Elliot Krieger, *A Marxist Study of Shakespeare's Comedies* (London, 1979), pp. 97–130.

NOTES

[Elliot Krieger presents a Marxist account of the play. In some ways his analysis follows in its practice a traditional, close reading of the play, but the overall perspective adopted is one that examines the class biases and differences between characters, seeing the play as controlled by 'ruling class ideology'. This leads Krieger on to redefining the theme of 'liberty' in the play by placing it in the context of material and economic factors, and how the ruling classes use 'fortune' as an evasion of their responsibility while fashioning the world to their advantage. All quotations are from *The Riverside Shakespeare*, ed. G. Blakemore Evans (Houghton Mifflin, 1974). Ed.]

1. C. L. Barber, *Shakespeare's Festive Comedy* (rpt. Cleveland, OH, 1963). [Subsequent page references are given in parentheses in the text. Ed.]

2. J. Hollander, '*Twelfth Night* and the Morality of Indulgence', in *Sewanee Review*, 68, rpt. in Alvin B. Kernan (ed.), *Modern Shakespeare Criticism* (New York, 1970), pp. 228–41. [Subsequent page references are given in parentheses in the text. Ed.]

3. M. P. Tilley, 'The Organic Unity of *Twelfth Night*', *PMLA*, 29 (1914), 550–66, 550–1.

4. J. Hasler, *Shakespeare's Theatrical Notation: The Comedies* (Bern, 1974), p. 161.

5. E. Welsford, *The Fool* (London, 1935), p. 248.

6. The Duke's servants in *Gl'Ingannati*, one of the sources for *Twelfth Night*, detest the newly arrived servant, Lelia, whose part is analogous to Viola's. 'He hath robbed me of my place', one complains, II.vi. See G. Bullough (ed.), *Narrative and Dramatic Sources of Shakespeare*, II (London, 1958), p. 309.

7. The context forces me to be unduly cursory in my discussion of bourgeois and Puritan characteristics. My discussion refers only to the received ideas, in their broad outline, associated with these economic and religious movements. The connection between Puritanism and the bourgeois virtues is discussed in great detail in R. H. Tawney, *Religion and the Rise of Capitalism* (New York, 1926) and Christopher Hill, *Puritanism and Revolution* (London, 1958); *The Century of Revolution* (London, 1961); *Society and Puritanism in Pre-Revolutionary England* (New York, 1964); *Intellectual Origins of the English Revolution* (Oxford, 1975); *Reformation to Industrial Revolution*, The Pelican Economic History of Britain, II (Harmondsworth, 1969); and *The World Turned Upside Down* (1972; rpt. Harmondsworth, 1975).

8. O. J. Campbell, *Shakespeare's Satire* (1943; rpt. Hampden, CT, 1963), p. 87. Campbell's argument that Malvolio represents a threat to the aristocrats because he emphasises that they will have to economise, change their ways, in order to survive as a class, anticipates the work of Lawrence Stone, *The Crisis of the Aristocracy* (Oxford, 1965). Stone of course challenged R. H. Tawney's long-held view that the aristocracy primarily feared displacement by a rising bourgeoisie (see *Religion and the Rise of Capitalism*). J. W. Draper, 'Olivia's Household', *PMLA*, 49 (1934), 797–806, and M. Van Doren, *Shakespeare* (1939; rpt. Garden City, NY, n.d.), applied Tawney's view to *Twelfth Night*, arguing that Malvolio has 'offended' the aristocracy 'as a class' (p. 140).

9. P. G. Phialas, *Shakespeare's Romantic Comedies* (Chapel Hill, NC, 1966), p. 270. See also H. Jenkins, 'Shakespeare's *Twelfth Night*', *Rice Institute Pamphlet*, 45 (1959), rpt. in *Shakespeare: The Comedies*, K. Muir (ed.) (Englewood Cliffs, NJ, 1965), p. 73; L. S. Champion, *The Evolution of Shakespeare's Comedies* (Cambridge, MA, 1970), p. 94; and Theodore Wiess, *The Breath of Clowns and Kings* (New York, 1971), p. 306, all of whom argue that *Twelfth Night* – or, more specifically, Viola – educates Orsino and Olivia.

10. J. Markels, 'Shakespeare's Confluence of Tragedy and Comedy: *Twelfth Night* and *King Lear*', *Shakespeare Quarterly*, 15:2 (1964), 75–88. Subsequent page references are given in parentheses in the text.

11. C. Dennis, 'The Vision of *Twelfth Night*', *Tennessee Studies in Literature*, 18 (1973), 63–74; 70, 72.

12. B. S. Field, Jr, 'Fate, Fortune, and *Twelfth Night*', *Michigan Academician*, 6 (1973), 193–9; 194, 196, 198–9.

13. A. Leggatt, *Shakespeare's Comedy of Love* (London, 1974), pp. 252–3.

14. L. G. Salingar, 'The Design of *Twelfth Night*', *Shakespeare Quarterly*, 10 (1958), 117–39; 128, 131, 132, 133.

15. F. B. Tromly, '*Twelfth Night*: Folly's Talents and the Ethics of Shakespearean Comedy', *Mosaic*, 7: 3 (1974), 53–68; 59, 68, 66.

16. L. Salingar, 'Design', p. 122.

17. Joan Hartwig, 'Feste's "Whirligig" and the Comic Providence of *Twelfth Night*', *ELH*, 40 (1973), 501–13; 506, 510.

3

The Festive Agon: The Politics of Carnival

MICHAEL D. BRISTOL

THEORETICAL PERSPECTIVE

Theatre is an art form; it is also a social institution. By favouring a certain style of representation and a particular etiquette of reception, the institutional setting of a performance informs and focuses the meaning of a dramatic text and facilitates the dissemination of that meaning through the collective activity of the audience.[1] The social and political life of the theatre as a public gathering place has an importance of its own over and above the more exclusively literary interest of texts and the contemplation of their meaning. Because of its capacity to create and sustain a briefly intensified social life, the theatre is festive and political as well as literary – a privileged site for the celebration and critique of the needs and concerns of the *polis*. The critical intensification of collective life represented and experienced in the theatre, and the possibility it creates for action and initiative, is the subject of this text.

The richest material for the elaboration of the argument pursued here is the dramatic literature of Renaissance England and its complex relationship to the traditions of Carnival. For most of its more recent history, theatre has functioned with a diminished capacity to achieve its social and political purpose. In Renaissance England, however, the theatre objectified and recreated broadly dispersed traditions of collective life that were also represented and disseminated through anonymous festive manifestations such as Carnival. The dramatic literature produced by this theatre retains much of the power and the durable vitality of these strong political forms. Unlike the theatre of later periods, that of Elizabethan and Jacobean England is not exclusively or even mainly a specialised institution of literary production and consumption. In this theatre, literature as *objet-d'art* or as ideological finished product is subordinated to more active, though more ephemeral forms of institution-making carried over into theatre from the traditions of popular festive form.

These collective traditions give rise to dramatic forms that are intensely critical and even experimental in their representation of social and political structure. There is, first, a negative critique that demystifies or 'uncrowns' power, its justificatory ideology, and the tendency of elites to undertake disruptive radicalisations of traditional patterns of social order, and to introduce novel forms of domination and expropriation. In addition, there is a positive critique, a celebration and reaffirmation of collective traditions lived out by ordinary people in their ordinary existence. That positive critique, which articulates the capacity of popular culture to resist penetration and control by the power structure, is a central theme of this text.

For the first few decades of its existence, the public playhouse of Elizabethan England was not yet fully differentiated from more dispersed and anonymous forms of festive life, play and mimesis. Theatrical spectacle and the theatricalisation of social and intellectual life were common to virtually all social groups, corporations, and communities in Renaissance England, primarily in informal, amateur organisations. The performance traditions of these homogeneous groups usually emphasised the immediate social purposes of theatre, in particular the enjoyment of corporate or communal solidarity, over the specialised appreciation of durable literary values. Theatre and popular festivity were closely related forms of social life, neighbouring institutions with similar patterns of representation and similar orientations to political and economic practice.

> In the months of June and July, on the vigils of the festival days, and on the same festival days in the evenings after the sun setting, there were usually made bonfires in the streets, every man bestowing wood or labour towards them; the wealthier sort also, before their doors near to the said bonfires, would set out tables on the vigils, furnished with sweet bread and good drink, and on festival days with meats and drinks plentifully, whereunto they would invite their neighbours

and passengers also to sit and be merry with them in great familiarity, praising God for his benefits bestowed on them. These were called bonfires as well of good amity amongst neighbours that being before at controversy, were there, by the labour of others, reconciled, and made of bitter enemies loving friends.[2]

The midsummer watch was a collective celebration, combining spectacle and festive abundance with the social and political functions of the town meeting and the family court. The practice was repeated 'time out of mind'; it took place outside any formal administrative apparatus.

The same functions, according to Stow, have been accomplished through other traditional sports and collective pastimes, and, in his own day, these functions have been extended into the new institution of the public playhouse.

These, or the like exercises, have been continued till our time, namely, in stage plays ... [and] of late time, in place of those stage plays, hath been used comedies, tragedies, interludes, and histories, both true and feigned; for the acting whereof certain public places, as the Theatre, the Curtain, etc. have been erected.[3]

Stow's brief account describes theatre as a continuation of popular festive activity in which the social purpose as well as the playful atmosphere of other popular sports and pastimes are sustained. The public playhouse, then, must be considered a politically significant *mise-en-scène*, where the energy and initiative of collective life are forcefully manifested in texts, in performance convention, and in the reception and appreciation of theatrical spectacle.

Renaissance drama is important in that it invites consideration of forms of collective life and of subjectivity other than those proposed and legitimated by a hegemonic culture. The problem of specifying the relationship among subjectivity, collective life and the structure of formally constituted or 'official' authority is obviously very complicated, and the difficulties are compounded by the accumulated prestige and literary authority of canonical texts by Shakespeare and his contemporaries. The present analysis proceeds against the grain of traditional literary scholarship and also of its more recent, radically critical variants. The problem addressed here is not whether Shakespeare's plays, for example, represent a traditional world picture of some kind, whether Christian humanist or its secular counterpart in the Tudor Myth, or, on the contrary, represent a critical and subversive demystifying of a dominant ideology. The second position is certainly an advance over the first, both in its emphasis on discontinuity and rupture within the Tudor consensus, and in its insistence that the problem of meaning cannot be considered independently of the problem of authority. But the larger issue of authority and its allocation between the centres of political power and exceptional individual subjects, such as Shakespeare, has been, even in the most strongly revisionist critical texts, analysed primarily in light of the image power has of itself as an infinitely resourceful centre of initiative, surveillance and control. The existence of a popular element in the cultural landscape of the period has either been ignored or been treated as yet another instrument of political and cultural domination. But the problem of authority cannot be fully elucidated by focusing exclusively on the relationship between what purports to be a virtual monopoly of significant political power and a few individual centres of avant-garde consciousness uneasily balanced between alternatives of affiliation or critical rejection of the imperatives of a ruling elite.

The problem of 'authors' and of their 'authority' is discussed here not only in the light of their relationship to de jure authority, but also and more centrally in the light of their relationship to a coherent, diverse and energetic popular culture that struggles to retain its own particular and local authority over the ordering of social and economic life. Before proceeding to any detailed analysis of that popular culture, however, it is useful to place the problem in a more fully developed theoretical context. That context has three significant elements. First, there is the problem of the literary text and how it is most effectively situated in relation to the non-literary. Though interpretation of literature is an important element in the discussions that follow,[4] it does not take precedence over other issues, nor is the 'reading of texts' invested with decisive teleological importance. For this reason the perspective developed in the work of Mikhail Bakhtin has been adopted as a primary 'literary' or interpretive strategy. Second, there is the general problem of festivity and ritual form, and its evidently conservative function in sustaining the continuity of social life. That problem has been most powerfully addressed in the sociology of Emile Durkheim, and in recent revisions of his theory in the work of René Girard and Victor Turner. Third, there is the problem of specifying exactly what is meant by popular or plebeian culture, the degree to which that culture retained any degree of independent initiative, and the ability of that culture to articulate and carry out its own partisan agenda in the face of a powerfully organised hegemony. This is recognisably the problem of class struggle, but it is also an aspect of the social 'architecture' proposed by Fernand Braudel, in which the history of the *longue durée* and its embodiment in the diverse patterning of everyday life proceeds in accordance with its own interior rhythms independently of any mobility in the political superstructure.

The project undertaken here is informed by a range of materialist critical traditions. It is also animated by the attitude of materialist 'sadness' described so eloquently by Walter Benjamin in his *Theses on the Philosophy of History*:

> this sadness stands out more clearly if one asks with whom the adherents of historicism actually empathise. The answer is inevitable: with the victor. And all rulers are the heirs of those who conquered before them. Hence, empathy with the victor invariably benefits the rulers. Historical materialists know what that means. Whoever has emerged victorious participates to this day in the triumphal procession in which the present rulers step over those who are lying prostrate. According to traditional practice, the spoils are carried along in the procession. They are called cultural treasures, and a historical materialist views them with cautious detachment. For without exception the cultural treasures he surveys have an origin which he cannot contemplate without horror. They owe their existence not only to the efforts of the great minds and talents who have created them, but also to the anonymous toil of their contemporaries. There is no document of civilisation which is not at the same time a document of barbarism. And just as such a document is not free of barbarism, barbarism taints also the manner in which it was transmitted from one owner to another.[5]

TWELFTH NIGHT

The critical recognition of misrule and Carnival provides an alternative to a political theodicy of the nation-state. Misrule is not a merely negative idea, however, as in Jan Kott's conception of an absurd 'Grand Mechanism'.[6] The rhythmic succession of Carnivalesque uncrowning and renewal, the 'pathos of radical change', is the 'second life' of the people, a form of real politics, an ethos, a 'mode of production' existentially prior to the state and its administrative apparatus. This second life is lived in the public squares and also in the theatre as a public space; it is mimetically represented in the forms of political drama. Bakhtin elaborates this 'second life' in his account of 'the folkloric bases of the Rabelaisian Chronotope', describing it as an alternative experience of time.

> This time is collective, that is, it is differentiated and measured only by the events of *collective* life; everything that exists in this time exists solely for the collective. The progression of events in an individual life has not yet been isolated (the interior time of an individual life does not yet exist, the individuum lives completely on the surface, within a collective whole). Both labour and the consuming of things are collective.
>
> This is the time of labour. Everyday life and consumption are not isolated from the labour and production process. Time is measured by labour events. ... This sense of time works itself out in a collective battle of labour against nature. ...
>
> This is the time of productive growth. It is a time of growth, blossoming, fruit-bearing, ripening, fruitful increase, issue. The passage of time does not destroy or diminish but rather multiplies and increases the quantity of valuable things. ... [The] single items that perish are neither individualised nor isolated; they are lost in the whole growing and multiplying mass of new lives. ...
>
> This time is profoundly spatial and concrete. It is not separated from the earth or from nature. It, as well as the entire life of the human being, is all on the surface.[7]

The culture of common people or plebeians in its political, social, philosophical and artistic manifestations is already everywhere; government and the nation-state as institutional forms are latecomers. Holiday, or holy-day, Carnival and misrule are not isolated episodes in a uniform continuum of regularly scheduled real-life: the experience of holiday pervades the year and defines its rhythm.[8]

The theatre in its 'mature' or 'developed form' is an institution 'invented' by Jonson and by many others to oppose and displace a theatre already practised and appreciated throughout plebeian culture. Jonson, as the exemplary 'institution maker' proceeds by making a series of exclusions, redefining activities characteristic of traditional theatricality as aberrant and marginal. This project is carried out against the background of a very much larger and even more protracted struggle, in which the centralised authority of the state comes into being against social and political life already lived, and by means of traditionally dispersed, collective authority. One of the many engagements in that struggle concerns the local tradition of midsummer watches in London.

This midsummer watch was thus accustomed yearly, time out of mind, until the year 1539, the 31st of Henry VIII, in which year, on the 8th of May, a great muster was made by the citizens of the Mile's End, all in bright harness, with coats of white silk, or cloth and chains of gold, in three great battles, to the number of fifteen thousand. ... King Henry, then considering the great charges of the citizens for the furniture of this unusual muster, forbade the marching watch provided for at Midsummer for that year, which being once laid down was not raised again till the year 1548.[9]

The midsummer watch was, among other things, a procession of armed citizenry organised at the initiative of the common people. It was suppressed once in 1539, and again after the term of office as Lord Mayor of Sir John Gresham, during the reign of Edward VI. The initiative for this practice did not die out entirely, however, and, according to Stow, attempts were made to revive it during Elizabeth's reign. The antiquity and the scope of participation of such a manifestly powerful and independent urban politics could not in the end be compatible with the coalition of interests that support the centralised state, whose representatives find reasons quietly to discourage such activities. But the political life of plebeian culture is not effaced by these tactics; it persists in other popular festive events, in processional life, and in the theatrical performance of dramatic texts where elements of a 'second life' in the pattern of misrule provide the organising scheme for exemplary, mimetic actions. A central instance of this Carnival or popular festive structuration of politically significant narrative is the use of characteristic festive personae and the festive agon or Battle of Carnival and Lent as a narrative scheme governing both comic and serious actions. The festive agon reinterprets political succession, and other transitional procedures, as the double and reciprocal thrashing and expulsion of the Carnivalesque and Lenten tendencies.

The festive agon is fully played out in *Twelfth Night*, as Carnival misrule in the persons of Toby and his companions – the gull, the clown and the mischievous servant – contends with Lent in the person of Malvolio. This is often referred to as the 'comic sub-plot' – a series of episodes that constitute a marginal, non-serious commentary on the main action. The position taken here, however, is that the festive agon *is* the 'main action', continuous with the wider world indicated in the clown's 'return from the outside' and in Malvolio's Parthian shot – 'I'll be revenged on the whole pack of you'. The confrontation between the Carnivalesque and the Lenten principles is represented in the long drinking scene, where Toby, Andrew, Feste and Maria gather to enjoy hospitality with drink, laughter and singing. The scene begins by transgressive rescheduling of the normal order of day and night typical of Carnival and other forms of misrule.

> Sir Toby   Approach, Sir Andrew. Not to be abed after midnight is to be up betimes; and 'diluculo surgere', thou knowst—
> Sir Andrew   Nay by my troth, I know not. But I know to be up late is to be up late.
> Sir Toby   A false conclusion. I hate it as an unfilled can. To be up after midnight, and to go to bed then, is early, so that to go to bed after midnight is to go to bed betimes. Does not our life consist of four elements?
> Sir Andrew   Faith, so they say, but I think it rather consists of eating and drinking.
> Sir Toby   Thou'rt a scholar. Let us therefore eat and drink.
>   (*Twelfth Night*, II.iii.1–14)

This symposium combines bodily satisfaction with philosophical debate and dialogue. The Carnivalesque principle of knowledge operates here, as both crudely material, literal description and ingeniously transgressive redescriptions are equally necessary to an adequate account of 'our life'. The simple-minded, tautological view that 'late is late' is a 'false conclusion' that is none the less compatible with the abusive casuistry that maintains that 'late is early'. The hateful 'unfilled' tautology of the simple-minded Andrew that seems to require habits more abstemious than Toby likes is 'filled up' by the same simple-minded character's view that man's life is 'eating and drinking', rather than the four elements. Harmonisable disagreement and the 'abundance of the material principle' are celebrated in jokes and song until the intervention of Malvolio, whose Lenten severity is mandated by his perfectly cogent understanding of precedence and due order.

> Malvolio   My masters, are you mad? Or what are you? Have you no wit, manners, nor honesty, but to gabble like tinkers at this time of night? Do ye make an alehouse of my lady's house that ye squeak out your coziers catches without any mitigation or remorse of voice. Is there no respect of place, persons, nor time in you?
>   (*Twelfth Night*, II.iii.92–9)

Irrespective of person, place or time, the rejoinder offered by
Carnival is, as always, a celebration of food and drink.

> **Sir Toby** ... Art any more than a steward? Dost thou think because
> thou art virtuous, there shall be no more cakes and ale?
>
> (*Twelfth Night*, II.iii.122–5)

As the festive agon unfolds, this acrimonious feeling gives rise to the
active persecution, humiliation and confinement of Malvolio. But
the pattern of festive agon is not compatible with asymmetrical,
one-sided and conclusive outcomes. The combatants, Carnival and
Lent, each have certain obligations, in particular the obligation to
be thrashed. Toby organises the persecution of Malvolio and then
in a more improvisatory entertainment orchestrates the farcical duel
between Andrew and Viola, the boy-woman. The compensatory
thrashing of Toby is given by Sebastian near the end of the play.
Toby, escorted by the clown, appears briefly to display his bloody
coxcomb and is then escorted to his bed. This brief appearance is
important, as it visibly and materially confirms the fact of Toby's
thrashing and also the importance of that wider world offstage
where significant events that have the potential to upset the plots
and the intentions enacted on the stage continually occur. Malvolio
also has some scores to settle which he will attend to offstage. 'And
thus the whirligig of time brings in his revenges.' The battle of
angry Carnival and sullen, vindictive Lent is not concluded in the
represented world of Illyria, nor is it ever concluded in the world
offstage.

From Michael D. Bristol, *Carnival and Theater: Plebian Culture
and the Structure of Authority in Renaissance England* (New York
and London, 1985), pp. 3–7, 200–4.

NOTES

[Michael Bristol's approach is 'carnivalesque', seeing theatre as a social institution and drama as having social functions. What separates him from
earlier 'cultural anthropologists' like Northrop Frye and C. L. Barber, is his
concentration, shared with the Russian formalist critic Mikhail Bakhtin,
on how a play like *Twelfth Night* can reflect a political structure in the
context of popular culture. All quotations are from *The Riverside
Shakespeare*, ed. G. Blakemore Evans (Houghton Mifflin, 1974). Ed.]

1. Muriel Bradbrook, *The Rise of the Common Player* (Cambridge, MA, 1964); Robert Weimann, *Shakespeare and the Popular Tradition in the Theater* (Baltimore, MD, 1978); Victor Turner, 'Variations on a Theme of Liminality', in *Secular Ritual*, ed. Sally F. Moore and Barbara G. Myerhoff (Amsterdam, 1977), pp. 35–57; Louis A. Montrose, 'The Purpose of Playing: Reflections on a Shakespearean Anthropology', *Helios*, 8 (1980), 51–74.

2. John Stow, *A Survay of London*, ed. H. Morley (London, 1890), p. 370.

3. Stow, *A Survay of London*, p. 119.

4. [Bristol is here referring to the rest of his book where he goes on to discuss other Shakespeare plays. Ed.]

5. Walter Benjamin, 'Theses on the Philosophy of History', in *Illuminations*, ed. Hannah Arendt (New York, 1969), p. 256.

6. Jan Kott, *Shakespeare Our Contemporary* (New York, 1966), pp. 3–57.

7. Mikhail Bakhtin, *The Dialogic Imagination* (Cambridge, MA, 1968), pp. 206–8.

8. Claude Gaignebet, 'Le Combat de carnaval et de carême de P. Breughel (1559)', *Annales: Economies, Sociétés, Civilizations*, 27 (1972), 313–43; K. Thomas, 'Work and Leisure in Pre-Industrial Society', *Past and Present*, 29 (1964), 67–84.

9. Stow, *Survay of London*, p. 115.

4

Power on Display: The Politics of Shakespeare's Genres

LEONARD TENNENHOUSE

That heroines possessing the power of patriarchy should regularly appear on the stage during the 1590s and not later, obviously had something to do with the fact that a female monarch was on the throne. By this I do not mean to suggest that these heroines stood in any allegorical relation to Elizabeth. I am only suggesting that during this period it became possible to imagine patriarchal power embodied in a female, which obviously opened a whole new set of possibilities for representing power on the stage. Each of Shakespeare's heroines indeed enacts, problematises, and resolves the issues of how power was distributed in England. This is no doubt one reason why such a politically literate audience as Shakespeare's attended the popular theatre in the first place. Even as it expanded the possibilities for imagining power, however, the public theatre actually served Elizabeth's interests by presenting visible and readily accessible signs of the metaphysics of blood.

In the concluding moments of *The Merchant of Venice*, Shakespeare seizes the occasion to bring forth the political configuration governing each of the romantic comedies. Portia gives her ring to Antonio, and he in turn gives it to Bassanio. Antonio promises to be the bond for Bassanio's fidelity, and Bassanio is once more given the patrimony left by Portia's father. For the third time in this play, then, we see the female invested with the patriarchal prerogatives of status, wealth, and power, and for the third time, too, we see the female transfer the patrimony to the man she desires. Her desire thus appears instrumental in the acquisition of such power. What is true of *The Merchant of Venice* in this regard is true of all of the romantic comedies. Each makes it seem that female desire for the male is the essential means of acquiring patriarchal power, and each comedy in turn poses a slightly different problem for which the self-subordination of an aristocratic woman offers the only comic (as opposed to violent) solution. To generalise further, at the beginning of each comedy it appears that power originates with the male. Portia's father, Petruchio, Don Pedro and Claudio, Duke Frederick and Oliver, are all cases in point. As my discussion of both *The Taming of the Shrew* and *The Merchant of Venice* has argued, there is a moment in every comedy which transfers this power to the aristocratic female. Portia restores – as if by magic – Antonio's ships and with them the proper order of political relationships. Rosalind [in *As You Like It*] apparently has the power to call down Hymen to sanctify her betrothal. Kate [in *The Taming of the Shrew*] is not only the very pattern of wifely obedience but also the one who enforces her model upon other women. But even though Shakespeare endows each of his heroines with certain patriarchal prerogatives, this move always constitutes one step in a double move which relocates power in the male by way of marriage. Shakespeare thus restores the natural hierarchy of social relations as the wife subordinates herself to her husband. Having been so transferred from male to female and back again, however, the very nature of power changes. Because she authorises the male, power appears to originate in the female. With her restoration of power to the male, furthermore, the social order becomes more flexible and inclusive. The comic form itself depends upon such a transformation which increases the aristocratic community through marriage without ever impugning the purity of its blood.

Shakespearean comedy thus materialises the double bind which organises many of the cultural products of Elizabeth's reign. This double bind sets the imperative to seek membership in the community of blood against the imperative to keep the community pure. It is this double bind, I have argued, which shapes the Petrarchan fantasy as well as the comedies which so regularly parody the representation of sexual desire among the elite. Petrarchan writing always situates us outside of the community of blood. By definition it always fixes the gaze on that which is meta-physically other than the gazer as the male attempts to make himself desirable to a female of a significantly higher station by representing his desire for her in extravagant terms. By way of contrast, Shakespearean comedy foregrounds the instrumentality of female desire. The multiple marriages at a comedy's conclusion make it seem as if desire had brought about a politically homogeneous community. At the same time, desire also preserves the sexual hierarchy, for the subordination of wife to husband invariably invokes that of subject to king. On stage, furthermore, the dress of the various candidates for the hand of the heroine would have indicated all the distinctions of rank and the matching and mismatching of partners in a visually political game.

Given that the transfer of power from aristocratic female to a male counterpart is such a crucial feature of these comedies, given too, that this transfer depends on the desire of the aristocratic female, it was perhaps inevitable that as Shakespeare worked and reworked with the materials of Elizabethan writing he would eventually focus exclusively on the nature and instrumentality of female desire itself. I would like to consider *Twelfth Night* as the play in which the playwright strips away other political issues to consider the dilemma arising when the aristocratic female lacks the kind of desire that elsewhere in the comedies provides the glue for a social world that is both homogeneous and hierarchical.

If nothing else, Petrarchan language authorises the metaphysics of blood. And therein lies the upside-downness of Orsino's position in *Twelfth Night*. As Duke of Illyria, he embodies all the magic of blood. In using the language of the aspiring courtier, then, Orsino uses figures of speech to negotiate sexual relations which completely overturn his position of political superiority in relation to Olivia. His opening speech, 'If music be the food of love, play on', aestheticises love by dislodging it from its political body. Thus Orsino's courtier dialect makes him appear as if he were politically disenfranchised. Though empowered politically by virtue of his noble birth, the joke is that Orsino finds himself in the female position of being the desired object, only lacking the female's power to inspire desire. That is to say, he finds himself in the position of not being the object of desire but the desiring subject. The relationship may fulfil the ideals of courtier writing, but it also demonstrates how restrictive that kind of writing is; it places one outside of the empowered community. The more Olivia withholds herself, the more

Orsino desires her, and thus he invests her with the power that should normally be his. This comic dilemma becomes demonstrably clear as Shakespeare marshals the clichés of the Petrarchan lover, to represent the state to which Olivia's withholding has reduced Orsino. It is as if Orsino were no more than a Lucentio upon first gazing at the silent Bianca:

> O, when mine eyes did see Olivia first,
> Methought she purg'd the air of pestilence!
> That instant was I turned into a hart,
> And my desires, like fell and cruel hounds,
> E'er since pursue me.
>
> (I.i.18–22)

Rather than occupying a position of political power where he would be the object of the gaze, Orsino has placed himself in the role of the gazer. He has put himself in a position where his value depends upon Olivia's desire, and given her the power to refuse him. It is of course foolish for an aristocrat to discount the value of his blood, and dangerous to imagine the aristocratic body divided in this manner. Orsino has allowed himself to become yet one more competitor. We might note that, despite Orsino's tendency to lose sight of this point, desire always has its political significance in this play. Shakespeare never allows his audience to forget that the absence of desire in Olivia is tantamount to political disruption. Her rejection of Orsino calls into question all the criteria for determining one's political station. Sir Toby explains, 'She'll none o' th' Count. She'll not match above her degree, neither in estate, years, nor wit; I have heard her swear't' (I.iii.109–11).

If Orsino perversely assumes the role of courtier at the beginning of the play where he should be the one to stand aloof, at play's end he fails to sue for the hand of Viola, a fact which has disturbed those modern critics who wish Shakespeare had written a sentimental romance rather than a Renaissance romantic comedy. Neglecting to display any sign of desire for his intended, Orsino merely says to Cesario, 'Boy, thou hast said to me a thousand times / Thou never shouldst love woman like to me' (V.i.267–8). It is Viola who then assumes the role of courtier in repeating her earlier professions of love:

> And all those sayings will I over swear,
> And all those swearings keep as true in soul

> As doth that orbed continent the fire
> That severs day from night.
> (V.i.269–72)

Though it flies in the face of our own sense of normal behaviour, Cesario's performance reinscribes sexual relationships within the prevailing hierarchy of political relations. At this moment in the play, one might say, Shakespeare has rewritten Olivia as the Viola who steps forth to fill the role of desiring subject. This gesture restores the social order as female desire authorises aristocratic blood.

Orsino is not Shakespeare's only means of inverting the courtier fantasy; Cesario does much the same thing. A young courtier in the service of the duke, Cesario has to speak the language of aristocratic love in order to win the desire of the previously unavailable lady, Olivia. In this case, however, courtier language again misfires as it succeeds in winning the love of a woman for a woman. Shakespeare uses the figure of the transvestite to question the role of female desire, its object, and thus by implication the nature of the bond uniting the aristocratic community itself. As a transvestite, Cesario embodies all the features of the trope which personifies the courtier. As Puttenham explains,

> the Courtly figure *Allegoria* which is when we speake one thing and thinke another, and that our wordes and our meanings meete not ... his principall vertue ... is when we do speake in sence translatiue and wrested from the one signification, neverthelese applied to another not altogether contrary. ...[1]

Indeed, Olivia falls in love with Cesario when she regards his allegorically: 'I am not that I play,' (I.v.184) and 'What I am, and would, are as secret as maidenhead: to your ears divinity' (I.v.215–17). Not only does he declare himself the figure of false seeming, Cesario also uses the Petrarchan strategy of appealing to the lady's pity. Cesario explains that were he so rejected by her as Orsino has been, he would respond with cantos 'of contemned love' to

> Hallo your name to the reverberate hills,
> And make the babbling gossip of the air
> Cry out 'Olivia!' O, you should not rest
> Between the elements of air and earth
> But you should pity me!
> (I.v.272–6)

Sounding very much like Sidney's Astrophel, Cesario offers Olivia a text which echoes her name. To accept this invitation to hear her name sounded in poetry is for Olivia to succumb to self-love. The courtier's verse allows her to imagine Cesario as the perfect mirror of herself, to wit, Shakespeare has the page protest once again 'I am not what I am'. And he has Olivia respond with a figure that similarly dissolves the boundary between self and other, not the boundary between the sexes, we should note, but that between different social positions: 'I would you were as I would have you be' (III.i.142). Under similar conditions, Sebastian agrees to marry Olivia as if he were being dreamed by another:

> For though my soul disputes well with my sense,
> That this may be some error, but no madness,
> Yet doth this accident and flood of fortune
> So far exceed all instance, all discourse,
> That I am ready to distrust mine eyes,
> And wrangle with my reason that persuades me
> To any other trust but that I am mad,
> Or else the lady's mad; yet if 'twere so,
> She could not sway her house, command her followers, ...
> With such a smooth, discreet, and stable bearing
> As I perceive she does.
>
> (IV.iii.9–20)

On the basis of this reasoning he willingly accepts Olivia's invitation to marry.

And in such fashion Olivia fulfils the comic heroine's function of empowering the object of her desire, first declaring love to Cesario, then marrying his twin brother. The fact she marries Sebastian does not pose a problem. For Shakespeare, at least, such doubling provides the corrective to the doubling of desire which courtly poetry engendered. Sebastian is, after all, of the same blood as Viola/Cesario and the original for whom Viola substituted herself when she assumed her disguise in the first place. When Olivia first falls in love with Cesario, furthermore, she reads the signs of this lineage in his lineaments. It is such a reading that draws out her desire. Mulling over the answer to her query about Cesario's parentage, she says,

> 'Above my fortunes, yet my state is well:
> I am a gentleman.' I'll be sworn thou art;

Thy tongue, thy face, thy limbs, actions, and spirit
Do give thee fivefold blazon.

(I.v.290–3)

Thus she reads the body as a genealogical text whose nature reveals a noble birth beneath a page's dress. To pursue this line of thinking is to credit Olivia with reading the body quite accurately in Elizabethan terms, for what makes it desirable is first and foremost the iconic value of blood. Clearly that is what is meant when she says,

Methinks I feel this youth's perfections
With an invisible and subtle stealth
To creep in at mine eyes.

(I.v.296–8)

Class matter
more than sex.

To fall in love with Cesario inverts the order of things only if Cesario is a page, but not if he is of noble lineage – even if he should be a she. With the discovery of her birth, the problem posed virtually disappears; not sex, but blood makes all the difference. Thus when Sebastian appears on the stage to reveal that Olivia has been 'betrothed to a maid and man', Orsino quickly assures the countess, 'Be not amaz'd, right noble is his blood' (V.i.264).

If it was Olivia's failure to value blood that initially disrupted social relations, then Malvolio's desire to marry above his rank dramatises the other side of the Elizabethan double bind. He reveals the paradox inherent in the Petrarchan fantasy. In doing so, furthermore, he draws punishment without pity because his willingness to believe he could improve his station through marriage challenges the basis of membership in the aristocratic community more surely than Olivia's failure to desire Orsino. Malvolio, more than Orsino or Cesario, has all the necessary social ingredients for a Petrarchan lover. From outside the empowered community, he fantasises that access to power depends on the arbitrary nature of a female's desire which appears to operate according to some logic other than the metaphysics of blood. He believes, as he says, "Tis but fortune, all is fortune.' He draws encouragement for the fantasy 'To be Count Malvolio' from an incident where female desire went against the rules of status: 'the Lady of the Strachy married the yeoman of the wardrobe' (II.v.35–40). But at the prompting of a counterfeit letter which makes Olivia resemble this lady, Malvolio undertakes a form of self-fashioning that clearly parodies rather than fulfils the Petrarchan fantasy:

> I will be proud, I will read politic authors, I will baffle Sir Toby, I
> will wash off gross acquaintance, I will be point devise the very
> man. ... I will be strange, stout, in yellow stockings and cross-
> garter'd. ...
>
> (II.v.161–71)

Olivia could misread Cesario and yet not err because she read the
lineage in his lineaments correctly. What she desired in him and
what she finally gained in Sebastian was her own aristocratic likeness. Malvolio misreads her desire, however, in comparing his
situation with that of the yeoman of the wardrobe who was beloved
of the Lady of the Strachy. He thinks the desire of such women
hinges upon the courtier's performance – his dissimulation – rather
than the value inherent in the performer himself. This, the play's
third dramatisation of the Petrarchan fantasy in the play, demonstrates that contrary to the logic of the courtier's self-fashioning, it
is the value inscribed at birth within the lover's body – more than
his style of self-presentation – which gives rise to desire. In this
respect, Malvolio is a counterfeit while Cesario is the genuine coin,
and one proof of his lack of gentle heritage resides in his inability to
understand himself as such. Malvolio's snobbery betrays his lack of
breeding as clearly as does his ability to carry off the courtier's
performance without making mockery of it.

Malvolio can only imagine the community to which he aspires as
one that arbitrarily excludes him. On this basis, he takes it upon
himself to enforce the principle of exclusion when acting as the
overseer of Olivia's household. Malvolio appropriates the voice of
the community to which he wants to belong, however, and uses it
to assault certain practices of courtly life. Intolerant of déclassé kin
such as Sir Toby, inhospitable to such guests as Sir Andrew, and
disapproving of the presence of Feste the clown, Malvolio threatens
to close down those ceremonies and processionals which celebrate
the aristocratic body. He would deny to the privileged community
the very forms of power which it uses to order society without recourse to violence.

Sir Toby Belch, Feste, Sir Andrew, and Maria in turn take up the
oppositional practices of disguise and inversion to drive Malvolio
out of the society. Their opposition is political rather than aesthetic.
They punish him for his presumption; they mock his seriousness;
and they turn his desire to madness. Here, as in the other comedies,
the carnivalesque operates in concert with the interests of an

idealised aristocratic community to punish the figures opposing that ideal. After doing its work, however, knavery must be contained and solemnised. For in this fashion can Shakespeare stage a purer, more idealised representation of the aristocratic community and also produce a larger, more expansive vision of society. Once their energy and aggression has demolished the element threatening the purity of the aristocratic body, namely, the presumptions of Malvolio, Shakespeare strips the disruptive features from Sir Toby and his crew. Sir Toby is ready to set aside carnivalesque practices for a more moderate mode of behaviour once Malvolio has been punished. 'I would we were well rid of this knavery,' he says of the mock imprisonment of Malvolio, 'If he may be conveniently deliver'd, I would he were, for I am now so far in offence with my niece that I cannot pursue with any safety this sport...' (IV.ii.67–70). When Sir Toby once more misreads Cesario's lineaments – taking Sebastian for the page – the fat knight is given a ritual beating about the ears. He finally renounces disruptive play to join the lovers in solemnising his own marriage to Maria.

Earlier romantic comedies imply what *Twelfth Night* makes explicit. The problem and resolution of each depends upon the transfer of patriarchal power to a woman. Nowhere is this comic move so bold as in the case of Cesario/Viola who wins Olivia's gaze where the page wished only to woo for his master. But this shift in power from male to female – Orsino to Olivia – is part of a circuit of exchange which relocates power in the male through the marriage ceremony which concludes all of the comedies. When the male figures – Petruchio, Theseus, Orsino, Bassanio – do come to embody patriarchal power, however, the power they embody has changed. In the transfer of this power from male to female and back again, romantic comedy transforms it. Having passed into the body of a woman, power becomes her gift to give. As such, it assumes a more humane and less violent form. The illusion that the edge of monarchy's sword has thus softened materialises upon the stage as the threat of civil violence gives way to ceremonies of state. These – the wedding dance and feast – are modelled upon and incorporate materials of popular festival indigenous to England. They invoke and contain the disruptive power of nature. For the reason that they bear traces of the spontaneous and joyful as well as transgressive elements of festival, they acquire the symbolic force of a natural hierarchy – or myth, if you will – where they originally appeared arbitrarily exclusive and opposed to human desire.

From Leonard Tennenhouse, *Power on Display: The Politics of Shakespeare's Genres* (New York and London, 1986), pp. 61–8.

NOTES

[Leonard Tennenhouse bases his analysis on the overriding fact of a female, Elizabeth I, occupying the throne when Shakespeare wrote his series of comedies which empower women. The system, Tennenhouse argues, may still be patriarchal (and power is returned to men by the end), but the instrumentality of power, the driving force in the play and outside it in the state, is female desire. Ed.]

1. George Puttenham, *The Arte of English Poesie* (Menston, 1968), p. 155.

5

Fiction and Friction

STEPHEN GREENBLATT

I

In September 1580, as he passed through a small French town on his way to Switzerland and Italy, Montaigne was told an unusual story that he duly recorded in his travel journal. It seems that seven or eight girls from a place called Chaumont-en-Bassigni plotted together 'to dress up as males and thus continue their life in the world'.[1] One of them set up as a weaver, 'a well-disposed young man who made friends with everybody', and moved to a village called Montier-en-Der. There the weaver fell in love with a woman, courted her, and married. The couple lived together for four or five months, to the wife's satisfaction, 'so they say'. But then, Montaigne reports, the transvestite was recognised by someone from Chaumont; 'the matter was brought to justice, and she was condemned to be hanged, which she said she would rather undergo than return to a girl's status; and she was hanged for using illicit devices to supply her defect in sex.' The execution, Montaigne was told, had taken place only a few days before.

I begin with this story because in *Twelfth Night* Shakespeare almost, but not quite, retells it. It is one of those shadow stories that haunt the plays, rising to view whenever the plot edges toward a potential dilemma or resolution that it in fact eschews. If we dwell on these shadow stories, we shall be accused of daydreaming (a serious charge, for some reason, against literary critics); the plays insist only that we register them in passing as we take in (or are taken in by) the events that 'actually' happen. What if Olivia had succeeded in marrying Orsino's page Cesario? And what if the scandal of a marriage contracted so far beneath a countess's station were topped by a still greater scandal: the revelation that the young groom was in fact a disguised girl? Such a marriage – if we could still call it one – would make some sense in a play that had continually tantalised its audience with the spectacle of homoerotic desire: Cesario in love with 'his' master Orsino, Orsino evidently drawn toward Cesario, Antonio passionately in love with Sebastian, Olivia aroused by a page whose effeminacy everyone remarks. But how could the play account for such desire, or rather, since an account is neither called for nor tendered, how could the play extricate itself from the objectification of illicit desire in a legal marriage?

The case recorded by Montaigne, let us recall, did not set off a psychological examination – the 'scientia sexualis' that Foucault finds at the heart of the modern history of sexuality – but a legal proceeding, a trial issuing in a condemnation not, it seems, for deception but for the use of prohibited sexual devices, devices that enable a woman to take the part of a man.[2] So too at the critical moment of misunderstanding in *Twelfth Night*, when Olivia urges the apparently timorous Cesario to take up his new status as her husband, the issue is defined not in psychological but in legal terms. A priest is brought in to testify to the procedural impeccability of the ceremony he has performed:

> A contract of eternal bond of love,
> Confirm'd by mutual joinder of your hands,
> Attested by the holy close of lips,
> Strength'ned by interchangement of your rings,
> And all the ceremony of this compact
> Seal'd in my function, by my testimony.
> (V.i.156–61)

This legal validity would clash violently with the gross impropriety of a homosexual coupling; presumably, there would have to be a ceremony of undoing to resolve the scandal. But then, of course, Olivia does not succeed; she actually marries Viola's twin who is, as it happens, a male. At the moment that Cesario discloses what lies beneath the 'masculine usurp'd attire' – 'I am Viola' – her twin Sebastian frees Olivia from the scandalous shadow story:

> So comes it, lady, you have been mistook;
> But Nature to her bias drew in that.
> (V.i.259–60)

What happened in Montier-en-Der was against nature; in *Twelfth Night* events pursue their natural curve, the curve that assures the proper mating of man and woman. To be matched with someone of one's own sex is to follow an unnaturally straight line; heterosexuality, as the image of nature drawing to her bias implies, is bent. Shakespeare's metaphor is from the game of bowls; the 'bias' refers not only to the curve described by the bowl as it rolls along the pitch but also to the weight implanted in the bowl to cause it to swerve. Something off-centre, then, is implanted in nature – in Olivia's nature, in the nature that more generally governs the plot of the comedy – that deflects men and women from their ostensible desires and toward the pairings for which they are destined.

This deflection can be revealed only in movement. As befits a play intended for performance, the metaphor for nature invokes not simply internal structure but a structure whose realisation depends upon temporal unfolding, or *rolling*. An enacted imbalance or deviation is providential, for a perfect sphere would roll straight to social, theological, legal disaster: success lies in a strategic, happy swerving. The swerving is not totally predictable because the bowl will encounter obstacles, or 'rubs', that will make its course erratic; if sometimes frustrating, these rubs are also part of the pleasure and excitement of the game. Licit sexuality in *Twelfth Night* – the only craving that the play can represent as capable of finding satisfaction – depends upon a movement that deviates from the desired object straight in one's path toward a marginal object, a body one scarcely knows. Nature is an *unbalancing* act.

Swerving is not a random image in the play; it is one of the central structural principles of *Twelfth Night*, a principle that links individual characters endowed with their own private motivations to the larger social order glimpsed in the ducal court and the aristocratic household.[3] The play's initiatory design invites the audience to envisage the unification of court and household through the marriage of their symbolic heads, Orsino and Olivia. This uniting, at once a social and psychological consummation, is blocked only by a vow that must be broken in the interest of both the political and the natural order of things. To intensify the narrative pressure behind this design, the play insists upon the perfect eligibility of Olivia: she is not only a great heiress but, in the wake of the deaths of her father and only brother, the sole ruler of her fortunes. Courtship need not be represented, as for example in *The Taming of the*

Shrew and *Much Ado about Nothing*, as (at least in part) a negotiation with the father or male guardian; the countess Olivia is a prize encumbered only by her devotion to her brother's memory. (Her uncle, who could have filled the role of her guardian, is a hopeless sot whose own candidate for his niece's hand is suitable only to be bilked and mocked.) The lady richly left was a major male wish-fulfilment fantasy in a culture where the pursuit of wealth through marriage was an avowed and reputable preoccupation. Here the fantasy is at its most dreamlike because it focuses not on a widow – the only group whose members actually corresponded on infrequent occasion to this daydream – but on 'a virtuous maid' (I.ii.36).[4]

The maid, however, is strong-willed and refuses perversely to submit to the erotic dance that would lead to the legitimate male appropriation of her person and her 'dirty lands' (II.iv.82). Indeed she appears to enjoy ruling her household – controlling access to her person, taking pleasure in her jester, managing her manager Malvolio, dispensing rewards and punishments. One extraordinary woman in the period provided, of course, a model for such a career, lived out to its fullest – the virgin queen, ageing and heirless and very dangerous. The queen had at once mobilised, manipulated, and successfully resisted decades of anxious male attempts to see her married; but this was a career that Elizabeth herself, let alone her male subjects, could not tolerate in any woman of lesser station.

There is then a powerful logic – social, political, economic, erotic – to the eligible, perfectly independent male ruler of the land taking possession of this eligible, perfectly independent maiden prize. The linked elements of this logic are suggested by Orsino's anticipation of the time

> when liver, brain, and heart,
> These sovereign thrones, are all supplied, and fill'd
> Her sweet perfections with one self king!
> (I.i.36–8)

All that stands in the way, the play makes clear in its opening moments, is the extravagant irrationality of her vow:

> The element itself, till seven years' heat,
> Shall not behold her face at ample view;
> But like a cloistress she will veiled walk,
> And water once a day her chamber round
> With eye-offending brine; all this to season

> A brother's dead love, which she would keep fresh
> And lasting in her sad remembrance.
>
> (I.i.25–31)

Olivia's swerving from this vow – absurdly ambitious in its projected duration, comically ritualised, perversely wedded to misery – is entirely predictable.[5] Indeed, in lines that play on the standard theological term for marital intercourse – 'to pay the debt' – Orsino takes her mourning less as an impediment to his love than as an erotic promissory note:

> O, she that hath a heart of that fine frame
> To pay this debt of love but to a brother,
> How will she love when the rich golden shaft
> Hath kill'd the flock of all affections else
> That live in her.
>
> (I.i.32–6)[6]

The surprise for Orsino is that the swerving, when it comes, is not in his direction. That it is not depends upon a series of events that the play also represents as swervings: a shipwreck that keeps Viola and Sebastian from reaching their destination, the blocking of Viola's initial intention to serve Olivia, Viola's relatively un-motivated decision to disguise herself in men's clothing, the mis-taking of Sebastian for the disguised Viola, and so forth. These apparently random accidents are at once zany deflections of direction, intention, and identity and comically predictable drives toward a resolution no less conventional than the one for which Orsino had longed. The plot initially invoked by Shakespeare's play is displaced by another, equally familiar, plot – the plot of cross-dressing and cross-coupling that had become a heavily overworked convention of Italian and Spanish comedy.[7]

Swerving in *Twelfth Night*, then, is at once a source of festive surprise and a time-honoured theatrical method of achieving a con-ventional, reassuring resolution. No one but Viola gets quite what she or he consciously sets out to get in the play, and Viola gets what she wants only because she is willing to submit herself to the very principle of deflection: 'I am not that I play' (I.v.184). She embraces a strategy that the play suggests is not simply an accident of circum-stance but an essential life-truth: you reach a desired or at least de-sirable destination not by pursuing a straight line but by following a curved path. This principle underlies Sebastian's explanation of Olivia's mistake: 'Nature to her bias drew in that.'

Sebastian glosses his own image with the comment, 'You would have been contracted to a maid' (V.i.261); that is, he invites Olivia to contemplate what would have happened had nature *not* drawn to her bias.[8] The line seems to call forth its complement – 'But now you are contracted to a man' – yet characteristically *Twelfth Night* does not give us such a sensible and perfectly predictable turn. Instead Sebastian concludes by renewing the paradox after it had seemed resolved:

> Nor are you therein, by my life, deceiv'd,
> You are betroth'd both to a maid and man.
> (V.i.262–3)

A man because Sebastian has beneath his apparel what Cesario lacks – 'Pray God defend me!' cries Cesario before the duel with Sir Andrew, 'A little thing would make me tell them how much I lack of a man' (III.iv.302–3); a maid because the term, by a quibble whose several sixteenth-century examples the OED records, could be applied to a male virgin.[9] Its use here refers wittily not only to Sebastian's virginity but to the homosexual coupling that Olivia has narrowly escaped. Only by not getting what she wants has Olivia been able to get what she wants and, more important, to want what she gets.

Nature has triumphed. The sexes are sorted out, correctly paired, and dismissed to bliss – or will be as soon as Viola changes her clothes. And nature's triumph is society's triumph, for the same clarification that keeps marriage from being scandalised by gender confusion keeps it from being scandalised by status confusion: no sooner has Sebastian explained to Olivia that he is both a maid and man than Orsino adds, as if he were in no way changing the subject, 'Be not amaz'd, right noble is his blood.' This is the first mention of the twins' nobility – previously we had only heard Cesario's declaration, 'I am a gentleman' – and Orsino's knowledge must stem from the same source that settled the question of identity: the name of the father.[10] Throughout the play we have been allowed to think that Viola and Sebastian are beneath Olivia's station – hence the spectral doubling of Malvolio's dream of social climbing – and consequently that the play's festive inversions have been purchased at the cost of the more perfect social alliance between the duke and the countess. Now, through the magical power of the name of the father, we learn that the threat to the social order and the threat to the sexual order were equally illusory. All's well that ends well.

'The most fundamental distinction the play brings home to us,' remarks C. L. Barber in his well-known essay on *Twelfth Night*, 'is the difference between men and women. ... Just as the saturnalian reversal of social roles need not threaten the social structure, but can serve instead to consolidate it, so a temporary, playful reversal of sexual roles can renew the meaning of the normal relation. One can add that with sexual as with other relations, it is when the normal is secure that playful aberration is benign. This basic security explains why there is so little that is queasy in all Shakespeare's handling of boy actors playing women, and playing women pretending to be men.'[11] Perhaps. Yet however acute these remarks may be as a humane vision of life, we must question them as a summary judgement of Shakespearian comedy in general and of *Twelfth Night* in particular. At that play's end, Viola is still Cesario – 'For so you shall be,' says Orsino, 'while you are a man' (V.i.386) – and Olivia, strong-willed as ever, is betrothed to one who is, by his own account, both 'a maid and man'. At the risk of intensifying our sense of the 'queasy' (a category that might reward some inquiry), I would suggest that *Twelfth Night* may not finally bring home to us the fundamental distinction between men and women; not only may the distinction be blurred, but the home to which it is supposed to be brought may seem less securely ours, less cosy and familiar, than we have come to expect.

But how can we unsettle the secure relation between the normal and the aberrant? How can we question the nature that like a weighted bowl so providentially draws to her bias and resolves the comic predicaments? I propose that we examine the bowl more carefully, search out the off-centre weight implanted in it, analyse why it follows the curve of gender. To do so we must historicise Shakespearian sexual nature, restoring it to its relation of negotiation and exchange with other social discourses of the body. For this task it is essential to break away from the textual isolation that is the primary principle of formalism and to move outside the charmed circle of a particular story and its variants. How can we do this? How but by swerving?

II

In 1601 in a small town near Rouen, a thirty-two-year-old widowed mother of two, Jeane le Febvre, had a very odd experience. For nearly five weeks she had been sharing her bed (not at all an odd experience) with a fellow servant, a woman in her early twenties who was recuperating from a long illness. Then one evening, while they were doing the laundry together, the bedmate, Marie le Marcis, whispered that she was in fact a man – a claim she (or rather he) graphically demonstrated – and precipitously proposed marriage. Jeane at first refused, but during the following weeks the two fell in love.

The couple did not intend to keep their relationship clandestine; they wished to get their parents' permission and have a proper wedding, sanctified by the church. Indeed, despite the wildly irregular circumstances in which they found themselves, they seem to have been immediately caught up in the ordinary social problems and strategies that attended marriage negotiations in the Renaissance. Jeane had been raised in the Reformed faith; Marie, though he had been converted to that faith by an employer, wished now to return, as his mother had long been urging, to the Catholic church. We may assume that Marie's parents were gratified, but there is no record of their reaction either to Marie's return to Catholicism or, strangely enough, to the revelation that their daughter was a son. We are told, however, that they strenuously objected to his decision to marry a penniless widow with two small children. The dutiful son at first consented not to see Jeane, but finding the separation unendurable, he returned to his beloved's bed. There, after making vows to one another, they consummated their passion – three or four times, we are told, on the first night alone.[12]

Not content with secret vows and private pleasures, Marie and Jeane remained steadfast in their desire for the public confirmation of a wedding. But to acquire this confirmation, Marie le Marcis needed to acquire a new sexual identity in the eyes of the community; he had been baptised, named, dressed, and brought up as a girl. Accordingly, he changed his clothing, asked that he be called Marin le Marcis, and publicly declared his matrimonial intentions. Not surprisingly (though the lovers themselves appear to have been surprised), there was an immediate public scandal; the two were arrested, tried, and condemned, Marin to be burned alive, Jeane to watch the execution, then to be beaten and banished from Normandy. (After an appeal for mercy, the sentence was humanely moderated: Marin was only to be strangled to death, Jeane merely to be whipped.) The crime of which they were convicted was sodomy, for both the wife and the mother of the man in whose household the couple had served testified that Marie le Marcis had regularly had her menstrual period ['ses purgations naturelles'] (p. 194), and a medical examination revealed no signs of masculinity. The accused maintained that as a consequence of the terror of imprisonment, his penis had retracted, but the court dismissed his claim. Marie, it was charged, was not a man but a 'tribade' – a homosexual seductress who had, with her unnaturally enlarged clitoris, abused the all-too-willing Jeane.

Marin appealed his conviction to the Parlement of Rouen, which appointed a panel of doctors, surgeons, and midwives to renew the medical examination. One of the doctors, Jacques Duval, had a learned interest in hermaphroditism, to which he saw this case as allied, and consequently he pursued the examination much further than his colleagues. Where they were willing to stay on the surface, Duval, recalling that Aristotle had reproached philosophers who foolishly held themselves aloof from those things vulgarly thought to be indecent, was determined to probe. This determination was rewarded: responding to his finger's pressure was 'a male organ, rather large and hard' (p. 403); a second examination left no doubt, for the friction of the doctor's touch caused Marin to ejaculate, and the semen, he reports, was not thin and watery like a woman's but, like a man's, thick and white (pp. 404–5).

On the strength of Duval's expert testimony (with which the rest of the medical panel did not concur), the lovers' conviction was overturned. Marin and Jeane were released. The court evidently remained guardedly sceptical: Marin was ordered to wear women's clothes until he reached the age of twenty-five and was forbidden, on pain of death, to have sexual relations during this time with either sex. What would happen thereafter – whether Marin would be allowed to marry Jeane or be forced to remain Marie – the court left undecided. Perhaps at the trial's end the judges had not the vaguest idea what Marin's sex really was. In any case, they did not feel certain enough to let him either marry or burn. If customary procedures for determining the gender of hermaphrodites were followed, at the end of the probationary period Marin would be permitted to choose once and for all a sexual identity.[13] Case closed.

This cheerfully grotesque story is recounted in a long book – Duval's *On Hermaphrodites, Childbirth, and the Medical Treatment of Mothers and Children* – and I want to propose that we may understand this book not as bizarre static on the margins of normative individualism – sexless, colourless, and above all culture-less – but as part of the particular and contingent discourse out of which historically specific subjects were fashioned, represented, and communally incorporated.

On Hermaphrodites participates in a larger field of sexual discourse – a field that in the early modern period includes marriage manuals; medical, theological, and legal texts; sermons; indictments and defences of women; and literary fictions. Rarely is any one text in this field decisively important – for even the strongest tradition generates counter-traditions – but taken as a whole, a culture's sexual discourse plays a critical role in the shaping of identity. It does so by helping to implant in each person a system of dispositions and orientations that governs individual improvisations, to implant, in other words, the defining off-centre weight: 'But nature to her bias drew in that.'[14]

The concrete individual exists only in relation to forces that pull against spontaneous singularity and that draw any given life, however peculiarly formed, toward communal norms. Even Marin le Marcis's highly original improvisation, we might note, had the most conventional of goals: a publicly recognised name and gender, an officially sanctioned marriage. Indeed the drive to be reabsorbed into the communal is sufficiently strong in his case to make us doubt that individualism, in the sense of freestanding and irreducible particularity, had any meaning or value to Marin or anyone involved with him. It has been traditional, since Jakob Burckhardt, to trace the origins of autonomous individuality to the Renaissance, but the material under consideration here suggests that individual identity in the early modern period served less as a final goal than as a way station on the road to a firm and decisive identification with normative structures.

Of these structures, the most powerful appear to have been those governing sexual identity. Male writers of the period regarded gender as an enduring sign of distinction, both in the sense of privilege and in the sense of differentiation. A man in Renaissance society had symbolic and material advantages that no woman could hope to attain, and he had them by virtue of separating himself, first as a child and then as an adult, from women. All other significant differential indices of individual existence – social class, religion, language, nation – could, at least in imagination, be stripped away, only to reveal the underlying natural fact of sexual difference. The Renaissance delighted in stories of the transformation of individuals out of all recognition – the king confused with the beggar, the great prince reduced to the condition of a wild man, the pauper changed into a rich lord.[15] Only the primary differentiation given by God himself – 'male and female he made them' – would seem to have been exempt from this swirling indeterminacy. Even here, of course, confusion was possible, for as the many stories of cross-dressing suggest, apparel may deceive the eyes of the most skilled observer. But beneath the apparel the body itself cannot lie – or so we might expect.

Yet in Renaissance stories, paradoxically, the apparently fragile and mutable social codes are almost always reinscribed – despite his savage upbringing, the true prince reveals his noble nature – while sexual difference, the foundation of all individuation, turns out to be unstable and artificial at its origin. To help us understand this paradox let us return to Duval's fascination with hermaphrodites. This fascination was not, for the late sixteenth century, eccentric but was an instance of a widespread cultural concern with prodigies. Prodigies could be viewed both as signs – monitory messages to be read by those who understood the art of divination – and as wonders – marvellous instances of the inexhaustible variety of things. Prodigies challenge the conventional classification of things, but they do not make classification itself impossible. On the contrary, as the voluminous accounts of monsters, earthquakes, eclipses, unnaturally heavy rains, physical deformities, and so forth affirm, these marvels give men a sense of the dynamic order of nature that constantly produces those differences – the gradations and distinctions and variations – by which men define themselves and their social and natural environment. Where the modern structuralist understanding of the world tends to sharpen its sense of individuation by meditating upon the normative, the Renaissance tended to sharpen its sense of the normative by meditating upon the prodigious.[16]

The presence of both male and female sexual organs in a single person is a resonant instance of that Renaissance meditation. Hermaphroditism was at once a bizarre anomaly, violating the most basic of natural categories, and a sign of the natural order whose underlying structure made possible the very generativity that produced the anomaly.[17] It is fitting then that Duval's book, in which the strange case of Marin le Marcis occupies so important a place, is not a mere compilation of the bizarre but a serious medical treatise on fertility, the care of pregnant women, and the safe delivery of babies. Discourse on hermaphroditism and discourse on normal sexuality and childbirth do not conflict for Duval; on the contrary, they are the same discourse, for the knowledge that enables one to understand the monstrous conjunction in one individual of the male and female sexes is the identical knowledge that enables one to understand the normal experience of sexual pleasure and the generation of healthy offspring.

Duval's task, as he understands it, is to display and explain the hidden riches of the human organs of generation and particularly of the womb, which he sees, in effect, as a fantastic treasure house to which he has acquired the key (p. 159). But why should the case of Marin le Marcis seem to give him this precious key? The answer lies in the event that saved Marin's life: empowered by the court of law, the physician reaches in behind the woman's secret fold of flesh and feels with his finger's end a swelling penis.

Marin is an oddity, but for Duval his body encodes in its strangeness a universal natural paradox: on the one hand, a single individual is in reality double, since all bodies contain both male and female elements; on the other hand, there are not two radically different sexual structures but only one – outward and visible in the man, inverted and hidden in the woman. Neither of these beliefs is unique to Duval; on the contrary, they reflect ancient anatomical wisdom, which Renaissance physicians at once elaborated and challenged. Like many of his peers, Duval is in the awkward position of accepting beliefs with which he is not altogether comfortable; the case of Marin le Marcis serves him by simultaneously reaffirming and marginalising these beliefs.

At least since the time of Galen it had been widely thought that both males and females contained both male and female elements (Duval goes so far as to posit male and female seed [p. 327]); the predominance, rather than the exclusion, of one or the other helped, along with the original position of the seed in the womb and other factors, to determine sexual identity and to make possible a harmonious accord between sex and gender. Predominance was never – or at least rarely – absolute, nor, in the opinion of most, was it established in final and definitive form in the womb. On the contrary, virtually all males experienced a transition during childhood from a state close to that of females – indeed often called 'effeminate' – to one befitting an adult man. Conversely, if less frequently, the predominance of the appropriate female characteristics could take some time to establish itself. Where the female elements were dominant but still insufficiently strong, the woman would be a virago; similarly, a man in whom male seed was weaker than it should be was likely to remain effeminate. And in those rare cases, as Duval notes, where the competition between male and female elements was absolutely undecided, a hermaphrodite could be formed.

All of this implies, as I have suggested, the persistent doubleness, the inherent twinship, of all individuals. But we should not conclude that the esoteric Neoplatonic speculations about androgyny in the Renaissance were in fact widespread; on the contrary, perceptions of gender doubleness were almost always closely linked to a belief in an internal power struggle between male and female principles. Proper individuation occurred as a result of the successful resolution of the friction between the competing elements, a resolution that was almost entirely bound up in medical manuals, as in theological tracts, with patriarchal ideology: 'By how much the more the Masculine Atoms abound in a Female Infant,' writes Nathaniel Highmore, a seventeenth-century English physician, 'by so much the more the Fetus is stronger, healthier, and more Man-like, a Virago. If the Female Atoms abound much in a Male Infant, then is that issue more weak and effeminate.'[18] One peculiar consequence of this view was that normal women had to submit to the weaker internal principle, to accept a certain debility, in order to achieve full female identity, an identity that itself entailed submission to a man; women were *by definition* the weaker sex. A further consequence is that women had momentarily to overcome their inherent defect, and hence their female nature, to produce the seed necessary for generation. Not surprisingly, this overcoming was thought to be difficult; accordingly, the medical texts prescribe extended foreplay as an integral part of sexual intercourse and, for cases where caresses and lascivious words fail, provide recipes for vaginal douches designed to 'heat' women beyond their normal bodily temperature.[19]

But if the Galenic heritage brought with it the notion that human singleness was achieved out of an inherent doubleness, it also brought with it a very different notion: since Galen it had been believed that the male and female sexual organs were altogether comparable, indeed mirror images of each other. Though Fallopius published in the 1560s his celebrated description of the female genitalia, and belief in female testicles gave way in the later seventeenth century to the discovery of the ovaries, the specific functioning of the ovaries was not well understood until the nineteenth century.[20] In the sixteenth and seventeenth centuries, physicians and laymen of sharply divergent schools agreed that male and female sexual organs were fully homologous. 'The spermatic vessels in women,' writes the celebrated French surgeon, Ambroise Paré, 'do nothing differ from those in men in substance, figure, composure, number, connexion, temper, original and use, but only in magnitude and distribution. ... For their Testicles, they differ little from mens but in quantity [that is, size]. For they are lesser and in figure more hollow and flat, by reason of their defective heat which could not elevate or lift them up to their just magnitude' (Paré, *Works*, p. 126). The womb seems unique to women, but in fact it is 'given by nature in stead of the *Scrotum*, as the neck there of, and the annexed parts in stead of the yard; so that if any more exactly consider the parts of generation in women and men, he shall find that they differ not much in number, but only in situation and use.'

Centuries earlier, Galen had invited his readers to engage in the topographical analysis implicit in Paré's description of the genitals: 'Turn outward the woman's, turn inward, so to speak, and fold double the man's, and you find them the same in both in every respect.'[21] If you imagine the male genitals inverted, you will find that the penis has become the cervix and the vagina, and the scrotum has been transformed into the womb with the testicles on either side. Conversely, Galen suggests, think of the 'uterus turned outward and projecting': 'Would not the testes (ovaries) then necessarily be inside it? Would it not contain them like a scrotum? Would not the neck (the cervix), hitherto concealed inside the perineum but now pendent, be made into the male member? ... In fact,' he concludes, 'you could not find a single male part left over that had not simply changed its position: for the parts that are inside in woman are outside in man.'

To be sure, this exact homology implies a difference that derives from the female's being colder, and hence less perfect, then the male. This defect keeps the female genitals from being born, as it were, a fate Galen images in an astonishing metaphor:

> You can see something like this in the eyes of the mole, which have vitreous and crystalline humors and the tunics that surround these ... and they have these just as much as animals do that make use of their eyes. The mole's eyes, however, do not open, nor do they project but are left there imperfect and remain like the eyes of other animals when these are still in the uterus.[22]

This double analogy gives a vertiginous twist to the topographical argument: not only are the female genitals an inverted version of the male genitals, but they are also like the perfectly formed but functionally useless eyes of the mole, which are in turn like the blind eyes of creatures that have not yet emerged from the womb. By invoking birth the metaphor implicitly acknowledges the functional utility it is intended to deny, and this paradox, far from embarrassing Galen, enables him to sustain a double vision of the female body, at once defective and perfectly suited to its function, a vision that endured for centuries. For Paré and most other Renaissance physicians, the delicate balance of sexual identity and difference expresses simultaneously the providential order of generation and the defectiveness of women, their failure to reach nature's goal: a penis. 'For that which man hath apparent without, that women have hid within, both by the singular providence of Nature, as also by the defect of heat in women, which could not drive and thrust forth those parts as in men.'[23]

One consequence of this belief in differential homology is a fascination with the possibility of sex change – almost always from female to male, that is, from defective to perfect. Paré recounts several such cases, including that of a fifteen-year-old peasant girl named Marie who one day was 'rather robustly' chasing her swine, which were going into a wheat field. As Marie in midpursuit leaped over a ditch, 'at the very moment the genitalia and male rod came to be developed'.[24] After consulting with physicians and the bishop, Marie changed her name to Germain and went on to serve in the king's retinue. On his way to Italy, Montaigne stopped to see Germain for himself – he had not married, Montaigne was told, but he had 'a big, very thick beard'. The prodigy was not at home, however. In the town, Montaigne noted in his journal, 'there is still a song commonly in the girls' mouths, in which they warn one another not to stretch their legs too wide for fear of becoming males, like Marie Germain'.[25]

Here again the prodigious is of interest because it reveals the natural. After all, such a spectacular change merely repeats or represents the normal development of males through the healthy operation of bodily heat. As with the two-seed theory, the implication of this developmental account is that men grow out of or pass through women, though now the formulation is reversed: where the two-seed theory imagines an individual identity emerging from the struggle between conflicting principles, the topographical account imagines gender as the result of the selective forcing out through heat of the original internal organ – like the reversal of a rubber glove – so that where there was once only one sex, there are now two.

Duval's work reflects this fascination with sex change, but it also registers and uneasily accommodates the anatomical discoveries that were beginning to cast serious doubts on the whole notion of homology. There cannot truly be a sexual metamorphosis, argues Duval, for despite the great resemblance between the male and female sexual organs, the latter cannot simply be converted into the former or vice versa. If you actually try to envisage such a transformation, you discover that it cannot be represented. 'If you imagine the vulva completely turned inside out ... you will have to envisage a large-mouthed bottle hanging from the woman, a bottle whose mouth rather than base would be attached to the body and which would bear no resemblance to what you had set out to imagine' (*On Hermaphrodites*, p. 375).

Like others of his generation, Duval is balanced uneasily between acceptance of the ancient concept of homology and a recognition that it does not quite work. This recognition does not lead him to give up a concept upon which a great deal depends, but it does shape his account of Marin le Marcis so that it illustrates not an instance of sexual metamorphosis but an embodied transvestism that momentarily confounds sexual categories only to give way in the end to the clarification of gender and hence to proper, communally sanctioned, identity.[26] Transvestism *represents* a structural identity between man and woman – identity revealed in the dramatic disclosure of the penis concealed behind the labia – but it does not *present* this identity as a reality. On the contrary, in some ways the case serves to marginalise, to render prodigious, the old wisdom. There has been no transformation from woman into man – Marie was always in some sense Marin, whose true gender was concealed by his anomalous genital structure – but the myth of such mobility is preserved in the very form of the account that denies its anatomical possibility.

The fascination with all that seems to unsettle sexual differentiation – hermaphroditism, gender metamorphosis, women who conceal the inward form of men and men who conceal the inward form of women – never decisively overturns in the Renaissance discourse of sexuality the proper generative order that depends upon a distinction between the sexes. To be sure, Duval writes, 'many women have been transformed into men'. But, he continues, it is more accurate to say that 'the male genitals, formerly hidden, have been discovered in many who were once thought to be women; whereupon they changed their names, clothing, and vocations' (p. 372). Even the much rarer cases of authentic hermaphroditism are not permitted to remain unresolved ambiguities; judges order that such people determine by which sex they are more aroused and on this basis choose – once and for all – their gender (p. 302). Thereafter any violation will be severely punished, indeed treated as a capital crime.

Despite this insistence on a determinate sexual identity, Duval and others cling to a notion of deep structural homology between male and female genitals, because without it the traditional psychology and physiology of sex would be thrown into confusion. Hence even when the belief that the woman was a defective male was abandoned by most physicians and the form of the female anatomy was attributed to function rather than inadequate heat, the notion of an alignment between the sexes proved surprisingly durable. It was supported by the drawings of the anatomists who found what they had expected to find: that the uterus was analogous to the scrotum and the vagina to the penis. And if by the early seventeenth century Duval, for example, recognised that this analogy was by no means perfect, he could easily shift the grounds of comparison to the clitoris, 'a particle in the shape of a small penis' ('une particule representant la forme d'un petit membre viril' [p. 63]).[27] By the close of the century, the immensely popular *Aristotle's Master-piece* informed its readers that 'to say that Woman has true Seed, is false and erroneous'; what Galen and Hippocrates had taken to be testicles are in reality ovaries.[28] But this does not mean, the manual argues, that there is a 'vast difference between the Members of the two Sexes' (p. 93); the clitoris is like a penis 'in Situation, Substance, Composition and Erection, growing sometimes out of the Body two inches' (p. 99). In some lascivious women, the clitoris swells to the size of a male organ and can be used to abuse women and girls – hence the suspicion that almost led to Marin le Marcis's execution.[29]

Like all of nature's gifts, this feminine penis could be abused, but its proper function was to help provide the 'delectable pleasure' necessary to enable the woman to 'yield forth' her seed. At least in the Galenic thought that dominated sixteenth- and seventeenth-century medicine, female ejaculation was at the centre of the homology between the sexes, for as Paré declared, 'generation or conception cannot follow without the concourse of two seeds, well and perfectly wrought in the very same moment of time' (p. 887). Everything in the process of conception hinges on sperm, which is the sole generative principle in a world without eggs, and sperm cannot be produced by either sex without intense sexual delight.

There is an elaborate medical literature on the purpose of erotic pleasure – as that which enables men to overcome their natural revulsion at the defectiveness of women; that which enables women to overcome their natural reluctance to endure the pain and put their lives at risk in childbearing; that which compensates for the Fall of Man. Sexual pleasure may be thought to link us to the beasts, writes Duval, but in fact in its specifically human form it is one of the marks of God's special favour. The Sovereign Creator was not content that his best beloved creatures mate as the other animals do, with the male mounting the female's back or, in the case of elephants, camels, and other heavy beasts, with the male and female turning their backs on one another (an ancient notion I find difficult to envisage). For human coition God ordained a different practice: men and women look into each other's faces – 'the beautiful lines and features' of the human face – so that they may be aroused to a more fervent desire to generate images of themselves and hence to make those beloved faces live again in their offspring. And as they look upon one another and make love, drawn into the genital 'labyrinth of desire' that God created specially for them and obeying the 'tacit commandments' engraved as a benediction in their very bodies, men and women avenge themselves upon their enemy death. For to leave behind one's own image – 'drawn to the life in one's child' ('vif & naivement representé en son successeur') – is not to die.[30]

Following an ancient medical tradition, Duval offers, simultaneously and bound together, two apparently contradictory accounts of the origin of gender: in one a determinate sexual identity emerges when a double nature becomes single, that is, when either male or female seed, co-present in every person, establishes dominance; in the other a determinate sexual identity emerges when a single nature becomes double, that is, when the unitary genital structure (identified as male in its perfect form) divides into two distinct forms, internal and external. Why two accounts? If there were only one authentic structure – outward and visible in the man, inverted and hidden in the woman – gender difference would be

reduced to a mere illusion, a trick performed with mirrors, and generation would be difficult to imagine. If there were two interlaced
structures – from which gender emerged only by domination and
submission – differentiation would also be threatened, since we
would always discover two persons where we thought to find one.
Identity is at once made possible and dissolved by the slippage
between these conflicting theories: to this extent, though gender for
the Renaissance has everything to do with determinate boundaries
(for the period – as the case of Marin indicates – was intolerant of
ambiguity), it has equally to do with the friction between
boundaries.

The link between these two accounts is heat: through heat the
struggle between the male and female seed is determined, and again
through heat the genital structure of the male emerges from its
hidden place, and again through heat ejaculation and orgasm are
produced. This caloric model of sexuality is not exclusively genital;
breast milk, for example, is also generated by the heating of the
blood, and blood itself is produced by the heating of food. Sexual
warmth does not differ essentially from other warmth; it is only a
particularly vehement instance of the principle of all animate life
and therefore can be generated to some degree by food, wine, and
the power of imagination.[31]

Duval is unusually idealising, but the essential elements of his
account of coition are widely shared: seed is produced and emitted
by the concoction, or cooking, of blood; this cooking is accomplished through erotic friction between men and women. Hence the
recurrent images in the medical literature of what a seventeenth-
century English gynaecologist calls 'the *Fervour* of a very
Libidinous Tickling'.[32] For as Thomas Vicary puts it in *The
Englishman's Treasure; or, the True Anatomy of Man's Body*
(1586), 'by the labour and chafing of the testicles or stones, [the
best and purest] blood is turned into another kind, and is made
sparme',[33] and by a still further chafing this 'sparme' is released into
the heated womb. Hence, too, Duval's account of the way in which
his rubbing in the course of the medical examination caused Marin
le Marcis's hidden penis to yield forth its seed and produce proof of
his sexual identity. And that chafing was an official, public
repetition and confirmation of the erotic friction, in bed with Jeane
le Febvre, that originated Marin's transformation from Marie.

Marin le Marcis is an object of public interest, concern, and
scrutiny because of this transformation. His socially articulated

individuality – his emergence from the anonymous mass of men and women into the light of representation – is for the Renaissance a moment of prodigious instability on the way to integration into the normal structures of gender and reproduction.[34] Those structures are not, however, the secure, ontologically grounded *bases* for identity; on the contrary, they are themselves necessarily built up out of sexual confusion, friction, and transformation. 'It is when the normal is secure that playful aberration is benign', writes C. L. Barber; Marin's case suggests that the palace of the normal is constructed on the shifting sands of the aberrant.

III

If we seem to have swerved far from the world of Shakespearian theatre, let us recall once again some of the features of the story of Marin le Marcis: a love that cannot at first declare itself and that encounters, when it finally does so, life-threatening obstacles; a dizzying confusion of identity centred on cross-dressing; an intense experience of desire – the biological imperative – that seeks to satisfy itself in a sanctified union; the intervention of authority initially to block this union but eventually to free the hero from the threat of death and remove the obstacle to marriage; the wildly unconventional drive toward conventionality. This is, of course, the plot outline of a prototypical Shakespearian comedy, and I want to propose briefly that the resemblance is more than fortuitous.

I hasten to disclaim any suggestion that Shakespeare took a lively interest in the medical discourse about sex, or that he favoured one theory of generation over another, or – most unlikely of all – that he had read Paré, let alone heard of Marin le Marcis and Jacques Duval. But the state of Shakespeare's knowledge of medical science is not the important issue here. The relation I wish to establish between medical and theatrical practice is not one of cause and effect or source and literary realisation. We are dealing rather with a shared code, a set of interlocking tropes and similitudes that function not only as the objects but as the conditions of representation. Shakespearian comedy constantly appeals to the body and in particular to sexuality as the heart of its theatrical magic; 'great creating nature' – the principle by which the world is and must be peopled – is the comic playwright's tutelary spirit. But there is no unmediated access to the body, no direct appropriation of sexuality;

rather sexuality is itself a network of historically contingent figures that constitute the culture's categorical understanding of erotic experience. These figures function as modes of translation between distinct social discourses, channels through which the shared commotion of sexual excitement circulates.[35]

How does a play come to possess sexual energy? What happens when a body is translated from 'reality' to the stage or when a male actor is translated into the character of a woman? What does it mean for a Renaissance comedy, that most artificial of forms, to invoke nature or for nature, in the reified form of medical discourse, to assume the artificial form of a Renaissance comedy? By focusing on the precise shape of certain cultural figures for the body – here the body as natural transvestite and as a generator of heat through friction – we can venture an answer to these questions. We can grasp the meaning of the natural swerving that resolves the plot complications of *Twelfth Night*. We can begin to understand why all memorable representation of individuality in Shakespeare – from the gross monumental fat of Falstaff to Richard III's hunchback, from Macduff's untimely birth to Viola's uncanny twinship – is marked by the prodigious. And we can comprehend why Shakespeare repeatedly calls attention to the playing of all the women's parts – Kate, Portia, Viola, Juliet, Cleopatra, all of them – by boys.

Accounts of Shakespeare's plays constantly appeal, most often at the climactic point in the argument, to natural forces that underlie both social customs and literary models and give the characters their special power. These critical invocations of nature are not themselves a misreading – on the contrary, the plays actively solicit them – but the mistake is to imagine that the natural forces invoked are timeless and free-floating. Between Shakespeare's culture and our own there has been at least a partial shift in male gender perception from a search for the hidden penis in women to a search for the hidden womb in men, and with this shift the 'natural forces' invoked in the representation of individuals have themselves changed. Moreover, a transformation of the way we understand the relation between sexual pleasure and generation has intensified this change. A culture that imagines – or, better still, knows as an indisputable biological fact – that women need not experience any pleasure at all to conceive will offer different representational resources than a culture that knows, as a widely accepted physical truth, that women have occulted, inward penises that for the survival of mankind must be brought, through the heat of erotic friction, to the point of ejaculation. More specifically, a conception of gender that is teleologically male and insists upon a verifiable sign that confirms nature's final cause finds its supreme literary expression in a transvestite theatre; by contrast, a conception of gender that is symbolically female insists upon a genetic rather than a teleological account of identity, interests itself in the inward material matrix of individuality, and finds its supreme literary expression in the novel.[36]

The medical texts that we have been examining suggest that the generative power of nature centres on fruitful, pleasurable chafing, and I want to propose that this notion – which functions less as a technical explanation than as a virtually irresistible assumption on which to build technical explanations – resonates in the fashioning of Shakespearian characters, particularly in comedy. The theatrical representation of individuality is in effect modelled on what the culture thought occurred during sexual foreplay and intercourse: erotic chafing is the central means by which characters in plays like *The Taming of the Shrew, A Midsummer Night's Dream, Much Ado about Nothing, As You Like It,* and *Twelfth Night* realise their identities and form loving unions.[37]

The enemies of the Elizabethan and Jacobean theatre charged that the playhouse was 'Venus' Palace', a place of erotic arousal.[38] For all its insistence upon the solemn ceremony of marriage, Shakespearian comedy curiously confirms the charge, not only by gesturing forward to the pleasures of the marriage bed but also by the staging of its own theatrical pleasures. 'Men and women,' wrote the great anatomist William Harvey, 'are never more brave, sprightly, blithe, valiant, pleasant or beautiful than when about to celebrate the act.'[39] Shakespeare's enactment of the celebration confers on his comic heroes and heroines something of the special beauty of sexual arousal.

More than any of his contemporaries, Shakespeare discovered how to use the erotic power that the theatre could appropriate, how to generate plots that would not block or ignore this power but draw it out, develop it, return it with interest, as it were, to the audience. And this Shakespearian discovery, perfected over a six- or seven-year period in the comedies from *Taming* to *Twelfth Night,* entailed above all the representation of the emergence of identity through the experience of erotic heat. This Promethean heat, which is, as we have seen, the crucial practical agent of sexuality in the

Renaissance, would seem to be precisely what is excluded from theatrical presentation – it takes place internally, out of sight, in the privileged intimacy of the body. But sexual heat, we recall, is not different in kind from all other heat, including that produced by the imagination. Shakespeare realised that if sexual chafing could not be presented literally onstage, it could be represented figuratively: friction could be fictionalised, chafing chastened and hence made fit for the stage, by transforming it into the witty, erotically charged sparring that is the heart of the lovers' experience.

By means of this transformation Shakespeare invested his comedies with a powerful sexual commotion, a collective excitation, an imaginative heat that the plots promise will be realised offstage, in the marriage beds toward which they gesture: 'We'll begin these rites,/ As we do trust they'll end, in true delights' (*As You Like It* V.iv.197–8). But if this promised end, like Viola's suit of women's clothes, holds out to the audience a fantasy of resolution, a genital, generative literalising of chafing, it does not simply collapse fiction into friction. On the contrary, the unrepresented consummations of unrepresented marriages call attention to the unmooring of desire, the generalising of the libidinal, that is the special pleasure of Shakespearian fiction. For the representation of chafing is not restricted to Shakespeare's lovers; it is diffused throughout the comedies as a system of foreplay. This diffusion is one of the creative principles of comic confusion: hence, for example, Viola/Cesario's cheeky replies to Olivia arouse the latter's passion in a way Orsino's sighs and groans cannot.

Moreover, for Shakespeare friction is specifically associated with verbal wit; indeed at moments the plays seem to imply that erotic friction *originates* in the wantonness of language and thus that the body itself is a tissue of metaphors or, conversely, that language is perfectly embodied. Take for a single instance the following unremarkable exchange between Viola and Feste the clown:

> **Viola** 'Save thee, friend, and thy music! Dost thou live by thy tabor?
> **Clown** No, sir, I live by the church.
> **Viola** Art thou a churchman?
> **Clown** No such matter, sir. I do live by the church; for I do live at my house, and my house doth stand by the church.
> **Viola** So thou mayst say the king lies by a beggar, if a beggar dwells near him; or the church stands by thy tabor, if thy tabor stand by the church.

Clown You have said, sir. To see this age! A sentence is but a chev'ril glove to a good wit. How quickly the wrong side may be turn'd outward!

Viola Nay, that's certain. They that dally nicely with words may quickly make them wanton.

Clown I would therefore my sister had had no name, sir.

Viola Why, man?

Clown Why, sir, her name's a word, and to dally with that word might make my sister wanton.

(III.i.1–20)

The brief, almost schematic, enactment of verbal friction leads to a perception of the suppleness of language, and particularly its capacity to be inverted, as imaged by the chev'ril glove. It is as if the cause of Marie le Marcis's sexual arousal and transformation were now attributable to the ease – the simple change of one letter – with which Marie is turned into Marin. 'Her name's a word, and to dally with that word might make my sister wanton.'

Dallying with words is the principal Shakespearian representation of erotic heat. Hence his plots go out of their way to create not only obstacles in the lovers' path but occasions for friction between them: to select but a single example, when Rosalind escapes from the danger posed by her uncle and finds herself on her own in the woods with Orlando, she does not throw herself into her beloved's arms but rather initiates an occasion for playful tension between them: 'I will speak to him like a saucy lackey, and under that habit play the knave with him' (*As You Like It*, III.ii.95–7). Critics have often remarked that the scenes of chafing that follow – Rosalind's supposed 'cure' for the madness of love – are a symbolic testing of the strength of Orlando's love, but that love is never really in doubt. The chafing functions rather as a symbolic enactment of the lovers' mutual desires and a witty experimental fashioning of Rosalind's identity. We should add that the unique qualities of that identity – those that give Rosalind her independence, her sharply etched individuality – will not, as Shakespeare conceives the play, endure: they are bound up with exile, disguise, and freedom from ordinary constraint, and they will vanish, along with the playful chafing, when the play is done. What begins as a physiological necessity is reimagined as an improvisational self-fashioning that longs for self-effacement and reabsorption in the community. This longing is the sign of a social system that marks out singularity, particularly in women, as prodigious, though the disciplining of singularity is most often represented in Shakespearian comedy as romantic choice, an act of free will, an expression of love.

Why should that fashioning be bound up with cross-dressing (Rosalind, you will recall, is pretending to be a boy named Ganymede)? In part, I suggest, because the transformation of gender identity figures the emergence of an individual out of a twinned sexual nature. That emergence, let us recall, begins in the womb, but it never results in the absolute exclusion of the other seed, and the presence of both genders remains evident through adolescence.[40]

Shakespeare's most ingenious representation of this twinned gender identity, which must have empowered the transvestite performances of his company's boy actors, is in *Twelfth Night*, with its fiction of male and female identical twins who are at the border of adulthood: 'Not yet old enough for a man, nor young enough for a boy' (I.v.156–7). With a change of a few conventional signals, the exquisitely feminine Viola and the manly Sebastian are indistinguishable: hence, perhaps, the disquieting intensity of Antonio's passion for Sebastian and the ease with which the confused Olivia is 'betroth'd both to a maid and man' (V.i.263). Near the play's opening, Orsino nicely captures the gender confusion in an unintentionally ironic description of his young page Cesario – actually Viola in disguise:

> thy small pipe
> Is as the maiden's organ, shrill and sound,
> And all is semblative a woman's part.
> (I.iv.32–4)

At the play's close, Orsino has not yet seen Viola – whom he intends to marry – in woman's clothes; she remains in appearance Cesario and therefore still the mirror image of her brother:

> One face, one voice, one habit, and two persons,
> A natural perspective, that is and is not!
> (V.i.216–17)

To be sure, the play suggests that beneath her 'masculine usurp'd attire' is a body in which the feminine elements are dominant, and the 'true' mettle of her sex resolves the play's ambiguities by attaching Orsino's desire to an appropriate and 'natural' object. Viola will in the end – that is, when the play is done – put off her assumed male role and become 'Orsino's mistress, and his fancy's queen' (V.i.388). But this transformation is not enacted – it remains 'high fantastical' – and the only authentic transformation that the Elizabethan audience could anticipate when the play was done was the metamorphosis of Viola back into a boy.

Though Shakespeare characteristically represents his women characters – Rosalind, Portia, Viola – as realising their identities through cross-dressing, this whole conception of individuation seems to me bound up with Renaissance conceptions of the emergence of male identity. Viola in disguise is said to look like one whose 'mother's milk were scarce out of him' (I.v.161–2); in effect a boy is still close to the state of a girl and passes into manhood only when he has put enough distance between himself and his mother's milk. If a crucial step in male individuation is separation from the female, this separation is enacted inversely in the rites of cross-dressing; characters like Rosalind and Viola pass through the state of being men in order to become women. Shakespearian women are in this sense the representation of Shakespearian men, the projected mirror images of masculine self-differentiation.[41]

Why should the comedies traffic in mirror images? Why don't they represent this male trajectory of identity through male characters dressing up as women? In part because women had less freedom of movement, real or imaginary, than men, and hence donning women's clothes would entail not the rolling on which the course of nature depends but rather a stilling of momentum. In part because a passage from male to female was coded ideologically as a descent from superior to inferior and hence as an unnatural act or a social disgrace. And in part because women were, as we have seen, already understood to be inverted mirror images of men in their very genital structure. One consequence of this conceptual scheme – 'For that which man hath apparent without, that women have hid within' – is an apparent homoeroticism in all sexuality. Though by divine and human decree the consummation of desire could be licitly figured only in the love of a man and a woman, it did not follow that desire was inherently heterosexual. The delicious confusions of *Twelfth Night* depend upon the mobility of desire. And if poor Antonio is left out in the cold, Orsino does in a sense get his Cesario. I should add as a corollary to this set of exchanges and transformations that men love women precisely *as representations*, a love the original performances of these plays literalised in the person of the boy actor.

For the Renaissance theatre there is a further dimension to transvestism, one that returns us for the last time to the case of Marin le Marcis. Within the imaginary women's bodies, there are other bodies – the bodies of the actors playing the parts of Shakespearian women. From the perspective of the medical discourse we have been exploring, this final transvestism serves to secure theatrically the dual account of gender: on the one hand, we have plays that insist upon the chafing between the two sexes and the double nature of individuals; on the other hand, we have a theatre that reveals, in the presence of the man's (or boy's) body beneath the woman's clothes, a different sexual reality. The open secret of identity – that within differentiated individuals is a single structure, identifiably male – is presented literally in the all-male cast.[42] Presented but not represented, for the play – plots, characters, and the pleasure they confer – cannot continue without the fictive existence of two distinct genders and the friction between them.

From Stephen Greenblatt, *Shakespearean Negotiations: The Circulation of Social Energy in Renaissance England* (Oxford, 1988), pp. 66–93.

NOTES

[Stephen Greenblatt, a self-styled 'New Historicist', examines *Twelfth Night* in the context of Renaissance beliefs about the physiology of sex, arguing that the play enacts many of these beliefs in the transposed medium of language. Characteristic of new historicism is the strategy of quoting anecdotes from historical sources as a point of entry into the drama, which is equally seen as an historical document negotiating many of the age's tensions, ideologies and anxieties. All quotations are from *The Riverside Shakespeare*, ed. G. Blakemore Evans (Houghton Mifflin, 1974). Ed.]

1. *Montaigne's Travel Journal*, trans. Donald M. Frame (San Francisco, 1983), p. 5. In his *Introduction av traité de la conformité des merueilles anciennes auec les modernes, ov traité preparatif à l'Apologie pour Herodate* (1579), Henri Estienne recounts a similar case which he says took place some thirty years earlier: 'C'est qu'vne fille natiue de Fontaines, qui est entre Blois & Rommorantin, s'estant desguisee en homme, seruit de valet d'estable enuiron sept ans en vne hostelerie du faux-bourg du Foye, puis se maria à vne fille du lieu, auec laquelle elle fut enuiron deux ans, exerceant le mestier de vigneron. Apres lequel temps estant descouuerte la meschanceté de

laquelle elle vsoit pour contrefaire l'office de mari, fut prise, & ayant confessé fut là bruslee toute viue' (pp. 94–5).

2. Michel Foucault, *The History of Sexuality*, vol. 1, trans. Robert Hurley (New York, 1978), pp. 53–73. Foucault argues for a large-scale shift in the modern period away from legal definitions of sexual roles to endlessly elaborated discursive revelations of the open secret of sexuality.

3. In one of Shakespeare's principal sources for *Twelfth Night*, Barnaby Riche tells his readers that in his story 'you shall see Dame Errour so plaie her parte with a leishe of lovers, a male and twoo femalles, as shall woorke a wonder to your wise judgement' (*Riche his Farwell to Militarie Profession* [1581], in *Narrative and Dramatic Sources of Shakespeare*, 8 vols, ed. Geoffrey Bullough [London, 1958–75], vol. 2, p. 345). 'Error' has, I think, some of its etymological force of divagation, or wandering, a version of what I am calling swerving.

4. John Manningham's early seventeenth-century summary of the play mistakenly refers to Olivia as a widow – a sign, I think, of the normalisation of the fantasy (in the Arden edition of *Twelfth Night*, ed. J. M. Lothian and T. W. Craik [London, 1975], p. xxvi).

5. In the image of the cloistress, Olivia's vow picks up for Shakespeare's Protestant audience associations with life-denying monastic vows, which must be broken to honour the legitimate claims of the flesh by entering into holy matrimony. When Theseus threatens the recalcitrant Hermia with the 'livery of a nun,/For aye to be in shady cloister mew'd' (I.i.70–1), we can be certain that *A Midsummer Night's Dream* will not close with her 'Chaunting faint hymns to the cold fruitless moon' (I.i.73). The comedy will instead celebrate the triumph of warm blood and fruitful union. Similarly, when Isabella actively seeks the cloister, wishing only 'a more strict restraint/Upon the sister-hood' (I.iv.4–5), we anticipate that the play will overrule her desires. Odd as is the close of *Measure for Measure*, with the Duke's peremptory and unanswered proposal – 'Give me your hand, and say you will be mine' (V.i.492) – it would be still odder in the context of English comic conventions if it consigned the heroine to the votarists of Saint Clare. And when at the start of *Love's Labour's Lost* the young French lords vow to abjure the sight of women for three years, we would be surprised if there were not an immediate announcement of the arrival of the princess and her ladies.

6. Here, as elsewhere at the opening of *Twelfth Night*; Orsino imagines a massive singleness in love, corresponding to the play's initial gambit of the union of duke and countess. And this singleness is focused conspicuously on the 'rich golden shaft' that has the power to destroy all competing emotions in the beloved. If any psychological progress is sketched for Orsino, it lies in his accepting multiple emotions. It is not

altogether clear that he progresses in this direction, though a skilled actor might be able to suggest at the close that Orsino splits his desire between Cesario/Viola and Olivia.

7. The lawyer John Manningham, who saw the play in February 1602, immediately recognised several of the antecedents: 'At our feast wee had a play called Twelue night or what you will, much like the commedy of errors or Menechmi in plautus but most like and neere to that in Italian called Inganni' (Arden edn, p. xxvi). Manningham's date 'Febr:1601' is old-style. Manningham sketched the Malvolio subplot, which evidently struck him as original – 'a good practise' – but said nothing further about the main plot: presumably, the simple notation of analogues seemed to him sufficient to recall the play's essential shape.

8. The modal 'would' in the verb form 'would have been contracted' lightly refers both to Olivia's mismatched desires and, had it not been for nature's bias, to the absurd consequences of those desires. The slight oscillation, though of miniscule dramatic effect, is worth noticing because it encapsulates the play's large-scale oscillation between will and passivity.

9. An epithalamion Donne wrote for the scandal-surrounded marriage of the Earl of Somerset to the divorced Countess of Essex (1613) includes the following stanza entitled 'Equality of Persons':

> But undiscerning Muse, which heart, which eyes,
>   In this new couple, dost thou prize,
>   When his eye as inflaming is
> As hers, and her heart loves as well as his?
>   Be tried by beauty, and then
> The Bridegroom is a maid, and not a man.
> If by that manly courage they be tried,
> Which scorns unjust opinion; then the Bride
> Becomes a man. Should chance or envy's art
> Divide these two, whom nature scarce did part?
> Since both have both th'inflaming eyes, and both the loving heart.

This miniature Shakespearian comedy would seem to be played, in part at least, for a king who had a marked erotic interest in his male favourites. (I am indebted for this reference to Paul Alpers.)

10. To Sebastian's question, 'What name? What Parentage?' Viola answers with the father's name (the mother in effect having no bearing on the question of parentage): 'Sebastian was my father' (V.i.231–2). At the first mention of Orsino's name, Viola had remarked, 'Orsino! I have heard my father name him' (I.ii.28). At the play's close, when we learn that this naming must have betokened a measure of social equality, the dialogue swerves from the natural back to the social. That is, in the face of the gender confusion, attention to social conflict had

apparently been deflected by a concern for the natural; now the social returns the favour by deflecting attention from the natural. The play hastens to its conclusion by matching Orsino to Viola while gesturing towards Malvolio's grievance. For a Lacanian analysis of the 'Nom-du-Père' in relation to trans-sexualism, see Catherine Millot, *Horsexe: Essai sur le transsexualisme* (Paris, 1983), esp. pp. 29–43.

11. C. L. Barber, *Shakespeare's Festive Comedy* (Princeton, NJ, 1959), p. 245.

12. Marie, subsequently renamed Marin, was a bit vague on the subject, but Jeane's recollection was that on the first night they made love four times: Jeane testified that she had more sexual pleasure – 'plus grand contentement,' – with Marin than with her late husband (Jacques Duval, *Des Hermaphrodits, Accouchemens des Femmes, et Traitement qui est requis pour les releuer en santé, et bien eleuer leurs enfans* [Rouen, 1603], p. 392). (The marginal note to Jeane's account of the first night is 'Belle confirmation de promesse de mariage'.) [All further page references are given in parentheses in the text. Ed.]

13. In the only remotely comparable case that I know of, the court seemed similarly perplexed, though its decision was significantly different (and, to my knowledge, unprecedented). This was the case of Thomasine Hall, born in the 1570s near Newcastle upon Tyne. At age twelve, Thomasine was sent by her mother to live with an aunt in London, where she remained for ten years. At the time of the Cádiz action, we are told, she cut her hair, renamed herself Thomas, and enlisted as a soldier; then returned to London and resumed her life as a woman; then abandoned her needlework again and sailed as a man to Virginia; then became Thomasine once more and served as a chambermaid. Hauled before the Council and General Court of Virginia in 1629 and asked 'why hee went in weomans aparell', Thomasine gave the unforgettable, if enigmatic, reply, 'I goe in weomans aparell to gett a bitt for my Cat'. The judges evidently felt that unresolved sexual ambiguity was more tolerable than dizzying sexual metamorphosis; they preferred a figure frozen in acknowledged androgyny to one who passed fluidly and unpredictably from one state to another. Accordingly, they ordered that it be published that Hall 'is a man and a woman', and they insisted upon this doubleness in the clothes they required him to wear: 'Hee shall goe Clothed in mans apparell, only his head to bee attired in a Cyse and Croscloth [?] wth an Apron before him' (*Minutes of the Council and General Court of Colonial Virginia, 1622–1632, 1670–1676*, ed. H. R. McIlwaine [Richmond, VA, 1924], p. 195).

14. Michell Z. Rosaldo, *Knowledge and Passion: Ilongot Notions of Self and Social Life* (Cambridge, 1980), p. 231; see also Pierre Bourdieu, *Outline of a Theory of Practice*, trans. Richard Nice (Cambridge, 1977):

Since the history of the individual is never anything other than a certain specification of the collective history of his group or class, *each individual system of dispositions* may be seen as a *structural variant* of all the other group or class habitus, expressing the difference between trajectories and positions inside or outside the class. 'Personal' style, the particular stamp marking all the product of the same habitus, whether practices or works, is never more than a *deviation* in relation to the *style* of a period or class so that it relates back to the common style not only by its conformity ... but also by the difference which makes the whole 'manner'. (p. 86)

15. Such stories are by no means limited to literary fictions. Thus, for example, the sixteenth-century chronicler Robert Fabian writes of three New World savages presented to Henry VII that they 'were clothed in beasts skins, & did eate raw flesh, and spake such speach that no man could understand them, and in their demeanour like to bruite beastes'. 'Of the which upon two yeeres after,' he continues, 'I saw two apparelled after the maner of Englishmen in Westminster pallace, which that time I could not discerne from Englishmen, til I was learned what they were' (quoted in Stephen Greenblatt 'Learning to Curse: Aspects of Linguistic Colonialism in the Sixteenth Century', in *First Images of America: The Impact of the New World in the Old*, 2 vols, ed. Fredi Chiappelli (Berkeley, CA, 1976), vol. 2, p. 563.

16. The modern interest, fuelled by sociology, in the structures that govern individual improvisations finds its paradoxical equivalent in the Renaissance interest in prodigies: prodigies function exactly like sociological structures – to make normative, individual variations possible. It is difficult in an inquiry such as this to hold on to the sense that individuals are variations on (or deviations from) a set of social structures. Pierre Bourdieu: ' "Interpersonal" relations are never, except in appearance, *individual-to-individual* relationships and ... the truth of the interaction is never entirely contained in the interaction' (*Outline of a Theory of Practice*, p. 81).

Nature in Renaissance thought is not a static entity but a life force that must constantly generate, create, reproduce individuals. If this force should cease for an instant, all life would cease, and matter would sink back into primal confusion and disorder. This ceaseless generativity is epitomised in the production of prodigies, which by their very existence affirm the variety of things and mark out ineradicable differences. At the same time, prodigies represent the disorder that their existence helps to negate. The monstrous is virtually defined by excess and by the improper, disordered fashioning of matter into misshapen lumps, strange conjunctions, gross and unnecessary excrescences. Hence even as they celebrate the inexhaustible fecundity of nature in producing prodigies, Renaissance scholars hasten to discover the principle of order that may be perceived behind even the most uncanny oddity (see Jean Céard, *La Nature et les prodiges: L'Insolie au 16e siècle en France* [Geneve, 1977]).

The prodigious functions as the extremest form of individuation – just as in modern sociology the quantifiable functions as the extremest form of the normative. This tendency of the individual, in its purest or logically extended form, to become the prodigious is supremely visible in Shakespeare, where the prodigious taints all decisive individuation. This is true, in different senses to be sure, in comedy as well as tragedy. Those comic characters who achieve the greatest level of individuation in effect pass through either a literal or metaphoric experience of the prodigious: Viola, Rosalind, Bottom the Weaver, Shylock, Falstaff, even Jaques and Malvolio. The prodigious (as physical grotesquerie, madness, or excess) is still more marked in the great tragic characters: Richard III, Macbeth, Hamlet, Othello, Antony and Cleopatra.

17. Hence the note of androgyny in Spenser's depiction of nature in the *Faerie Queene*:

> Then forth issewed (great goddesse) great dame *Nature*,
> With goodly port and gracious Maiesty;
> Being far greater and more tall of stature
> Then any of the gods of Powers on hie:
> Yet certes by her face and physnomy,
> Whether she man or woman inly were,
> That could not any creature well descry:
> For, with a veile that wimpled euery where,
> Her head and face was hid, that mote to none appear.
>
> (VII.7.5)

18. Nathaniel Highmore, *The History of Generation* (London, 1651), pp. 92–3.

19. See, for example, *The Workes of that Famous Chirurgian Ambrose Parey*, trans. Thomas Johnson (London, 1634):

> When the husband commeth into his wives chamber hee must entertaine her with all kinde of dalliance, wanton behaviour, and allurements to venery: but if he perceive her to be slow, and more cold, he must cherish, embrace, and tickle her, and shall not abruptly, the nerves being suddenly distended, breake into the field of nature, but rather shall creepe in by little and little intermixing more wanton kisses with wanton words and speeches, handling her secret parts and dugs, that she may take fire and bee enflamed to venery, for so at length the wombe will strive and waxe fervent with a desire of casting forth its owne seed, and receiving the mans seed to bee mixed together therewith. But if all these things will not suffice to enflame the woman, for women for the most part are slow and slack unto the expulsion or yeelding forth of their seed, it shall be necess-

ary first to foment her secret parts with the decoction of hot herbes made with Muscadine, or boiled in any other good wine, and to put a little muske or civet into the neck or mouth of the wombe. (p. 889)

This book will be referred to in the text of my essay as Paré, *Works*.

20. For an important and fascinating account of the changes in the understanding of female sexuality, see Thomas Laqueur, 'Orgasm, Generation, and the Politics of Reproductive Biology', in *Representations*, 14 (1986), 1–41.

21. Galen, *On the Usefulness of the Parts of the Body*, 2 vols, ed. and trans. Margaret May (Ithaca, NY, 1968), vol. 2:14.297, pp. 628–9.

22. Ibid., vol. 2:14.297–8, p. 629. Elsewhere in his work, Galen observes that while the mole's inability to bring forth its eyes is entirely a defect, the female's comparable inability to bring forth her genitals is of great use, since it enables her to bear children (Galen, *De semine*, vol. 2:5, in *Libri Novem* [Basle, 1536], pp. 173–4).

23. Paré, *Works*, p. 128. It is important to grasp that Paré does not connect his two explanations and argue for a 'providential defect'. Instead the contradictory theories exist side by side and speak to different aspects of the same problem.

24. Ambroise Paré, *On Monsters and Marvels* (1573), trans. Janis L. Pallister (Chicago, 1928), pp. 31–2.

25. *Montaigne's Travel Journal*, p. 6. Montaigne (or his secretary) adds, 'They say that Ambroise Paré has put this story into his book on surgery'.

26. Hence Duval's fascination with Marin expresses his own uneasiness with the inherited medical traditions that Marin seems at once to confirm and to push toward grotesquerie.

27. The clitoris is, Duval says, such a violent source of sexual pleasure that even the most modest of women will, if once they agree to allow it to be touched by the finger's end, be overcome with desire: 'amorcées & rauies, voire forcées au deduit veneréen' (*Des Hermaphrodits*, p. 63). ('Donnant l'exact sentiment de cette partie, pour petite qu'elle soit, vne tant violente amorce au prurit & ardeur libidineux, qu'estant la raison surmontee, les femelles prennent tellement le frain aux dents qu'elles donnent du cul à terre, faute de se tenir fermes & roides sur les arcons' [pp. 63–4].) Hence in French, Duval writes, the clitoris is popularly called 'tentation, aiguillon de volupté, verge femininine [sic], le mespris des hommes: Et les femmes qui font profession d'impudicité la nomment leur *gaude mihi*' (p. 64).
 On the displacement of the structural homology from the uterus to the clitoris, see Ian Maclean, *The Renaissance Notion of Woman: A*

Study in the Fortunes of Scholasticism and Medical Science in European Intellectual Life (Cambridge, 1980), p. 33.

28. *Aristotle's Master-piece or the Secrets of Generation Displayed* (London, 1690), p. 15. The first known English edition of this incessantly reprinted anonymous work is 1684, though the work was probably circulated in English considerably earlier; it was still circulated widely in the nineteenth century.

29. The notion of the enlarged clitoris is alive and well in the seventeenth and early eighteenth centuries: 'Sometimes it grows so long,' writes the midwife Jane Sharp in 1671, 'that it hangs forth at the slit like a Yard, and will swell and stand stiff if it be provoked, and some lewd women have attempted to use it as men do theirs ... but I never heard but of one in this Country' (quoted in Audrey Eccles, *Obstetrics and Gynaecology in Tudor and Stuart England* [Kent, OH, 1982], p. 34). See also Hilda Smith, 'Gynecology and Ideology in Seventeenth-Century England,' in *Liberating Women's History: Theoretical and Critical Essays*, ed. Berenice A. Carroll (Champaign, IL, 1976), pp. 97–114.

30. The interest and complexity of this account depends on the lovers' looking at the other as they strive to re-create images of themselves; or perhaps they are simultaneously looking at the other and at their own reflection in each other's eyes. In either case, the representation of oneself – one's reproduction and hence triumph over death – depends upon self-abandonment, upon giving oneself over to the image of the other. One might recall the moment in Milton when God draws Eve away from her narcissism – that is, her potentially dangerous and prodigious individuation – toward a proper bonding with another. The narcissism is symbolised by her peering in the water at her reflection, unstable and perpetually unsatisfying, and the proper bonding by her steady gazing into the face of another – Adam – and by the production of other images in the offspring they will generate.

31. The medical literature offers considerable speculation on the place of the imagination in the process of sexual consummation and conception, in the work of the German physician Paracelsus, for example, especially 'Das Buch von der Gebärung der empfindlichen Dinge in der Vernunft' (*c.* 1520), in Theophrastus von Hohenheim gen. Paracelsus, *Medizinische Naturwissenshaftliche und Philosophische Schriften*, ed. Karl Sudhoff (Munich, 1925), vol. 1, pp. 243–83. I owe this fascinating reference to Jane O. Newman.

32. John McMath, *The Expert Midwife* (1694), quoted in Eccles, *Obstetrics and Gynaecology*, p. 40.

33. Thomas Vicary, *The Anatomie of the Bodie of Man*, ed. Frederick J. Furnivall and Percy Furnivall, Early English Text Society, Extra Series 53 (London, 1888), p. 79. I should add, of course, that there are

endless references in the erotic poetry of the period to this heat, for example, in Marlowe's *Hero and Leander*:

She, fearing on the rushes to be flung,
Striv'd with redoubled strength; the more she strivèd,
The more a gentle pleasing heat revivèd,
Which taught him all that elder lovers know.
And now the same 'gan so to scorch and glow,
As in plain terms (yet cunningly) he craved it.
                                                    (II.66–71)

Similarly, the whole of Shakespeare's *Venus and Adonis* is dominated by the language of heat.

34. We might find in Hobbes a theoretical equivalent, outside the medical tradition, of Duval's sense of the importance of friction in the origin of human differentiation. For Hobbes all human thought emerges from sense, and sense emerges from what I have been calling chafing: 'The cause of Sense is the External Body, or Object, which presseth the organ proper to each Sense, either immediately, as in the Tast and Touch; or mediately, as in Seeing, Hearing, and Smelling; which pressure, by the mediation of Nerves, and other strings, and membranes of the body, continued inwards to the Brain, and Heart, causeth there a resistance, or counter pressure, or endeavour of the Heart, to deliver it self' (*Leviathan* 1:1).

If the sense of outward forms originates for Hobbes in 'counter pressure', then the sense of 'inward forms' likewise originates in this experience.

35. I borrow the term *commotion* from Leo Bersani, 'Representation and Its Discontents', in *Allegory and Representation*, ed. Stephen Greenblatt (Baltimore, MD, 1981), pp. 145–62. 'How are cultural activities,' Bersani asks in another essay, ' "invested" with sexual interests?' His answer, following Melanie Klein, is that there is in sexual excitement a supplement that exceeds any particular representation attached to it and that therefore becomes 'as it were, greedily, even promiscuously, available to *other* scenes and *other* activities' (Leo Bersani, ' "The Culture of Redemption": Marcel Proust and Melanie Klein', *Critical Inquiry*, 12 [1986], 410).

36. On the feminisation of the male subject, see Terry Eagleton, *The Rape of Clarissa* (Minneapolis, 1982), pp. 13ff.; Anne Douglass, *The Feminisation of American Culture* (New York, 1977); George S. Rousseau, 'Nerves, Spirits, Fibres: Towards the Origins of Sensibility', in *Studies in the Eighteenth Century III: Proceedings of the David Nichol Smith Conference*, ed. R. F. Brissenden and J. C. Eade (Canberra, 1976), pp. 137–57; John Mullan, 'Hypochondria and Hysteria: Sensibility and the Physicians', *Eighteenth Century: Theory and Interpretation*, 25 (Spring 1984), 141–74; and now Terry Castle,

'The Female Thermometer', *Representations*, 17 (1987); 1–27. I am indebted to Castle's article for several of these references.

The feminisation of the male subject is linked with a change in the conception of homosexuality, or rather with the development of the whole category of homosexuality as a distinct sexual status out of (and ultimately opposed to) earlier notions of unnatural acts. Unnatural acts – perversion – become explicable as inversion: the deviant performance of the inner nature, which is feminine. Important work in progress by Christopher Craft has helped to illuminate this conceptual shift.

37. I think Shakespeare first realised the erotic energy of chafing in the wooing scene in *Richard III*. In *The Rape of Lucrece* and *The Taming of the Shrew*, he went on to explore (and exploit) this energy in the form of violence and aggression, but the aggression is itself tamed in *A Midsummer Night's Dream* and *Much Ado about Nothing*.

38. The phrase 'Venus' Palace' is from Philip Stubbes, *The Anatomie of Abuses* (London, 1595), p. 104. On attacks on the theatre, see Jonas Barish, *The Antitheatrical Prejudice* (Berkely, CA, 1981), chs 3–6.

39. *The Anatomical Lectures of William Harvey*, ed. and trans. Gweneth Whitteridge (Edinburgh, 1964), p. 175. For Harvey the beauty conferred by sex is something man shares with the rest of the animal world. Harvey's own great work on roosters and hens began the shift, after Shakespeare's lifetime, toward an understanding of the ovum, yet even his account of animal behaviour conveys a sense of both the sexual energies that I find transfigured in the comedies and the melancholy darkness that lies just beyond the transfiguration:

> When males prepare themselves for coitus and, swelling with desire, are stimulated by the fire of venery, how wondrously does Cupid reigning within them heighten their inflamed spirits! how proudly do they parade themselves, bedecked with ornaments, how vigorous they are and how prone to do battle! But when this office of life is once ended, alas! how suddenly does their vigor subside and their late fervour cool, their swelling sails hang loose, and they lay aside their late ferocity. Indeed, even while this gay dance of Venus yet lasts, the males are straightway sad after coitus, and are seen to be submissive and pusillanimous as if mindful that, while they are bestowing life on others, they are hastening apace to their own decease. Only our cock, full of seed and spirits, lifts himself with greater sprightliness, and with beating wings and triumphant voice sings his hymeneal at his own nuptials. Yet even he flags after long use of venery and like a soldier time expired grows weary, and the hens too, like plants, become past laying and are exhausted. (William Harvey, *Disputations Touching the Generation of Animals*, trans. Gweneth Whitteridge [Oxford, 1981], p. 151)

40. The English stage, unlike the Chinese or Japanese, never developed a tradition of adult female impersonation; only boys could, as it were, naturally play the woman's part. (Or perhaps – and, if so, equally significant – the English called anyone who played a woman's part a boy.)

41. For a similar argument about stories of cross-dressing in medieval saints' lives, see Caroline Walker Bynum, 'Women's Stories, Women's Symbols: A Critique of Victor Turner's Theory of Liminality', forthcoming in *Anthropology and the Study of Religions*, ed. Frank E. Reynolds and Robert Moore [pub. 1981–Ed.]. See also the suggestive observations in Nancy K. Miller, ' "I"s in Drag: The Sex of Recollection', *Eighteenth Century*, 22 (1981), 47–57.

42. For the idea of the 'open secret' I am indebted to a superb essay on *David Copperfield* by D. A. Miller: 'Secret Subjects, Open Secrets', *Dickens Studies Annual*, 14 (1985), 17–38. This essay will appear as a chapter in Miller's forthcoming *The Novel and the Police*, to be published by the University of California Press.

There is a further, paradoxical, function to the open secret of theatrical cross-dressing since the all-male cast is used to excuse the theatre from any imputation of erotic *reality*: all of the wooing has been an imaginary pageant since the 'natural' end of that wooing – the union of a man and a woman of the generation of offspring – is impossible.

6

'And all is semblative a woman's part': Body Politics and *Twelfth Night*

DYMPNA CALLAGHAN

I

Once a marginalised object in traditional literary scholarship, the body has emerged as a crucial category of critical inquiry. In Renaissance studies, it has become the focus of attention as the site of emergent notions of the modern subject and attendant concepts of privacy and intimacy hitherto viewed as natural and trans-historical. Transformations wrought by the Reformation and the shift from feudalism to capitalism rendered the body subject to what Norbert Elias has called 'the civilising process'.[1] More specifically, Renaissance theatre itself had a corporeal, sexual identity. It was a place where, to use Dekker's redolent term, 'stinkards' gathered, where patrons engaged in those sexual practices so often vilified by anti-theatricalists: arousal, prostitution, perhaps even copulation itself.[2] The Renaissance body, then, especially in the arena of theatre, has been recognised as political, that is, as a site for the operation of power and the exercise of meaning, and one 'fully social in its being and in its ideological valency'.[3]

That the Renaissance seems peculiarly concerned with the somatic might seem justification enough for a study of the body in Shakespeare. We might concur with Carroll Smith-Rosenberg who argues, 'During periods of social transformation, when social forms crack open ... ideological conflict fractures discourse ... sexuality and the physical body emerge as particularly evocative political symbols.'[4] But the resurgence of the body in Renaissance studies (and elsewhere) is not a perennial, cyclical phenomenon. Rather, the intensity of focus on the body is related to very specific, historically situated developments in poststructuralist theory.

In *The Ideology of the Aesthetic*, Terry Eagleton draws attention to the politics of current concern with the body:

> few literary texts are likely to make it nowadays into the new historicist canon unless they contain at least one mutilated body. A recovery of the importance of the body has been one of the most precious achievements of recent radical thought. ... At the same time, it is difficult to read the later Roland Barthes, or even the later Michel Foucault, without feeling that a certain style of meditation on the body, on pleasures and surfaces, zones and techniques, has acted among other things as a convenient displacement of a less immediately corporeal politics, and acted also as an *ersatz* kind of ethics. There is a privileged, privatised hedonism about such discourse, emerging as it does at just the historical point where certain less exotic forms of politics found themselves suffering a setback.[5]

The body is simultaneously situated here as *de facto*, 'exotic', 'precious achievement', and 'displacement' of serious politics. The emancipatory potential projected on to the body (by feminist and Queer theorists as much as the doyens of poststructuralism) versus the political limitations of current fetishisations of the body seem to put the 'undecidable' and the 'dialectical' perilously close. None the less, Eagleton draws our attention to the fact that the body in much critical discourse becomes the site of 'micropolitics' (in centrist or 'ludic' readings of the postmodern as opposed to resistance postmodernism),[6] which is believed to have replaced the grand conceptual, liberatory narratives of political economy. Ludic postmodernism produces a naïve notion that social transformation can be articulated at the local level of the corporeal. Foucault falls into this utopian vision of the body at the end of *The History of Sexuality*. The body, as a site of opacity almost exempt from meaning, becomes the privileged locus of resistance: 'The rallying point for the counterattack against the deployment of sexuality ought not to be sex-desire, but bodies and pleasures.'[7] While 'bodies and pleasures' mark Foucault's distance from Derridean and Lacanian desire, in the end the ideological effect is the same, namely one of 'privileged, privatised hedonism'. Similarly Bakhtin, whose rhetoric is more that of mouth and anus than zone and surface, none the less deploys a populist, utopian view of the disruptiveness of the grotesque body.[8]

Paradoxically too, micropolitical analyses are frequently presented as 'materialist'. For example, both Foucault's techniques of the subject and Bakhtin's grotesque realism have been viewed as such, in what Eagleton dubs 'the modish, purely gestural uses of that most euphoric of radical buzz-words'.[9] In some instances, popular and politically specific uses of the term materialism are employed as if they were synonymous. Lucy Gent and Nigel Llewellyn, for example, in their fairly traditional, thematic approach to *Renaissance Bodies*, argue for the sheer material reality of the body, as opposed to 'abstraction and distance', that is, the discursivity of the 'figure': ' "Body", by contrast, suggests the solidly central unrepresented fact of existence, a materiality that is of itself inarticulate. It is the mute substance of which "figure" is a more nervous and expressive shadow.'[10] Yet, this appearance of substance occurs only because this is how, within the transactions of discourse, the body is rendered intelligible in our culture. When Gent and Llewellyn refer to the body's 'sheer physicality', the mute facticity of its materiality, they reduce the material to the elemental. This is a classically humanist definition of the material as the density of things you can touch. Mas'ud Zavarzadeh explains:

> In the discourses of ludic postmodernism, 'politics' is an exemplary instance of totalitarian 'conceptuality'. The micropolitics of the body, on the other hand, is politics without concepts: the local politics of material experience. However *material* in these theories ... means the immediate elements of the medium of the political, that is to say, the discourses that articulate subjectivities and thus produce the micropolitical. It is, in other words, a materialist politics only in the sense that, for example, focusing on the 'photochemical reality' of film makes the film maker a 'materialist' film maker. An idealist materialism isolates single issues and their mode of enunciation from the global structures of the political economy.[11]

Such critical discourses, then, invoke the body as substantive, ontologically grounded *raw* material devoid of any agenda for social transformation. Alternatively (and sometimes simultaneously) in its textualist rendition, the material is defined *as* discourse, as the material part of the sign, to which the body contributes, as Barthes has proposed, through the phatic dimension of speech.[12] Thus, a characteristic deconstructionist manoeuvre places the opacity of both the signifier and the body as the 'material' dimensions of the production of meaning. This depoliticised materialism conveniently coincides with both post-Marxism and those reactionary elements of the (ludic) postmodern to which it is also causally related. In this way, contemporary discourse on the body, as Eagleton argues, has become alienated from the 'more traditional political topics of the state, class conflict and modes of production', that is, from historical materialism as it has been previously and more rigorously understood.[13] The body, then, even when it is understood not as simple transhistorical fact but as 'a relation in a system of liaisons which are material, discursive, psychic, sexual, but without stop or centre',[14] may signal, none the less, the displacement of the political defined as the global, totalising agendas relegated to obsolescence in much postmodern theory. Thus, while ludic postmodern discourses of the body offer substantially different accounts of the body from humanist understandings, finally, their ideological effects are disarmingly similar.

Materialism, as I have argued, can be reduced neither to raw physicality nor to the so-called materiality of signs; both constitute 'idealist materialism'. In terms of discourse on the body, this is to deny neither the 'real' ontological existence of the body nor the materiality of discourse.[15] However, the material should not be confined to the binarism brute-material/discursive, but rather considered as the way the social and cultural always *exceed* the discursive. For this is precisely what is at stake over the question of the material. An example may clarify the point: that certain classes of women were particularly marked out as rape victims in the Renaissance (servants, for example), and that women continue to be viewed as sexual terrain to be possessed, violated, and commodified, constitute physical, social and cultural aspects of rape as opposed to purely physical or 'textual' ones.[16] (Thus, women are no more vulnerable to rape as an inherent fact of biology than men are to castration.) Rape has, then, both a physicality and a politics that in a patriarchal culture concerns relations *between men* in which women are property, and as such it cannot be separated from issues of class and ownership. That is, the discursive construction of the gendered body is implicated in the materiality of the non-discursive; and the latter is not simply raw materiality, but also the social and cultural.

I have chosen an example pertinent to feminist struggle because the politics of the body are exacerbated and more urgent there: as the object of patriarchal subjugation women are uniquely identified

with their anatomy, which has been simultaneously and problematically marked as the ground of feminist resistance. The problem is
whether the body intrinsically constitutes an appropriate and effective site of resistance to the increasingly dense, subtle, and comprehensive conceptual trap of late capitalist patriarchy. The danger
is that 'its pre-existing meanings, as sex object, as object of the male
gaze, can always prevail and reappropriate the body.'[17] It is not
clear that we reclaim women's bodies – especially denigrated female
genitals which get culturally marked as the source of women's
oppression – without regressing into biological essentialism (the
very rationale for women's subordination), the phenomenology of
lived experience, or the political evasions of poststructuralism.[18]
Nor can we reclaim past representations of female corporeality in
any simple, celebratory way.

In what follows, I want to use a more politically effective understanding of materialism than the one current in cultural criticism of
the body in order to focus on the absent-presence of female genitals
in *Twelfth Night*. My analysis of the play's representations of the
female body works within global rather than local structures and
resists the characteristic poststructuralist notion that undecidability
is liberating. Further, I want to resist the pervasive tendency in
Shakespeare criticism, in both its humanist and poststructuralist
manifestations, to conflate 'matter' and materialism, a trivialisation
that blocks the emancipatory potential of this radical concept.[19] For
the female body, while not literally present on the Renaissance
stage, was constantly and often scabrously constructed in masculine
discourses in ways that reinforced larger patriarchal institutions and
practices.[20]

II

Boys dressed up as women!

In Shakespearian comedy the female body is most obviously a
problem at the (secondary) level of the text's fiction where female
characters like Viola and Rosalind disguise themselves as eunuchs
and lackeys. But the female body is also problematised at the
primary level of Renaissance theatre practice in which boys played
'the woman's part'. Lisa Jardine argues: ' "Playing the woman's
part" – male effeminacy – is an act for a male audience's appreciation' and that 'these figures are sexually enticing *qua* trans-
vestised boys, and that the plays encourage the audience to view

them as such.'[21] As the complexity of this state of affairs has been emphasised, however, there has been something of a displacement of the initial feminist recognition that transvestism is an aspect of misogyny based on the material practice of excluding women from the Renaissance stage – the 'boy actress' phenomenon.[22] Thus, while Stephen Orgel in a brilliant contribution to *South Atlantic Quarterly's* special issue on homosexuality contends like Jardine that homosexuality was the dominant form of eroticism in Renaissance culture, he also argues (and this is indeed a crucial recognition) that the homoeroticism of the Renaissance stage was not inevitably misogynist.[23] Transvestism could not have had particularly insidious implications for women, he argues, because plays depended for their success on the large numbers of female playgoers. None the less, the *exclusion* of women from the stage and their simultaneous *inclusion* as customers – the fundamental characteristic (contradiction) of the institution of theatre in early modern England – does not exculpate theatre from charges of misogyny. This should not lead us to conclude, of course, that women's appearance on the stage at the Restoration should be read simply as 'progress'. In those countries where female players were allowed on stage, women were no less oppressed than in England.[24] Rather, the point here is to recognise the flexibility, the historically and geographically variable nature of patriarchy, while insisting on the exclusion of women from the Renaissance stage as the determinate material condition in the theatre's production and representation of femininity.

Catherine Belsey's essay, 'Disrupting Sexual Difference: Meaning and Gender in the Comedies', a feminist-deconstructionist reading of the comedies, where any destabilisation of meaning is in and of itself 'political', urges the positive play of transvestism only by ignoring the fact that it is founded on the systematic and structural oppression of women. She reads the endless play of meaning inherent in transvestism as inherently subversive; it becomes undecidable and therefore, 'for us to decide'. But since, as she points out, all meanings in language are inherently unstable, it is hard to see why transvestite destabilisations should offer any particularly liberating possibilities for feminism.[25] None the less, for Belsey, comic transvestism, particularly in *Twelfth Night*, which 'takes the most remarkable risks with the identity of its central figure' permits us 'to glimpse alternative possibilities'. But it is very likely that the new possibilities Belsey envisages would equally provide the basis for control and self-surveillance.[26]

In contrast to this strain of criticism, I want to argue that in the carnivalesque world of *Twelfth Night* the female body's capacity for resistance and disruption is severely curtailed by the fact that the transvestite actor is 'as likely to be portraying women with contempt as with respect'[27] and where the male body, 'the very instrument of the art of the theatre',[28] repeatedly and ritually enacts the displacement, exclusion, and discipline of its female counterpart.

III Historical views of cross dressing

In the Renaissance, mimicking social superiors by wearing their clothes was as much a violation of natural order as the assumption of a sexual identity other than that dictated by one's anatomical destiny. Antitheatricalists tirelessly inveighed against the latter. A fairly typical example of such an attack is to be found in Philip Stubbes's infamous book, whose very title, *The Anatomy of Abuses*, invokes the corporeality of deviance:

> Our apparell was given as a sign distinctive, to discern betwixt sexe and sexe, and therefore one to wear the apparell of an other sex, is to participate with the same and to adulterate the veritie of his own kinde.[29]

Gender cross-dressing is an obvious target for antitheatricalists given the biblical injunction against it: ' "the Lord forbideth men and wemen to chaunge raiment" ', and the 1620 pamphlet controversy about androgynous dress, *Hic Mulier* and *Haec Vir*.[30] Nevertheless, *two* types of transvestism prevailed: that which violated the boundaries of gender demarcation and that which violated class hierarchy. On this matter, Jonas Barish summarises the representative view of Puritan cleric William Perkins: 'Distinctions of dress, however external and theatrical they may seem to us, for Perkins virtually belong to our essence, and may no more be tampered with than that essence itself.'[31] Thus, for the likes of Perkins and Stubbes, essence resides in apparel rather than in what lies beneath it. To divest oneself of the appropriate social signifiers is to alter one's essence, to adulterate God-given nature. From this point of view, the soul resides in the clothes, not just for Parolles, but for all humanity.

That there is a structural identity between gender and class transvestism is demonstrable in the fact that the profound hostility to transvestite actors was related to the revival of medieval sumptuary

laws which prohibited the confusions of 'degrees' and 'callings'
ordained by God.[32] This is so much the case that Malvolio's
obedience to the injunction contained in a forged letter that he wear
yellow stockings and cross-garters, all but overwhelms the
Viola/Sebastian plot from which it singularly diverts the audience's
attention.[33] Malvolio's cross-gartering, his 'transvestism' is, then,
structurally and symbolically related to gender inversion, and it is
no further removed from anatomical inscription than is Viola's disguise. Malvolio adopts attire that might be suitable if worn by a
young gentleman suitor to Olivia, but incongruous and ridiculous
when worn by a servant who sees himself fit to be her husband.[34]
As the Elizabethan 'Homily Against Excess of Apparell' contended,
such behaviour constitutes a violation of both decorum and decree:

> many a one doubtless should be compelled to wear a russet coat
> which now ruffleth in silks and velvets, spending moe by the year in
> superfluous apparell than their fathers received for the whole revenue
> of their lands.[35]

Having indulged in these improprieties, in a sense, Malvolio really
is mad because it is, as Raymond Ruyer remarks, such eccentricities
and deviations from the naturalised orthodoxy of decorum which
are 'the small change of madness'.[36]

Notably, the only record we have of a Renaissance performance
of the play does not so much as mention Viola's transvestism.[37]
John Manningham's contemporary response places Malvolio at the
play's core:

> At our feast we had a play called Twelfth Night or What You Will,
> much like the Commedy of Errors or Menechmi in Plautus, but most
> like and near to that in Italian called Inganni. A good practise in it to
> make the Steward believe his Lady Widdowe was in love with him by
> counterfeyting a letter from his Lady in general terms, telling him
> what shee liked best in him and prescribing his gesture in smiling his
> apparaile etc, and then when he came to practise making him beleeve
> they tooke him to be mad.[38]

Similarly, Charles I, embracing the title's invitation to tag the play,
'What You Will', inscribed *Malvolio* opposite the title of the play in
his second folio. A 1623 performance of the play also refers to it by
that title.[39] Although we cannot account for all the changes that
may have occurred from the time of the first recorded performance
to the text we have received (Olivia is not a widow for instance,

and we have no way of knowing whether this represents Manningham's error or a reference simply to the costume of a widow, or to a change in the text), there is good reason to concur with Margaret Maurer who contends, 'Frankly he [Malvolio] has upstaged the twin device.'[40] However, Malvolio does not merely upstage the comedy of the main plot: he notoriously disrupts the festive spirit of *Twelfth Night*. The unrecuperable 'I'll be reveng'd on the whole pack of you' (V.i.377) troubles all the charm and delight that critics and audiences have found in the play. It is also possible that Malvolio's desire for revenge is directed at women, and at Olivia quite specifically for her 'Alas, poor fool, how they have baffled thee!' (V.i.368). It would seem, then, that class transvestism is more threatening than that of gender, which can be resolved rather more readily.[41] In this respect, Malvolio's cross-gartering is more subversive than any instance of gender cross-dressing because it is Malvolio who disturbs the romantic coupling with which the play concludes.

Because traditional criticism has often been at pains to gloss over or dissolve the discordant tone produced by Malvolio's promise of revenge, it has never been linked to the other major source of disharmony, namely the ' "discord" between the romance and the broader comedy of the play'.[42] The dimensions of significant corporeality enacted in both gender and class transvestism and the feminised carnal excesses constitutive of the play's bawdy are crucially interarticulated. Recognising this interconnectedness, the way the female body is imbricated in complex ways with other social categories, especially class, renders the female body in *Twelfth Night* not as a merely localised phenomenon but as a pervasive cultural one. Specifically here I want to contest the notion put forth by Kathleen McLuskie that 'The primary, physiological, distinction could not, of course, be represented on the stage.'[43] In other words, in my reading, what is at issue is not *whether it could be* represented but *how it is* represented. That is, the monstrous female genitalia in the play's representational register is not merely a localised 'theme', but rather depends upon and produces the exclusion and denigration of women, and the ridicule and punishment of men who attempt to change their status in the social hierarchy. This is nothing less than the maintenance and reproduction of patriarchy.

Let me elaborate first on the text's bawdy, the raw physical humour that often disconcerts critics who favour the ethereal lyricism held to be the definitive characteristic of romantic comedy. Eric

Partridge in a revised edition of his famous book, *Shakespeare's Bawdy*, is obliged to retract an earlier declaration that *Twelfth Night* is 'the cleanest comedy except for *A Midsummer Night's Dream*'.[44] Further, since *Twelfth Night* is by critical consensus the culmination of Shakespeare's work in the genre, when he 'completely masters and exhausts the possibilities of this form of drama',[45] and since comedy is inherently corporeal, that range of possibilities necessarily includes the 'bawdy body'. Stephen Greenblatt observes: 'Shakespearian comedy constantly appeals to the body and in particular to sexuality as the heart of its theatrical magic; "great creating nature" – the principle by which the world is and must be peopled.'[46] Such a view, although it once again ignores the exclusion of real female corporeality, none the less grates against Granville-Barker's contention that Shakespeare's was a celibate stage devoid of physical representations of sexuality where transvestism functioned as an aesthetic device to foreground theatrical artifice.[47] For all the critical reluctance to address it, the 'broad humour' of the play is perfectly appropriate to its celebration of Twelfth Night, the Feast of Misrule, when licensed inversion is the order of the day; as Feste remarks: 'To see this age! A sentence is but a chev'ril glove to a good wit – how quickly the wrong side may be turned outward!' (III.i.11–12). Here the fleshy grotesque body reigns supreme. Stallybrass and White describe the symbolic components of this structural inversion as follows:

> Grotesque realism images the human body as multiple, bulging, over- or under-sized, protuberant and incomplete ... with its orifices (mouth, flared nostrils, anus) yawning wide and its lower regions (belly, legs, feet, buttocks and genitals) given priority over its upper regions (head, 'spirit', reason).[48]

The play's laughter is thus produced by such comic violations of social and somatic decorum integral to the culture of 'cakes and ale', 'masques and revels', which has its most ardent devotees in Sir Toby Belch and Sir Andrew Aguecheek. Sir Toby, who epitomises the corpulent excess of the carnival grotesque, vows to remain a drunkard as long as there is passage in his throat and drink in Illyria (I.iii.39–40). Should he renege on this oath, Sir Toby avers, 'call me cut' (II.iii.186). In the spirit of carnivalesque inversion, such derogatory references to the female genitals constitute much of the play's humour – not to mention its misogyny – thwarting the attempt of hegemonic, twentieth-century criticism to find in the

Malvolio — feminised

play the good clean fun of benign (verging on the beneficent) comedy romance.

Malvolio's class transvestism, as I have argued, is the central inversion of the play and is closely related to the play's representation of femininity, as well as its bawdy humour. In accordance with its carnival theme, female genitals are at the heart of Malvolio's gulling, the play's most famous scene:

> **Malvolio** (*Taking up the letter*) By my life, this is my lady's hand: these be her very C's, her U's, and her T's, and thus makes she her great P's. It is in contempt of question her hand.
> **Sir Andrew** Her C's, her U's, and her T's: Why that?
> **Malvolio** (*Reads*) *To the unknown beloved, this, and my good wishes.* Her very phrases! By your leave, wax. Soft! and the impressure her Lucrece, with which she uses to seal: 'tis my lady! To whom should this be?
>
> (II.v.87–96)

Sir Andrew's exclamation is in part a rhetorical question emphasising the scandalous pun, which Malvolio spells out in slow, excruciating detail: 'cu[n]t'. On another level the query justifies this crude jest because, of course, no C, U, or T exist in the superscription of the letter.[49] At that literal, textual level we never really do know why there is a 'CU[N]T' in *Twelfth Night*. Symbolically, however, Malvolio, in taking seriously the possibility of trading a steward's servility for sexual service with his mistress – 'She that would alter services with thee' (II.v.157–8) – has, as Maria promised, been gulled into a 'nayword' (II.iii.135–6). That is, he has become, 'liver and all', feminised, ridiculed, castrated; his corporeal being in its entirety has been reduced to the most denigrated body part – a 'cut'. Malvolio is already primed for this by his earlier fantasies of social advancement, which begin to forge the connection between debased femininity and class aspirations: 'To be Count Malvolio' (II.v.35). 'Count' and 'cunt' were probably homonymic in Elizabethan English as we see from Katherine's translation of 'la robe' in *Henry V*, III.iv as the '*mauvais, corruptible, gros, et impudique*' '*le count*'. Malvolio's is a stern lesson on the dangers of wish fulfilment. His degeneration into femininity is a reversal of the transformation from female to male thought biologically feasible in the Renaissance on the grounds that nature strove for perfection. In short, Malvolio's gender reversal constitutes an unnatural act. Thus his social ambitions implicate him, albeit inadvertently, in a species of deviance far more dangerous than Viola's deliberate transgression.[50]

The resonance of the female genitalia, however, is more comprehensive than that. It signifies Maria's ambivalent sexual identity as Amazon Queen, Penthesilea (prefiguring in the denouement's genitally undecipherable 'fancy's Queen') and as the text's author, and Olivia's private parts. The audience is thus presented with the dynamic between Olivia's political authority and the (mis)representation of her body. To some extent, the letter reveals all representation of the aristocratic body, which Leonard Tennenhouse has shown is necessarily female in the Elizabethan era,[51] as untrustworthy mimesis. Olivia's authority is undercut by her status as semi-petrarchan object of diverse passions – Orsino's idealising and Malvolio's idiocy – and compounded by the letter's further dislocation of her power.

That Malvolio's 'CUT'[52] does indeed have implications for Olivia's power is established by the banter with Cesario about how, without ceding her virginity, Olivia might leave some copy of her beauty in the world. In the wordplay on (corporeal) reproduction and (discursive) representation, Olivia works to retain at least linguistic sovereignty over her body. In one sense she plans to extend this control even to the grave, but in another, female sovereignty of the body is merely dominion over a corpse: 'I will give out divers schedules of my beauty. It shall be inventoried, and every particle and utensil labelled to my will. As, item, two lips indifferent red; item, two grey eyes, with lids to them; item, one neck, one chin, and so forth' (I.v.247–51). Olivia's inventoried body is its representation after her decease in her *will*. 'Will' signifies both sexual desire and, literally, the legal document containing instructions about the disposal of her property. Command over one's body consists of command over its representations, its reproductions – something that would have resonated with Elizabethans, whose queen carefully supervised the reproduction and dissemination of her authority by controlling the use of her image as stringently as she controlled marriage plans prepared on her behalf.

Of course, Olivia cannot know that in the very next Act, without her consent, her private parts will be on display for everyone's amusement. It is significant, too, that Olivia is the object of this form of ridicule since she is clearly the female figure with most authority in the play and the one with the most inclination to use it independently of men. Not only is the sexual function of the pudendum ridiculed but also its urinary one in the jest on Olivia's micturition – 'her great P's'. The allusion to Olivia's copious urination further deforms veiled, cloistered, aristocratic femininity into the grotesque and, paradoxically, more suitable object of Malvolio's sexual and social ambitions. 'Her great P's' also bring us closer to the source of Olivia's excitement, 'folds adjacent to the meatus urinarius on the female', which when tumescent can result in tribadism, as Ambrose Paré's *On Monsters and Marvels* fearfully points out: 'they grow erect like the male rod, so much so that they can disport themselves with them, with other women'.[53] Olivia's private parts, preposterously resembling the phallic proportions of a full-grown man, make her ridiculous (as female character, as boy actor, and as wooer of Cesario). The clitoris, the site of female desire, is in a sense a phallic imposter, as Jane Sharp's midwifery guide asserts: 'It will stand and fall as the yard [penis] doth and makes women lustful and delight in copulation.'[54] Olivia as the 'phallic' woman in her advances towards Viola has a cultural parallel in homophobic accounts of women whose clitoral hypertrophy made them similarly aggressive suitors of other women.[55] Thus, Nicholas Tulp's treatise on anatomy gives an account of a German woman's predilection for exposing her clitoris, which extended some way from the vulva, in order to engage in 'licentious sport with other women'.[56] The boy actress Olivia thus becomes the 'hypersimulation' of a woman[57] because despite the allusions, there is, of course, no female body as such in the 'C.U.T' passage (just as there is none in the play).

It is worth exploring the cultural resonance of women's genitals, particularly in the arena of theatre. Andrew Gurr offers one of Henry Peacham's anecdotes from *The Compleat Gentleman*, which has a certain positive, erotic connotation, rather than one aimed at violence or ridicule. None the less, it suggests that the most important thing about both a woman's 'cut' and a woman's purse (metaphorically related in contemporary psychoanalytic theory), is that both belong to her husband and can therefore be stolen by other men:

> A tradesman's wife of the Exchange, one day when her husband was following some business in the city, desired he would give her leave to go see a play; which she had not done in seven years. He bade her take his apprentice along with her, and go; but especially to have care of her purse; which she warranted him she would. Sitting in a box, among some gallants and gallant wenches, and returning when

the play was done, returned to her husband and told him she had
lost her purse. 'Wife, (quoth he,) did I not give you warning of it?
How much money was there in it?' Quoth she, 'Truly, four pieces,
six shillings and a silver tooth-picker.' Quoth her husband, 'Where
did you put it?' 'Under my petticoat, between that and my smock.'
'What, (quoth he,) did you feel no body's hand there?' 'Yes, (quoth
she,) I felt one's hand there, but I did not think he had come for
that.'[58]

Thus, even if as Leah Scragg suggests, the 'C.U.T.' of *Twelfth Night*
is an admonition to the audience to beware pickpockets; to feel
themselves up and pat themselves (or their neighbours) down, its
implications may not be so innocent as an issue of warning about
potential financial loss. (This is particularly the case when we
recollect that the appellation Moll Cutpurse in *The Roaring Girl*,
connotes her identity as both thief and 'codpiece daughter'
[II.ii.89]).[59] Given the prevalence of pleasure in critical discourse at
present, perhaps we should also consider the possibility that this
admonition may signal that 'cut' is not entirely pejorative; it may
have erotic connotations. Indeed, while the public exposure of
female genitals by women was rare, it was an explicit invitation to
sexual activity. That Malvolio comically presents himself as having
familiarity with Olivia's private parts, can also be read as a claim to
have engaged in mutual masturbation, which seems to have been a
very common form of premarital sex, as in the case of one virgin
whose intimacies entailed the woman lying on the bed while her
partner 'combed her private member'.[60] While we may read the
potential eroticism of the suggestion of mutual masturbation in
Twelfth Night as positive, it is counterbalanced by the con-
travention of social hierarchy, which, as it relates to Malvolio and
Olivia's 'relationship', is resoundingly negative. The argument for
the scene as a benign jest on women's sexual pleasure – which could
be rationalised in terms of Laqueur's claim that female pleasure,
specifically orgasm, was thought to be necessary for conception – is
severely compromised by the fact that this was also used as
a way of dismissing rape charges.[61] Magistrates were advised that
women who were impregnated during rape must have been
pleasured and therefore must have consented.[62] This points up not
only the difficulty of reading the gulling scene in terms of
female pleasure, but also the fact that the episode depends
for its humour on the conspicuous absence of Olivia's
'consent'.

The 'C.U.T.' scene is connected with the social enactment of women's oppression. Numerous women brought legal complaints about men trying to touch and manipulate their genitals: 'Whiles he was thus soliciting her, his hand was always grappling about her plackett, striving to have felt her privy part.' Many of these incidents have been usefully assembled from court records in G. R. Quaife's *Wanton Wenches and Wayward Wives*. One man apparently told his friends of how he had groped a woman's genitals, and told the woman herself, 'Faith Mary, thou hast a soft cunt.' Another case, perhaps even more pertinent to that of Olivia, is that of one Margaret Woods who was held by the privates so long that she urinated in the man's hands.[63] Further, the public exposure of women's genitals could have unambiguously violent meanings and effects. One man from Batcombe 'did violently take up the clothes of Elizabeth Numan and showed her nakedness to many', and a husbandman from Halse

> made an offer to divers then present that for a penny a piece they should see his wife's privities and there withal did take her and throw her upon a board and did take up her clothes and showed her nakedness in most beastly and uncivil manner.[64]

Predictably, however, *men* are recorded as having found such violence both comic *and* erotic. One inn servant jumped in terror from a window after being thus abused, but it is quite clear from the account of a fellow female servant that her drunken assailants felt otherwise:

> throwing her down Jay, Willis and Sherwood holding her legs and arms down by force did one after another lift her clothes up to her girdle and then thrust their hands shamefully between her legs and feel her privities and look upon them. After which done Jay (who named himself the knight of the castle) sat upon a bench, taking and holding Edith between his legs, placing a stool before her face, and holding her arms fast. And then and there drawing their wicked rapiers and laying them upon the table made proclamations in these or the like words viz: 'Oyes, whosoever dareth to break down the walls of grimcunt castle let him approach ... Henry Sherwood come forth and appear at grim-cunt castle.' Whereupon Sherwood came forth with a glass of beer in his hand and taking up Edith's coats above her knees felt her privities and then threw the glass of beer at the same.[65]

The histrionics of this incident share certain features of the 'C.U.T.' scene in *Twelfth Night*. There is a fantasy of exalted social status (knighthood), male bonding (recall that Maria exits directly before the gulling and re-enters directly after it), and abuse directed quite specifically at the pudenda. Also, like Olivia's household, this gathering was amused by the graphic exposure of the woman's genitals and relished it as a focus of their theatrics.

The 'graphic' display in *Twelfth Night* is, of course, precisely that, a written representation, linguistic rather than somatic, allowing the company to be hugely entertained. The elusiveness of 'graphic' display renders female genitalia present in pornographic detail, and absent as the 'real' beyond representation.[66] What is palpably present, however, is 'anatomised' femininity. Olivia's 'hand' is both a limb and writing; in this case a blatant misrepresentation – a forgery. There is also the figure of Lucrece, who would seem to interject this scene with a more sober rendition of the feminine as object of male violence. The usurped seal ring depicts Lucrece, probably portrayed in the 'noble' act of stabbing herself, the self-penetrating re-enactment of her violation that constitutes the only recourse of the ravished woman who seeks to preserve her moral integrity.[67] Lucrece is an appropriate figure for a seal, made to be ruptured by the letter's recipient in an act loosely analogous to sexual violation. To 'open' a letter – to read it, to interpret it, is in some sense to breach its integrity. We are thus left with images of comically debased and tragically valorised femininity, each of which are specifically associated with writing as a mode of representation. In fact, the 'licence of ink' with which Sir Toby urges Sir Andrew to taunt Cesario (III.ii.42–3) is precisely the liberty taken by Maria's missive. For writing offers freedom from anatomical and class designations. Its manoeuvrable discursivity is emblematic of the power of (mis)representation which constitutes theatrical licence itself, and does so most vividly in the various forms of transvestism we have detailed here.

In order to consolidate (and complicate) the connection between the business of representing corporeality and the overall implications for a reading of *Twelfth Night*, I want to turn briefly to Stephen Orgel's comments on the play. He writes:

> Viola announces in the final moments of *Twelfth Night* that she cannot become a woman and the wife of Orsino until her woman's clothes have been recovered – a dress borrowed from Olivia or a new one purchased for the occasion apparently are not options – and that this will require the release of the sea captain who alone can find them, which in turn will necessitate the mollification of the enraged

Malvolio, who has had the sea captain incarcerated: this all *materialises out of nowhere* in the last three minutes of the play. And Malvolio at the play's end offers no assistance but runs from the stage shouting 'I'll be revenged on the whole pack of you.' For Viola to become a woman requires, in short, a new play with Malvolio at its centre [my emphasis].[68]

Orgel is right that the play's production of femininity is dependent upon Malvolio, but it is so in more ways than he imagines. For as I have argued, we do not need a new play because we already have Malvolio at the centre of a plot where femininity is little less than an impossible condition, and female authority a ridiculous one. For if the play, as Leonard Tennenhouse argues, involves the explicit transfer of patriarchal power into the body of a woman, who then returns it, now in 'a more humane and less violent form' via marriage,[69] the play must persuade us of the urgency of the final transaction.

Twelfth Night, then, treats the corporeal representation of sexuality, which was equated with femininity. Sue-Ellen Case summarises the cultural rationale for this manoeuvre as follows:

> The female gender had become the custodian of male sexual behaviour, which it instigated and elicited. The female body had become the site for sexuality. If women performed in the public arena, the sexuality inscribed upon their bodies would elicit immoral sexual responses from the men, bringing disorder to the social body.[70]

Thus, the very thing that justified women's exclusion from the stage is graphically foregrounded in this play. But the play does not therefore subversively evade the strictures against female bodies on stage; rather it adds weight to them by presenting the female body in its most biologically essential form – the cunt.[71] For the critic, *Twelfth Night* illustrates the problem of recovering the female body for feminism. We cannot make a female body 'materialise' from nowhere; we can only register the complexity of its exclusion.

IV

Jane Gallop recalls that in *Les Bijoux Indiscrets* the protagonist is given a magic ring in order to confer the power of speech, and thence sexual revelation, upon female nether parts. Diderot's narrative, recounted by Gallop in 1989, almost exactly parallels her own rendition of the rank, raucous pudendum in *The Daughter's Seduction*, where, taking her cue from Freud's remarks on the odour of menstrual blood, she constructs an opposition between vaginal aroma and the veiled impassive specularity of the phallus: 'the cunt clamours for attention, makes a big stink'.[72] In the later analysis of *Les Bijoux Indiscrets* she elaborates on the protagonist's desire for a female pudendum that will speak with the 'feminist' fantasy of one possessing powers of intellection – a shift from the stinking to the talking/thinking cunt. Gallop's is a fascinating effort to disrupt the mind/body dualism structuring Western thought. But as I noted at the start, the articulation of corporeal female desire is always open to appropriation by patriarchy.

Twelfth Night, as we have seen, invokes the raucous articulation of desire in the process of its ritualised de-regulation. In its world, if you are fortunate enough to evade the castrating effect of the letters 'C.U.T.' (as Malvolio cannot), you may become or possess 'What You Will'. 'Will', as is apparent in the sonnets, is bawdy for both penis and pudenda. Its bawdy humour derives from the articulation of inappropriate desire, especially female desire. Female desire is not clearly affirmed in this inverted world, just as in actual social sites of symbolic inversion such as carnivals, women were as likely to be sexually abused as given sexual licence. Thus, there is as much violence against women in the tradition of carnivalesque trans-gression as in the authoritarian suppression to which it was formulated as a response.[73]

None the less, the corporeality of sexual desire, which tends to be identified with the feminine, is articulated in this play as food, olfaction, noise, plague and pestilence. To give but a brief example from the 'C.U.T.' scene, Malvolio's desires make him a 'brock', a badger, a stinking beast. Eating and hunting as emblems of the erratic course of sexual desire open the play, as Orsino is alternately pleasured and tormented by all his sensory capacities:

> If music be the food of love, play on,
> Give me excess of it, that, surfeiting,
> The appetite may sicken, and so die.
> That strain again, it had a dying fall:
> O, it came o'er my ear like the sweet sound
> That breathes upon a bank of violets,
> Stealing and giving odour. Enough, no more;

'Tis not so sweet now as it was before ...

Curio Will you go hunt, my lord?

(I.i.1–9, 16ff)

Olivia is identified with a scent, both that of the hunted hart (into which Orsino rhetorically metamorphoses when pursued by his own uncontrollable desires) and that which 'purg'd the air of pestilence' (I.i.20). She is the food which whets his appetitive sexual desire, and sates it all too quickly, 'Enough, no more.' Orsino maintains his dignity by responding with lethargy to the onslaught upon his senses.[74] This corresponds with the notion that sexual attraction was immanent in the body of the desired object. It is an illusion which characterises itself, 'a wish to locate the arousal, the erotics, in some object rather than in an intersubjective dynamic'.[75] And of course, Olivia does not actually desire Orsino, any more than she does Malvolio. None the less, she manages to usurp her own dignity and 'a smooth, discreet, and stable bearing' (IV.iii.19) of her authority by marrying an effeminate boy of dubious social standing.

In the letter that dupes Malvolio, the 'dish of poison' that is set for him by Maria, we come closest to Gallop's fantasy of the thinking, (almost) vocal cunt:

(*He opens the letter.*)

Fabian   This wins him, liver and all.
Malvolio   (*Reads*) *Jove knows I love:*
                                        But who?
                                        Lips, do not move.
                                        No man must know.
'No man must know'! What follows? The numbers altered! 'No man must know – If this should be thee, Malvolio!
Sir Toby   Marry, hang thee, brock!
Malvolio   (*Reads*) *I may command where I adore:*
                                        But silence, like a Lucrece knife,
                                        With bloodless stroke my heart doth gore:
                                        M.O.A.I. doth sway my life.

(II.v.96–109)

In one sense the letter has itself become a cunt clamouring its desire, but forced either to feign passivity or actually be quiescent, 'Lips, do not move'. The bawdy implications of the earlier 'C.U.T.' are not abandoned either; as both 'lips' and 'know' have carnal connotations, as Paré observes:

> Moreover, at the beginning of the neck of the womb is the entrance and crack of the woman's 'nature', which the Latins call *Pecten*; and the edges, which are covered with hair, are called in Greek Pterigomata [*sic*] as if we were to say wings, or lips of the woman's crown, and between these are two excrescences of muscular flesh, one on each side, which cover the issue of the urine conduit; and they close up after the woman has pissed.[76]

The woman's part also requires considerable powers of exegesis: 'No man must know ... The numbers altered!' Voracious female sexuality, it would appear, despite the injunction to silence, speaks for itself and yet demands the careful attention of interpretation, referring us also to the extra-diegetic reality of the boy actress's sexual equipment. Similarly, Viola's dubious sexual identity appears to give itself away, to sound off:

> For they shall yet belie thy happy years,
> That say thou art a man; Diana's lip
> Is not more smooth and rubious: thy small pipe
> Is as the maiden's organ, shrill and sound,
> And all is semblative a woman's part.
> (I.iv.30–4)

The maiden's organ is both voice and genital femininity. Thus for Viola: 'A little thing would make me tell them how much I lack of a man' (III.iv.307–8). Here, however, contrary to the feminist fantasy of the inherently disruptive qualities of the female genitals in the phallocentric order, Viola must speak on behalf of her sexual parts because, ambivalent as they are, they incite her to discourse. Kathleen McLuskie writes of the endless complications of signifying woman on the Renaissance stage, 'The frustrated critic may wish, like the puppet in *Bartholemew Fair*, simply to lift the skirts and expose the reality behind the signification, but the result, as in Jonson's play, would simply be a disconcerted silence.'[77] In *Twelfth Night*, however, we have anything but that; we have an elaborate, fanciful instance of patriarchal ventriloquism.

   I have attempted here to give a theoretical and critical context for my partial reading of the female body in *Twelfth Night*. In it, I have insisted on the materiality of woman's exclusion from the stage even while examining the representation of her private parts. To do so is to some extent to halt the play of possibilities envisaged by much contemporary cultural analysis of transvestism in order to take a political position which works to open up new space for the

purposes of resistance postmodernism rather than leaving us sus-
pended in the poststructuralist space of the undecidable.[78] I have
also tried to confront the exclusion of women from the Renaissance
stage without denying the complexity of the representation of the
female body. This claim requires some small elaboration; for we
have reached a moment when 'complexity' is now routinely
invoked as a reactionary formulation of 'undecidability' in order to
claim that things were not so bad for women in the Renaissance
after all.[79] What is complex is the way in which apparently benign
representations of women operate as regulatory fictions for the suppression, exclusion and containment of those who, in their corporeality, lived the Renaissance condition of femininity. In this, I
hope that my analysis constitutes an intervention for current
feminist politics by using the body in a Shakespeare text as a way of
articulating the problems of its reclamation at this historical
juncture for a materialist feminist agenda.[80]

V

It has become a commonplace of criticism, one that recurs in
interesting ways in analysis of Renaissance transvestism, that the
anarchic, transformative possibilities of Renaissance Drama,
especially those relating to the status of women, were foreclosed by
the Puritan-motivated closing of the theatres.[81] However, there is
no evidence that the closing of the theatres can be identified as a
major component of either the progressive deterioration of
women's status during the seventeenth century or the subsequent
post-Enlightenment regime that now recruits our subjectivities.[82]
For it was not, of course, the Puritans who were the agents of the
then emergent politics and sensibility that we now live, although it
is possible that the closing of the theatres offers some a sign of why
the revolution failed. Rather, the Puritans were the radical forces of
change whose revolution was foreshortened by Royalist victory.

This confusion coincides with a persistent tendency to conflate
women cross-dressers abroad in the streets of London and the institutional practice of theatrical transvestism necessitated by the
exclusion of women from the stage. The issue about women in
men's clothing is one to which the romantic comedies only
obliquely refer.[83] While the phenomena of stage and social transvestism are connected, they are not identical. Thus, even the case of

The Roaring Girl does not involve a woman cross-dressing on stage – it entails that only as part of the plot's fiction, not as a systematic aspect of the operation of theatre. Further, no antitheatricalist would have been mollified by the suggestion that if female actresses played women, the evil of stage transvestism might happily be avoided. This simply is not an option available within the conceptual horizon of early modern England. For it is the presence of women in any and all its manifestations that poses a problem either horrifying or unthinkable. Further, in social life women dressed as men, but in theatre men dressed as women, and the latter is to *some degree* an arena for licensed inversion.[84] No matter how heinous antitheatricalists found theatrical transvestism, they never found it necessary to inveigh against men gadding about London dressed as women. That men did not dress as women in social (as opposed to theatrical) practice is a phenomenon not contended with by those who argue for theatre as pre-eminently a site of gender instability.[85] Nor did the political radicals of early modern England share the enthusiasm of contemporary 'radical' critics about theatrical transvestism. Jean-Christophe Agnew remarks:

> What is clear from the protracted debate over stage transvestism ... is the Puritans' utter disbelief in the traditional corrective virtues of travesty. How could they countenance a remedy that was so difficult to distinguish from the disease?[86]

From the perspective of my analysis, the Puritans had a point.[87]

From *Textual Practice*, 7 (1993), 428–52.

NOTES

[Dympna Callaghan, like Stephen Greenblatt (essay 5), historicises the play by examining contemporary ideas about transvestism and sexuality, employing an approach which deals with 'body politics'. This emphasises not only the centrality of the body in its dramatic presence, but also sees the body as a site for ideological discourse. Callaghan's special contribution is to set these approaches in a consistently feminist argument. All quotations are from *The Riverside Shakespeare*, ed. G. Blakemore Evans (Houghton Mifflin, 1974). Ed.]

This essay was completed with the help of a Monticello College Foundation Fellowship at the Newberry Library, Chicago.

1. Norbert Elias, *The Civilizing Process*, vols I and II (1939; Oxford; 1982). See also Lucy Gent and Nigel Llewellyn (eds), *Renaissance Bodies: The Human Figure in English Culture c.1540–1660* (London, 1990), pp. 1–10.

2. Andrew Gurr, *Playgoing in Shakespeare's London* (Cambridge, 1987), p. 38.

3. Francis Barker, *The Tremulous Private Body: Essays on Subjection* (London and New York, 1984), p. 13.

4. Carroll Smith-Rosenberg, 'The Body Politic', in Elizabeth Weed (ed.), *Coming To Terms: Feminism, Theory, Politics* (London and New York, 1989), p. 103. One important strain of analyses of the body in Renaissance Studies has been that of the body politic. For a recent Shakespearean example see Zvi Jagendorf, 'Coriolanus: Body Politic and Private Parts', *Shakespeare Quarterly*, 41: 4 (1990), 455–69.

5. Terry Eagleton, *The Ideology of the Aesthetic* (Oxford, 1990), p. 7.

6. See Mas'ud Zavarzadeh, *Seeing Films Politically* (Albany, NY, 1991). On the political necessity of asserting women's physiological specificity, see Emily Martin, *The Woman in the Body: A Cultural Analysis of Reproduction* (Boston, MA, 1987). On resistance postmodernism, see Teresa L. Ebert, 'Political Semiosis in/of American Cultural Studies', *American Journal of Semiotics*, 8: 1/2 (1991), 113–35.

7. Michel Foucault, *The History of Sexuality, Vol. One: An Introduction*, trans. Robert Hurley (Harmondsworth, 1981), p. 157. For a trenchant critique of Foucault's 'body politics', see Nancy Fraser, *Unruly Practices: Power, Discourse and Gender in Contemporary Social Theory* (Minneapolis, MN, 1989), pp. 62–3. See also Judith Butler, *Gender Trouble: Feminism and the Subversion of Identity* (London and New York, 1990), pp. 128–41.

8. See Peter Stallybrass and Allon White, *The Politics and Poetics of Transgression* (Ithaca, NY, 1986).

9. Terry Eagleton, *Against the Grain: Essays 1975–1985* (London, 1986), p. 80.

10. Gent and Llewellyn, *Renaissance Bodies*, p. 2.

11. Zavarzadeh, *Seeing Films Politically*, p. 48.

12. For an excellent account of this phenomenon see Donald Morton, 'Texts of Limits, the Limits of Texts, and the Containment of Politics in Contemporary Critical Theory', *Diacritics*, 20:1 (1990), 57–75.

13. Eagleton, *Ideology of the Aesthetic*, p. 7.

14. Barker, *Tremulous Private Body*, p. 12.

15. See Michèle Barrett, *Women's Oppression Today: The Marxist/ Feminist Encounter* (1980; London, 1988), p. xxviii; Janet Wolff, 'Reinstating Corporeality: Feminism and Body Politics', in *Feminine Sentences: Essays on Women and Culture* (Berkeley, CA, 1990), p. 133.

16. See Nazife Bashar, 'Rape in England between 1550 and 1700', in London Feminist History Group (ed.), *The Sexual Dynamics of History* (London, 1983), pp. 28–46.

17. Wolff, 'Reinstating Corporeality', p. 121.

18. There are other important and related debates which I do not have space to engage in here. There has been a lot of rethinking around biological essentialism, especially as it has been articulated in response to Irigaray's 'womanspeak' and Cixous' *écriture féminine*. Also there has been considerable debate as to whether the body exists outside discourse. Elizabeth Grosz argues, for example, that 'the body can be seen as the primary object of social production and inscription' in her 'Notes Towards a Corporeal Feminism', *Australian Feminist Studies*, 5 (Summer 1987), 1–16. See also Wolff who argues 'the critique of essentialism does *not* amount to proof that there *is* no body' (p. 135). Both Wolff and Elizabeth Dempster try to locate new, liberatory understandings of the body in dance, but the result is a feminist rendition of the utopian excesses of the theorised bodies of Barthes and Foucault. Elizabeth Dempster, 'Women Writing the Body: Let's Watch a Little How She Dances', in Susan Sheridan (ed.), *Grafts: Feminist Cultural Criticism* (London, 1988), pp. 35–54.

   See also Denise Riley, '*Am I That Name?*' *Feminism and the Category of 'Women' in History* (Minneapolis, MN, 1988), pp. 96–114. She remarks that 'the very location of "the sexual" in the body is itself historically mutable' (p. 104).

19. See for example Gail Kern Paster, 'Leaky Vessels: The Incontinent Women of City Comedy', in Mary Beth Rose (ed.), *Renaissance Drama As Cultural History: Essays From Renaissance Drama 1977 to 1987* (Evanston, IL, 1990), pp. 211–33, which, though an elegant and useful reading, takes urine as the 'raw material' of its 'materialist' analysis. See also Valerie Wayne (ed.), *The Matter of Difference: Materialist Feminist Criticism of Shakespeare* (Ithaca, NY, 1991).

20. See Sheila Fisher and Janet E. Halley (eds), *Seeking the Woman in Late Medieval and Renaissance Writings* (Knoxville, TN, 1989).

21. Lisa Jardine, *Still Harping on Daughters: Women and Drama in the Age of Shakespeare* (Brighton, 1983), pp. 31; 29. Stephen Orgel contends, like Jardine, that homosexuality was the dominant form of eroticism in Renaissance culture. 'Nobody's Perfect: Or Why Did the English Stage Take Boys for Women?', *South Atlantic Quarterly*, 88: 1 (Winter 1989), 7–29. See also Linda Woodbridge, *Women and the*

English Renaissance: Literature and the Nature of Womankind, 1540–1620 (Urbana, IL, 1984), pp. 154; 327.

22. See Kathleen McLuskie, *Renaissance Dramatists* (Atlantic Highlands, NJ, 1989), pp. 100–57 and her 'The Act, the Role, and the Actor: Boy Actresses on the Elizabethan Stage', *New Theatre Quarterly*, 5 (1987), 120–30; Kiernan Ryan, *Shakespeare* (Atlantic Highlands, NJ, 1989), pp. 88–9; Sue-Ellen Case, *Feminism and Theatre* (London and New York, 1988), pp. 26–7; Woodbridge, *Women*, p. 327.

23. Orgel, 'Nobody's Perfect', p. 17. Phyllis Rackin draws attention to the homophobic satire of Jonson's *Epicoene*, thus demonstrating the important point that not all instances of transvestism were homoerotic. Phyllis Rackin, 'Androgyny, Mimesis, and the Marriage of the Boy Heroine on the English Renaissance Stage', *PMLA*, 102: 1 (1987), 29–41; 31. Jean Howard points out that the social transgressions entailed in women attending the theatre may well have been more directly related to the goings on in the auditorium than to the content of the plays. See 'Scripts and/versus Playhouses: Ideological Production and the Renaissance Public Stage', in Wayne (ed.), *Matter of Difference*.

24. In a different vein, Juliet Dusinberre observes: 'Restoration drama boasts neither female heroes nor male heroines. But the woman actor offers no challenge to the dramatists to understand femininity beyond surface appearance.' Juliet Dusinberre, *Shakespeare and the Nature of Women* (London, 1985), p. 271.

25. Catherine Belsey, 'Disrupting Sexual Difference: Meaning and Gender in the Comedies', in John Drakakis (ed.), *Alternative Shakespeares* (London and New York, 1985), pp. 190; 166–90. See Ryan, *Shakespeare*, p. 9 for an account of the limitations of deconstruction in Shakespeare studies. Ironically, Ryan proceeds to valorise the play of instabilities in his subsequent analysis of the comedies, pp. 88–9.

26. Belsey, 'Disrupting', pp. 185; 166–7. See Wolffe, 'Reinstating Corporeality', p. 127.

27. Wolff, Reinstating Corporeality', p. 129.

28. Brian Gibbons (ed.), *Romeo and Juliet* (London and New York, 1980), p. 64.

29. Philip Stubbes, *The Anatomy of Abuses* (London, 1583), p. 38.

30. Jardine, *Still Harping*, pp. 14; 155–6.

31. Jonas Barish, *The Antitheatrical Prejudice* (Berkeley, CA, 1981), p. 92. See also Jonathan Dollimore, *Sexual Dissidence: Augustine to Wilde, Freud to Foucault* (Oxford, 1991); J. W. Binns, 'Women or Transvestites on the Elizabethan Stage?: An Oxford Controversy', *The Sixteenth Century Journal*, V: 2 (1974), 95–120; Sandra Clark,

' "*Hic Mulier, Haec Vir*" and the Controversy over Masculine Women', *Studies in Philology*, 82: 2 (1985), 157–83; Rudolf Dekker and Lotte C. Van de Pol, *The Tradition of Female Transvestitism in Early Modern Europe* (New York, 1989); Laura Levine, 'Men in Women's Clothing: Anti-theatricality and Effeminization from 1579 to 1642', *Criticism* (Spring 1986), 121–43.

32. Orgel, 'Nobody's Perfect', p. 15.

33. Malvolio similarly occupied the attention of critics of the play until in the surge of recent interest in gender, cross-dressing focused instead on Viola's disguise.

34. On Malvolio's class status, see Cristina Malcolmson, ' "What you will". Social Mobility and Gender in *Twelfth Night*', in Wayne (ed.), *Matter of Difference*, pp. 29–57. [reprinted in this volume – Ed.]

35. *Certain Homilies Appointed to be Read in Churches in the Time of Queen Elizabeth* (London, 1908), pp. 334–5.

36. Quoted in Peter Stallybrass, 'Patriarchal Territories: The Body Enclosed', in Margaret W. Ferguson, Maureen Quilligan, and Nancy J. Vickers (eds), *Rewriting the Renaissance: The Discourse of Sexual Difference in Early Modern Europe* (Chicago, 1986), p. 123; see also Leonard Tennenhouse, 'Violence Done to Women on the Renaissance Stage', in Nancy Armstrong and Leonard Tennenhouse (eds), *The Violence of Representation: Literature and the History of Violence* (London and New York, 1989), p. 67.

37. There is perhaps a 'coded' reference to transvestism in the mention of the play's Italian parallel. If as Margaret Maurer suggests, the play is a 'trick' play, Manningham might not have wanted to give the game away. None the less, the emphasis is all on the 'device' against Malvolio, which reinforces the sense that this is the trick of the play. Margaret Maurer, 'Coming of Age in Illyria: Doubling the Twins in *Twelfth Night*' (unpublished).

38. T. V. King, *Shakespearean Staging* 1599–1642 (Cambridge, MA, 1971), p. 97.

39. Criticism since the Renaissance has also been preoccupied with Malvolio. See T. W. Craik and J. M. Lothian (eds), *Twelfth Night* (1975; London and New York, 1981), pp. lxxix–xcviii.

40. Maurer, 'Coming of Age', p. 2.

41. Malcolmson, 'Social Mobility', p. 51, argues that social estate in *Twelfth Night* is 'a matter of desire or will rather than birth or title' in order to praise willing service, as that of Viola to Orsino, and to condemn self-interest represented by Malvolio.

42. Craik and Lothian (eds), *Twelfth Night*, p. liv; Levine, 'Men in Women's Clothing'; Joseph Westlund, *Shakespeare's Reparative*

Comedies: A Psychoanalytic View of the Middle Plays (Chicago, 1984).

43. McLuskie, *Renaissance Dramatists*, p. 110.

44. Eric Partridge, *Shakespeare's Bawdy: A Literary and Psychological Essay and the Comprehensive Glossary* (1947; London, 1968).

45. Mary Beth Rose, *The Expense of Spirit: Love and Sexuality in English Renaissance Drama* (Ithaca, NY, 1988), p. 41.

46. Stephen Greenblatt, 'Fiction and Friction', in *Shakespearean Negotiations: The Circulation of Social Energy in Renaissance England* (Berkeley, CA, 1988), p. 86 [reprinted in this volume – Ed.]; see also Craik and Lothian, p. lii.

47. Harley Granville-Barker, *Prefaces to Shakespeare*, vol. 1 (Princeton, NJ, 1952), p. 15.

48. Stallybrass and White, *Transgression*, p. 9.

49. Craik and Lothian (eds), *Twelfth Night*, p. 67.

50. Malvolio's connection with bawdy is consolidated by the fact that despite his Puritan leanings, he isn't immune from making a lewd jest himself, as when he describes Orsino's messenger to his mistress:

> Not yet old enough for a man, nor young enough for a boy; as a squash is before 'tis a peascod, or a codling when 'tis almost an apple. 'Tis with him in standing water, between boy and man. He is very well-favoured, and he speaks very shrewishly. One would think his mother's milk were scarce out of him.
>
> (I.v.158–64)

'Peascod' and 'codling' refer to his genitals. It would seem too, that he participates in the solitary pleasures of masturbation – playing with his jewel; a pretty common double entendre (II.v.60–1) – despite editors' efforts to sanitise his lines.

51. Tennenhouse, 'Violence', p. 79.

52. Partridge argues that in this 'nursery spell-out' of *cunt* and *piss* that 'Shakespeare has not, after all, omitted the *n*; it occurs in "and no T's" [*sic*] as several discerning scholars have noted' (*Shakespeare's Bawdy*, p. 160). 'N, innuendoes or concealed or – especially in *and* (pronounced "n") – representing *in*; connected with the ways in which words or sounds are – for instance, with suggestive pauses – delivered on stage ... Mr Aylmer Rose, in a long and valuable letter dated 2 October 1955, writes thus, concerning *Twelfth Night*, II.v.87–9: ' "Her very C's, her U's, and [pronounced 'n', i.e. N] her T's; and thus makes she her great P's [where, he implies, there is a significant pause before P's]. If my suggestion about the innuendoed N is correct, it draws attention to the necessity of considering the sound of words and

the way in which they are delivered on stage" ' (*Shakespeare's Bawdy*, pp. 151–2).

53. Ambroise Paré, *On Monsters and Marvels* (1573), trans. Janis L. Pallister (Chicago, 1982), p. 188. Paré was first translated into English in 1634 by Th. Johnson; Thomas Laqueur, *Making Sex: Body and Gender from the Greeks to Freud* (Cambridge, MA, 1990), pp. 116; 188.

54. Quoted in Thomas Laqueur, 'Amor Veneris, vel Ducedo Appelatur', in Michael Freher, Ramona Naddaff and Nadia Tazi (eds), *Fragments for a History of the Human Body: Part Three* (New York, 1989), p. 105.

55. Valerie Traub offers an important critique of the heterosexist bias of the assumption 'that love between women was readily available as a source of both humour and humiliation for members of Shakespeare's audience'. (Valerie Traub, 'Desire and the Difference it Makes', in Wayne [ed.], *Matter of Difference*, p. 83.) And indeed, while misapprehension of any sort may be a source of ridicule, this does not exclude the production of homoerotic play here.

56. Quoted in Laqueur, 'Amor Veneris', p. 115.

57. I have borrowed this term from Sue-Ellen Case's 'Toward a Butch-Femme Aesthetic', in Lynda Hart (ed.), *Making A Spectacle: Feminist Essays in Contemporary Women's Theatre* (Ann Arbor, MI, 1989), pp. 282–99; especially p. 297.

58. Gurr, *Playgoing*, pp. 6–8.

59. See Rose, *Expense*, p. 78; Leah Scragg, 'Her C's, Her U's, Her T's', *Review of English Studies*, 42 (1991), 1–16; 15–16 especially. A contemporary pun with a similar effect is 'snatch' which can mean theft (as in purse snatching), or can mean a woman's crotch. Jane Gallop's *Thinking Through the Body* (New York, 1988) uses 'snatches of conversation' as a subtitle in one of its chapters in order to suggest both female crotch and partial apprehension.

60 G. R. Quaife, *Wanton Wenches and Wayward Wives: Peasants and Illicit Sex in Early Seventeenth Century England* (New Brunswick, NJ, 1979), p. 169. This is a possibility not entertained by Gail Kern Paster's reading of this episode. Paster claims that Malvolio's verbal transgression is constituted by the fact that he appears to have contravened the norms of urinary segregation ('Leaky Vessels', p. 213). I am indebted to Fran Dolan for the reference to Quaife.

61. Laqueur, *Making Sex*, pp. 2–3; 161; 182.

62. Quaife, *Wanton Wenches*, p. 172.

63. Ibid., p. 168.

64. Ibid., p. 168.

65. Ibid., p. 170.

66. Further, the emphasis on the linguistic dimension of the sexualisation and denigration entailed in the process of enforcing social hierarchy, links both Olivia and Viola, whose names, as Jonathan Goldberg has pointed out, are anagrammatic mirrors of one another and links both with Malvolio, to whose names his adds a negative prefix. Jonathan Goldberg, 'Textual Properties', *Shakespeare Quarterly*, 37: 2 (1986), 216.

67. For a fascinating analysis of the image of Lucrece in Shakespeare's narrative poem, see Nancy J. Vickers, 'This Heraldry in Lucrece's Face', in Susan Rubin Suleiman (ed.), *The Female Body In Western Culture: Contemporary Perspectives* (Cambridge, MA, 1985), pp. 209–22.

68. Orgel, 'Nobody's Perfect', p. 27.

69. Leonard Tennenhouse, *Power on Display: the Politics of Shakespeare's Genres* (London and New York, 1986), p. 68.

70. Case, *Feminism and Theatre*, p. 20.

71. 'Everything pertaining to the female genitalia is comprehended in the term "of nature" [*phuseos*], and the obscene term cunt [*cunnus*]', wrote Caspar Bauhin, Professor of Anatomy and Botany at Basel (1560–1624). Laqueur, 'Amor Veneris', p. 107.

72. Jane Gallop, *The Daughter's Seduction: Feminism and Psychoanalysis* (Ithaca, NY, 1982), p. 32; *Thinking Through the Body*.

73. See Peter Stallybrass, ' "Drunk with the cup of liberty": Robin Hood, the Carnivalesque, and the Rhetoric of Violence in early modern England', in Armstrong and Tennenhouse (eds), *Violence of Representation*, pp. 45–76; and Stallybrass and White, *Transgression*.

74. As Leonard Tenenhouse puts it, Orsino 'aestheticises love by dislodging it from its political body', *Power On Display*, p. 63.

75. Gallop, *Thinking*, p. 139.

76. Paré, *Monsters*, p. 188.

77. McLuskie, *Renaissance Dramatists*, p. 111.

78. See Case, 'Toward a Butch-Femme Aesthetic', pp. 282–99; Butler, *Gender Trouble*, p. 136; Marjorie Garber, *Vested Interests: Cross-Dressing and Cultural Anxiety* (London and New York, 1992).

79. See Dympna Callaghan, *Woman and Gender in Renaissance Tragedy* (Atlantic Highlands, NJ, 1989), ch. 2.

80. It is not, in my view, that materialism has become impossible, but that it is perhaps not quite so self-evident as it was, say in 1982 (see Barrett, *Women's Oppression*), or even in 1985 (see Judith Newton

and Deborah Rosenfelt [eds], *Feminist Criticism and Social Change: Sex, Class and Race in Literature and Culture* [London and New York, 1985]).

81. See for example, Case, *Feminism and Theatre*.

82. Rackin argues, 'The Puritans closed the theatres and a multitude of causes, which we are only beginning to understand, closed off many of the opportunities and possibilities that had been open to women at the beginning of the modern age' ('Androgeny, Mimesis', p. 38).

83. See Rose, *Expense*, p. 91.

84. Greenblatt points out in relation to Arnaud du Tilh's impersonation of Martin Guerre, 'What is entirely unacceptable – indeed punishable by death in the everyday world – is both instructive and delightful in spaces specially marked off for the exercise of impersonation. For in these spaces, and only in these spaces, there is by a widely shared social agreement no imposture.' Stephen Greenblatt, 'Psychoanalysis and Renaissance Culture', in Patricia Parker and David Quint (eds), *Literary Theory/Renaissance Texts* (Baltimore, MD, 1986), pp. 219–20.

85. This remains true of Dollimore's recent chapter on cross-dressing in early modern England in *Sexual Dissidence*.

86. Jean-Christophe Agnew, *Worlds Apart: The Market and the Theatre in Anglo-American Thought, 1550–1750* (Cambridge, 1986), p. 131. Dollimore argues: 'But what kind of resistance, if any, does a materialist criticism discover in Renaissance tragedy? I argued in *Radical Tragedy* that we find in this theatre not so much a vision of political freedom as a knowledge of political domination. But we simply cannot slide between the two, or assume that the second easily produces the first. This knowledge *was* challenging: it subverted, interrogated, and undermined the ruling ideologies and helped precipitate them into crisis. But history tells us time and again that from such crisis there may emerge not freedom but brutal repression. And such repression emerges not because the subversive was always contained, subversion being a ruse of power to consolidate itself, but because the challenge really *was* unsettling.' Jonathan Dollimore, 'Shakespeare, Cultural Materialism, Feminism and Marxist Humanism', *New Literary History*, 21:3 (1990), 471–93; 482.

87. Phyllis Rackin, who, in a fascinating comment, argues for the positive nature of the transvestism none the less points out that it is the stuff of male fantasy rather than women's historical experience: 'Thus, in Jonson's play [*Epicoene*], which subscribes to the neoclassical ideal of art as an imitation of life, gender also imitates life – both in a limited, literal sense, since the sex of Epicoene is finally revealed as male (the sex of the actor who played the part), and in a broader sense, since

women in the play are subjected to the same calumny, stereotyping, and social restrictions that real women suffered in Jonson's world. For Lyly and for Shakespeare, the relation between art and life is complementary as well as reflective. ... Thus, in these plays the true gender of the transvestite figure turns out to be feminine, the opposite of the real sex of the boy who played her part. Similarly, the dynamics of the plots make femininity a desideratum rather than the liability it was in actual life' (Rackin, 'Androgyny, Mimesis', p. 33).

7

'What You Will': Social Mobility and Gender in *Twelfth Night*

CRISTINA MALCOLMSON

When Sebastian enters the last scene of *Twelfth Night* and begins to untangle the various intricacies of the plot, Duke Orsino describes his vision of Sebastian and Viola together in these words:

> One face, one voice, one habit, and two persons –
> A natural perspective that is and is not.

Orsino refers to a set of Renaissance artifacts, including complicated mirrors, which highlighted the effect of perspective on human vision. With some of these 'perspectives', a confusion of images would resolve themselves into clarity if viewed from one indirect position. In others, like Holbein's famous painting of 'The Ambassadors', two images could only be seen clearly from two entirely different points of view. Orsino's reference to a 'natural perspective that is and is not' implies not only that he thinks nature has produced before him what is usually the work of art by bringing two mirroring figures on the stage at once; he also suggests that one of these figures, Viola or Sebastian, is a confusion to the eye, and if one took the proper point of view, the confusion would be cleared. But the play reveals that things are more complicated than he would like: there is no view from which Viola will blend into Sebastian; the play proves that Orsino must learn to accept the confusion or the deeper clarity of two, equally viable, points of view.[1]

Orsino's reference to the 'perspective' reproduces the problem of gender in the play (are women and men twins in their mental and emotional abilities? do they have fundamentally different perspectives?). But it also evokes the play's twin issue: the relationship between gender and status. The play in fact treats these issues as reflections of each other: Viola's relationship to Orsino includes both that of woman to man and that of servant to master. More complexly, Viola's relationship to Orsino mirrors Malvolio's relationship to Olivia: both servants want to marry their masters; both men in these pairs are self-obsessed; both women seem far more intelligent than their male counterparts. Shakespeare considers the compatibility of servants and masters as he considers the comparability of men and women. When Orsino recognises the 'impropriety' of Viola's service to him, he puts it in terms of gender and status:

> So much against the mettle of your sex,
> So far beneath your soft and tender breeding.
> (V.i.322–3)

The artful rather than natural perspective of the play moves us to compare men and women, servants and masters, gender and status, and to ask if one can ever get all these issues clearly into view, while respecting their differences and understanding their connections.

The questions evoked by Orsino's reference to the 'perspective' are remarkably similar to those posed by the historian Joan Kelly in her article on gender and class, called 'The Doubled Vision of Feminist Theory'. Kelly urges feminist historians to recognise that a *woman's place is not a separate sphere or domain of existence but a position within social existence generally*. She claims that feminists can see 'the relations of the sexes as formed by both socio-economic and sexual-familial structures *in their systematic connectedness*'. She posits a critical method which would acknowledge the differences of feminism and Marxism, and yet recognise that the issues of gender and class can only be clearly understood in their relation to each other: 'From this perspective, our personal, social and historical experience is seen to be shaped by *the simultaneous operation* of relations of work and sex; relations that are systematically bound to each other – and always have been so bound.'[2]

Twelfth Night was written during a period before a woman's place was imagined as a separate sphere, since, for the Renaissance, a woman was considered to be analogous to other social inferiors in a hierarchical society. The Anglican homily on obedience substantiates its political claims through a mirroring set of obligations: 'some are in high degree, some in low, some Kings and Princes, some inferiors and subjects, Priests and laymen, Maisters and servauntes, Fathers and children, Husbands and Wives.' English society linked gender and status in its own, Renaissance version of Kelly's 'systematic connectedness'. The homily on marriage teaches wives to 'cease from commanding, and performe subjection' by using the same set of analogies: 'For when we ourselves doe teach our children to obey us as their parents, or when we reforme our servants, and tell them that they should obey their masters ... If they should tell us againe our dueties, we should not thinke it well done.'[3] The homilies testify to the flexibility of this system of correspondences, since women can be included as parents when it serves the purpose (in the homily on marriage) but excluded when it does not: the homily on obedience prefers 'Fathers and children'. Shakespeare, and other authors, constructed literary representations of these mirroring social estates sometimes to reinforce the ideology preached in the homilies, sometimes to challenge it, but primarily by evoking and manipulating what amounted to a cultural language of the analogies of subordination.

Kelly's article suggests that we need to include a historical perspective of both gender and class in our analysis of literature. My thesis is a development of hers: we can understand how gender operates in Renaissance literature only if we consider its relationship to status or class, and only through focused historical research about socio-economic structures, as Kelly puts it, as well as sexual-familial structures. We have to uncover, first, how representations of gender and status in a particular work operate within the Renaissance language of interconnection, and, second, how these representations express or elide actual conditions. Materialist feminists and, actually, all literary historicists have to create a 'perspective' of their own, in which gender and status, literature and history can be perceived in a modern account of their 'systematic connectedness'.[4]

Twelfth Night dramatises the issue of social mobility through women who, though servants, are as capable as their male masters, and who rise out of their role as servants to become their master's mistresses. Our problem is to tease out the ideological significance inherent in the play's version of the cultural mirroring process, a version which links women and aspiring servants, marriage and social mobility. *Twelfth Night* considers advancement in terms of a marriage market which in the play is much more open to personal choice and status exogamy than it is in traditional society, and which also firmly closes down at particular moments. In the play, both men and women improve their lot through this open market, but the play explicitly compares the success of its women to the failure of particular men, who are excluded from the gifts of fortune for reasons which are culturally significant. Not only are female triumphs compared to male inadequacies; the proper attitude towards marriage becomes the mirroring reflection of the proper attitude towards social advancement.[5] The play therefore transfers anxieties about fluid social relations onto gender relations, and solves the problem through its ideal of marriage. I will argue that the play dramatises the superiority of women to men in order to call into question the rigid structures of the traditional order, and, in the process, to validate certain forms of social mobility. Nevertheless, such questioning is contained through the play's model of marriage, which requires a 'loving' commitment to others. The ideology of the play resides in its formulation of love, which includes both dominant, traditional notions of interdependence, and newly emerging attitudes towards individual choice and personal desire, or, as the play puts it, 'will'.[6]

As all critics of the play have noticed, desire or 'what you will' is the motivating force in the play, but this will or appetite is often hungry not only for music, drink or love, but for an improved social position. Maria's forged letter of love from Olivia to Malvolio, which promises him that 'thou art made, if thou desir'st to be so', is a jesting version of the projects of the other characters (II.v.150–1). Sir Toby Belch seeks to better Sir Andrew Aguecheek's estate and his own by marrying Sir Andrew to his niece, Olivia. After Olivia marries Sebastian, and meets the unknowing Cesario in Act V, Olivia says:

> Fear not, Cesario; take thy fortunes up,
> Be that thou know'st thou art, and then thou art
> As great as that thou fearest.
>
> (V.i.147–9)

Olivia points out the social distinction between Cesario and Duke Orsino, but exhorts the servant to embrace his new position as her husband, an estate which makes him as 'great' as his master. Marriage may be the goal of desire in the play, but these marriages can also elevate one of the partners to a higher social estate. Love and desire participate in the process of social mobility made most visible in Cesario's association with the Duke. Valentine says, 'If the Duke continue these favours towards you, Cesario, you are like to be much advanced' (I.iv.1–2). Orsino says:

> Prosper well in this,
> And thou shalt live as freely as thy lord
> To call his fortunes thine.
>
> (I.iv.38–40)

Viola herself has explicitly chosen her place in the play: 'I'll serve this Duke' (I.ii.55); her marriage to him at the end of the play turns Cesario's advancement into a love-match.

The notion that one's social estate could be subject to one's will or a matter of desire underlies the play's simultaneous consideration of the relation of man to woman, and of master to servant. When Viola woos Olivia for Orsino, but wins her heart for herself, the wonder of it lies not only in that a woman has been mistaken for a man, but that a woman has been mistaken for a gentleman. When alone, Olivia repeats to herself her questioning of Cesario, and reveals her attraction to what she takes to be his 'gentility':

> 'What is your parentage?'
> 'Above my fortunes, yet my state is well.
> I am a gentleman.' I'll be sworn thou art.
> Thy tongue, thy face, thy limbs, actions, and spirit
> Do give you fivefold blazon. Not so fast; soft, soft,
> Unless the master were the man. How now?
> Even so quickly may one catch the plague?
> Methinks I feel this youth's perfections
> With an invisible and subtle stealth
> To creep in at mine eyes.
>
> (I.v.287–96)

Olivia feels the inappropriateness of falling in love with a servant, but we see that she has in fact fallen for a cleverly created illusion, Viola's capable representation of the attributes of an upper-class young man, with his tongue, face, limbs, actions and spirit. As Sir Andrew puts it, 'That youth's a rare courtier' (III.i.88). The argument of some critics that Viola's nobility shines through her disguise must be qualified by the emphasis that the play puts on manipulating illusions and fashioning appearances.[7] Viola's success at this task is measured by Sir Andrew Aguecheek's failure; he is both male and knight, but his inadequate wit and verbal awkwardness ensure that he will be 'put down' by both Maria and Sir Toby (I.iii.79).

In the play, a gentleman is 'made' and made lovable not by his title or blood, but by his (or her) will. Olivia makes it quite clear that she cannot love Duke Orsino simply for his aristocratic blood, though he is 'noble' and of 'great estate', 'a gracious person' both 'in dimension and the shape of nature' (I.v.255–60). Cesario instead wins Olivia's heart when he plays the wilful lover:

> **Viola**   If I did love you in my master's flame,
>   With such a suff'ring, such a deadly life,
>   In your denial I would find no sense;
>   I would not understand it.
> **Olivia**   Why, what would you?
> **Viola**   Make me a willow cabin at your gate
>   And call upon my soul within the house;
>   Write loyal cantons of contemnèd love
>   And sing them loud even in the dead of night;
>   Hallo your name to the reverberate hills
>   And make the babbling gossip of the air
>   Cry out 'Olivia!' O, you should not rest
>   Between the elements of air and earth
>   But you should pity me.
> **Olivia**   You might do much. What is your parentage?
>   (I.v.262–75)

Viola's reference to and demonstration of her verbal talents reveal that a gentleman's 'tongue' and 'spirit' are the result of intelligence and will, rather than gender or the 'great estate' that supports Orsino. Olivia in fact only becomes interested in Cesario's parentage after she is impressed with his linguistic potency. Viola is as able as the clown, whom she commends for the skills that she, he and a successful courtier share:

> He must observe their mood on whom he jests,
> The quality of persons and the time.
>   (III.i.63–4)

A good wit can turn a sentence inside out, like a 'chev'ril glove' (III.i.12); he can turn a woman into a man or a servant into a master. Viola and Maria are twinned in the play because, whereas Viola can produce the appearance of a man, Maria can produce the appearance of her mistress, not only through the similarity of their handwriting, but through the use of language that convinces Malvolio that this is indeed 'my Lady's hand' (II.v.84). The skilful intelligence of Viola and Maria wins for them marriages which improve their social estate: clearly for Maria, whose role as a gentle-woman-in-waiting places her beneath Sir Toby, kinsman to Olivia; and mostly likely for Viola, whose father's noble position is never precisely identified, and is probably beneath the rank of Duke Orsino.[8] When Sir Toby marries Maria in recompense for her 'device', the play represents through the advancement of a woman by marriage what was occurring for ambitious men in society: verbal agility could turn a servant into a master, make a gentleman into a peer or send a commoner into the ranks of the upper classes.

Commentators on the social order speak frequently and heatedly during this period about a fluidity in the status structure which they take to be common knowledge and objective fact. William Harrison claims that merchants 'often change estate with gentlemen, as gentlemen do with them, by a mutual conversion of the one into the other'. According to Harrison, many obtain gentility through attending the Inns of Court or the University, gaining the money and leisure to 'bear the port, charge, and countenance of a gentleman', and purchasing a coat of arms from the heralds; by this process, they, 'being made so good cheap, bee called master ... and reputed for a gentleman ever after'. Thomas Smith agrees with Harrison on this point, comments that the prince can 'make' gentlemen, esquires or peers, and, in a section entitled 'Whether the maner of England in making gentlemen so easily is to be allowed', decides that such changes of status are good for the realm, especially for the treasury. He also considers quite sympathetically the yeomen who 'doe come to such wealth, that they are able and daily doe buy the landes of unthriftie gentlemen'. By sending their sons to school and freeing them from manual labour, yeomen 'doe make their saide sonnes by these meanes gentlemen'. Thomas Wilson concurs that gentlemen have been 'overreched' by yeomen, and adds that city lawyers are in pursuit of a country seat: 'they undoe the country people and buy up all the lands that are to be sold.' Smith is less sympathetic to the phenomenon, as are a multitude of preachers and satirists. However, even a churchman like Robert Sanderson, middle-of-the-road Anglican minister, could in 1621 announce that such fluidity was not only the status quo, but to be preferred to a closed system of rank. In a sermon on vocation, Sanderson urges idle 'gallants' to find their own work:

> observe by what steps your worthy Progenitors raised their houses to the height of *Gentry*, or *Nobility*. Scarce shall you find a man of them, that gave an accession, or brought any noted Eminency to his house; but either serving in the *Camp*, or sweating at the *Bar*, or waiting at the *Court*, or adventuring on the *Seas*, or trucking in his *Shop*, or some other way industriously bestirring himself in some settled Calling and Course of Life.

Only by equal labours can these young heirs merit 'those Ensigns of *Honor* and *Gentry* which [their ancestors] by industry atchieved'.[9]

Modern historians who study social mobility agree in general with these views, but argue that the movement actually taking place was far less extensive than these comments imply. In his original account of the situation, Lawrence Stone represented the social mobility of the period as 'a seismic upheaval of unprecedented magnitude', and his figures suggest as much: between 1500 and 1700, the number of the upper classes trebled during a time when the population doubled; the number of peers rose from 60 to 160, of knights from 500 to 1400, and of armigerous gentry from 'perhaps 5000 to 15,000'.[10] In his later work, Stone severely restricts his earlier assessment by claiming that newcomers were largely younger sons of the gentry, who, through the professions or trade, re-established their gentility. Nevertheless, he does admit to 'the influx of mercantile wealth into land in the late sixteenth and early seventeenth century'.[11] Keith Wrightson states that 'social mobility was a constant phenomenon in English society', since gentility was based on 'the acquisition and retention of landed wealth' rather than birth. He also claims that the later sixteenth and seventeenth centuries 'produced a quickened pace of upward and downward social mobility'. He cites a study of Lancashire where 278 families lost their place among the gentry between 1600 and 1642, and 210 families (and perhaps 79 more) moved up into it. The rising families were in part those of wealthy townsmen, which Wrightson argues were largely younger sons of the gentry; nevertheless, by far the majority of newcomers were prosperous yeomen.[12] Although Stone had originally defined marriage as 'the easiest road to riches', Wrightson concludes, as does Stone elsewhere, that very few marriages took place across status lines. There were, however, some

gender roles re

connections made between those in positions close to each other in rank or wealth: the peerage intermarried with the upper gentry, rich merchants and lawyers; the gentry with mercantile or yeoman families.[13] Both of these historians agree that there was significant movement between ranks; they also believe that contemporary accounts of its range and frequency were exaggerated.

In *Twelfth Night*, Shakespeare creates a unique version of the age's commentary about social mobility, since the play represents as primarily a female achievement the advancement noted by his contemporaries. One would like to classify this as pure myth; on the other hand, there is very little historical evidence about the social mobility of women. According to David Cressy:

> widows and women who were heads of households were the only women assumed to have any independence, but the polity was normally assumed to exclude women of all sorts ... While a wife in England was accorded the rank or status of her man, she was, nonetheless '*de jure* but the best of servants'.[14]

The analogies of English social theory were quite inaccurate in their identification of wives with male children or male servants, since women were prohibited from most avenues for advancement. There is evidence that some daughters of rich merchants married into the gentry or peerage, but most marriages occurred within particular status groups.[15] It is clear that studies of social mobility are severely lacking in evidence on women; more work needs to be done to investigate whether or not women improved their position through marriage or through trade. We can assume, however, that the play's representation of the mobility of its society through women is historically inaccurate, and curiously and significantly skewed in a way unlike the exaggerations of commentators.

Twelfth Night sets free a fluidity between the roles of man and *Malvol*
woman, and master and servant in the case of Viola and Maria, but limits it severely and abruptly in the case of Malvolio. In *A Marxist Study of Shakespeare's Comedies*, Elliot Krieger argues that Malvolio's aspirations are ridiculed and exorcised by the play not in order to preserve the true 'liberty' of saturnalia, but 'to allow the aristocracy to achieve social consolidation'. He claims that whereas identity is generally mutable in the play, Malvolio's attempt to cross the line between servant and master is condemned as transgressive. Whereas Viola's enactment of gentility is rendered legitimate by our discovery at the end of the play of her 'noble' blood, Malvolio's

inferior status ensures that his ambition will be viewed as presumption.[16]

Krieger is quite right to point out that the play balances the freedom of Viola's fluid identity against the strictures on Malvolio, and that such strictures finally reinforce class prejudice. But in this play such prejudice is more complex than Krieger suggests. The play includes a tentative but radical disruption of conventional categories of identity which is checked but not erased by its ending, and checked in a complicated way. Reducing Viola's astute role-playing to an expression of her nobility ignores the part she plays in this limited but tangible disruption as well as in its containment. Viola's performance as a courtier wins her prestige and potential financial rewards from Orsino and a proposal of marriage from Olivia; her noble breeding may make such success more likely, but her female gender makes it remarkable. Viola is never simply a noble person masquerading as a gentle person without wealth; her rendition of masculine gentility subtly suggests that all social roles can be impersonated. The play treats Viola very differently from Perdita in *Winter's Tale*, since *Twelfth Night* emphasises Viola's performative talent rather than her 'authentic' nobility. We may be convinced in Viola's first scene that she is no commoner: she speaks to the Captain and his sailors with authority, they defer to her, she pays them 'bounteously' (I.ii.52). Yet the scene raises questions about whether Orsino's 'name' accurately represents his 'nature', or whether the Captain's 'outward character', either as behaviour or title, is related to his 'mind' (ll.25, 50–1). These questions prepare us for Viola's experiments with appearance, partially because she has to negotiate in a world where titles may not be trustworthy, and partially because she herself will manipulate the relationship between seeming and being. The scene does not explicitly define Viola's status as either noble or gentle; rather, her rank is veiled from us just as Viola veils it from the people she will meet. Such masking has a purpose: we, and the characters, will know her through her role-playing and her 'intent':

> O that I served that lady,
> And might not be delivered to the world,
> Till I had made mine own occasion mellow,
> What my estate is ...
> Conceal me what I am, and be my aid
> For such disguise as haply shall become
> The form of my intent.
>
> (ll.41–4, 53–5)

In these passages, to will or choose her way allows Viola to disrupt conventional definitions of identity: 'my estate', 'what I am'. Not to be 'delivered to the world' is to withhold the details of one's family origins, gender and present situation until one can give birth to oneself at the most propitious moment. Such a self-protective delay replaces birth and status with a flexible identity, since not only can outer appearance be subject to one's will, but this will can also be influenced by the practice of acting: Viola's disguise 'haply shall become / The form of my intent'. The word 'form' reproduces the riddles about inner and outer identity that pervade the scene, and the word 'become' increases the dilemma: will the disguise 'become' or be used as the outward form of her inward intent? Will the 'matter' of her external costume represent decorously the inner structuring 'form' or principle of her willed purpose? Will this disguise itself become or begin to dictate her desires? To what extent do clothes make the man? Not only is rank replaced by intent in Viola's plot, but also the focus of the scene on a correspondence between outer and inner quality is complicated by the suggestion that external forms can determine internal states. When her estate is 'delivered' to us in the last act, it is only after we have seen to what an extent her skilful use of disguise becomes her.

Malvolio also does not fit within Krieger's rigid schema. The play manipulates Malvolio's status titles for dramatic purposes: when Malvolio is to appear presumptuous in his disciplining of Sir Toby, Toby cries, 'Art thou more than a steward?' (II.iii.113). When we are to recoil and laugh at Malvolio's desire to wed Olivia, his analogy tricks us into overestimating the lowliness of his rank: 'There is example for't. The Lady of the Strachy married the yeoman of the wardrobe' (II.v.39–40). We find out only in the late prison scene, when our sympathy is needed, that Malvolio is in fact not a commoner but a gentleman (IV.ii.85; see also V.i.277, 280). He is therefore not disenfranchised in any technical sense; he has already crossed over the most significant boundary line in the society, and is already a legitimate member of the ruling classes. It is true that a marriage between Malvolio and the Countess Olivia would be viewed as unconventional – it would be analogous to the marriage between the Duchess of Malfi and her steward Antonio.[17] But Malvolio's dream of marrying Olivia is in principle no more socially disruptive than Olivia's dream of marrying what she takes to be the gentleman Cesario. Shakespeare seems less intent on stigmatising characters for behaviour outside their rank than on emphasising status differences at particular moments for particular purposes. The play veils and manipulates the rank of Malvolio and Viola in order to encourage the audience to compare their relative success at winning their desired marriages. When their status is identified, it seems unlikely that the ideological point would be that women of undefined noble blood can marry dukes, whereas gentlemen cannot marry countesses. We must search more deeply for Malvolio's offending characteristic.

The play presents the problem most forcefully in two conjoining scenes: Act II, scene iv, in which the Duke and Cesario debate whether or not a woman's love is equal to a man's, and scene v, in which Malvolio imagines himself to be equal to Olivia and superior to Sir Toby through the marriage that would make him 'Count Malvolio'. It is here that the play's interest in twin characters and twin issues becomes most complex: Cesario is like Malvolio because both are servants who wish to marry their masters; Viola is like Maria because both use language and counterfeited appearances to manage their chosen male subjects; Malvolio is like Orsino because both are self-absorbed men for whom mastery consists in the exercise of power and the exclusion of any consideration of the perspectives of others. The play calls attention to its twin issues by repeating lines: when the Duke asks Cesario what sort of woman he has fallen in love with, Cesario replies, 'Of your complexion' (II.iv.26). When Malvolio imagines Olivia's love for him, he remembers Olivia's previous remark that, should she love, 'it should be one of my complexion' (II.v.23–4). The play invites us to consider love from two angles: Viola's self-abnegating, amorous desire and Malvolio's self-deluded dream of power. It also encourages us to consider Orsino's inadequate sense of women in terms of Malvolio's more explicitly identified 'self-love'. It is in the simultaneous exploration of the worthiness of women and the inadequacy of Malvolio that we find the play's ideological bias: the desire of an inferior to be matched with a superior is acceptable as long as it is motivated by love; to the extent that desire is self-interested, it is foolish and dangerous. In the world of the play, Malvolio represents ill will or bad will (*mal*: evil; *voglio*: I will or desire). He pursues his ends for the wrong reasons rather than the right. Viola's name, on the other hand, suggests a female, positive version of Malvolio, one whose will has become, let us say, musical, and capable of harmonising society rather than disrupting it. In this play, desire replaces reverence as the basis of the bond that links master and servant, man and woman; we could say that loving and erotic desire mediates the issue of social mobility in the play, since loving desire acknowledges choice and human will, but it also ensures devotion or a commitment to others. In *Twelfth Night*, ambition is acceptable, as long as it is the ambition to love. Our question is, why is such devoted desire identified with a woman rather than a man? What does such an identification make possible for the play and what does it obscure?

In *Twelfth Night*, the current and popular controversy over women mediates the dilemmas about social mobility. This allows the play to question quite fully the traditional ideology that those who rule are mentally or morally superior to those who are ruled, but it holds such questioning in check through an ideal of marriage and a model of marital contract which guards against the dangers of personal independence. The romantic love in the play acknowledges the power of desire, but ensures that such desire will flow into the channels of traditional, socially instituted bonds.

Act II, scene iv, allows Viola to confront the Duke with the value and power of female intelligence, but such intelligence is only discussed in terms of a woman's capacity to love.[18] The erotic power of this scene consists not only in the Duke's ignorance that his man-to-man talk with Cesario about love finally allows Viola to express what she feels, but also in the fact that the scene stages between two potential lovers the debate about women which usually took place within the confines of contemporary treatises. Shakespeare stages the debate with a bias: Viola's concealed identity and love for Orsino ensure our sympathy for her point of view. The Duke claims that women cannot love as deeply as he does, but the scene suggests that his love for Olivia is superficial, inconstant and finally repressive, since he seems unwilling to imagine or believe that a woman could initiate a love of her own. The Duke's 'self-love' has already been revealed in the first scene of the play, when he proclaims that, after Olivia's grief over her brother dies out, the Duke himself will take his place as the new male sovereign, the 'one self king' reigning in Olivia's affections (I.i.40). In their conversation in Act II, scene iv, Viola reminds the Duke that he may not be so successful, and offers him the possibility of seeing things from a woman's point of view:

> **Viola** Say that some Lady, as perhaps there is,
>   Hath for your love as great a pang of heart
>   As you have for Olivia. You cannot love her.

You tell her so. Must she not then be answered?
Duke   There is no woman's sides
Can bide the beating of so strong a passion
As love doth give my heart; no woman's heart
So big to hold so much; they lack retention.
(II.iv.89–96)

The Duke refuses to imagine that a woman could initiate desire as he does, and so he loses the point of the scene communicated to us: a woman, Viola, loves as deeply as a man, and recognises that she cannot control her beloved's point of view.

The debate about love in this scene is a submerged exploration of the extent to which Renaissance masculinity depends on denying women a will of their own, and the independent perspective that goes with it. Viola deflates this masculine conceit by her words and her presence:

Duke   Make no compare
Between that love a woman can bear me
And that I owe Olivia.
Viola   Ay, but I know –
Duke   What dost thou know?
Viola   Too well what love women to men may owe.
In faith, they are as true of heart as we.
(ll.101–6)

When Viola interrupts the Duke's masculine and mastering order, 'Make no compare', she asserts that her knowledge and experience constitute an identity comparable to his own: 'Ay, but I know.' But what she knows is her erotic attachment to the Duke, 'what love women to men may owe', an attachment that ensures her willing participation in a marital system which fears more deeply the unattached woman than the brilliant wife. Viola's debate with the Duke exposes as masculine tyranny his desire to be Olivia's 'one self king', but protects him and the audience against the play's deeper fear of female independence, expressed in the Duke's reference to the story of Diana and Actaeon:

O, when mine eyes did see Olivia first,
Methought she purged the air of pestilence,
That instant was I turned into a hart,
And my desires, like fell and cruel hounds,
E'er since pursue me.
(I.i.20–4)

female subservience/inde

The Duke speaks in the fanciful language of a poetic love, but his words reveal that he already fears rejection, since Olivia, like Diana, might refuse to be married; such a fear must be repressed because it would result in the dismemberment of a sense of masculinity which depends on female subservience. Again, the play questions Orsino's association of masculinity and power, but provides a new protection against the dangers of Diana: women will marry because they want to. When Sir Toby praises Maria for her victory over Malvolio, he calls her 'Penthesilea', the Amazon warrior with whom Achilles fell in love just before he killed her. These dangerous extremes of female independence and masculine tyranny are modified by Toby's affirmation that Maria is 'one that adores me' (II.iii.176–9).

Viola's response to Orsino in their debate about love is similar to that of Jane Anger in the treatise 'Her Protection for Women' (1589), which answers a lost pamphlet by 'the surfeiting lover'. These two treatises took part in a series of exchanges which fuelled the controversy about women during the period.[19] Like Viola, 'Her Protection for Women' declares that women should be recognised for their 'trueness of love' (p. 181), but the difference between the treatise and the play is registered in the difference between the name Jane Anger and that of Viola. Like Viola, Anger counters male views of female love, but less as a preface to marriage than as a reproof of men, uttered, as she says, in a 'choleric vein' (p. 173). Answering an opponent whose treatise seems to have renounced love and women as well, Anger uses the author's term for himself as 'surfeiting' to consider the destructive effects on women of defining male desire as an appetite. Orsino proclaims his inability to 'suffer surfeit' in his appetite for love, since he 'is all as hungry as the sea / and can digest as much' (II.iv.100–1), but Anger points out the problem with the metaphor: men 'become ravenous hawks, who do not only seize upon us, but devour us' (p. 178). Her treatise clarifies the contradictory nature of Orsino's love, which he describes as both 'so strong a passion' that 'no woman's heart' is 'so big to hold so much', and as 'more longing, wavering, sooner lost and worn, / Than women's are' (II.iv.94–6, 33–4). His desire for Olivia is described as infinite, like the sea, but he uses words which suggest that marriage itself would be no solution:

> Nought enters there,
> Of what validity and pitch so ever,

But falls into abatement and low price
Even in a minute.

(I.i.11–14)

The Duke's description of desire implies that whether the lover
surfeits or never surfeits, the fate of his wife will be the same:

> For women are as roses, whose fair flow'r,
> Being once displayed, doth fall that very hour.

Viola's reply is full of pathos:

> And so they are; alas, that they are so;
> To die, even when they to perfection grow.

(II.v.38–42)

Such a reply is quite different from Jane Anger's comment on the
subject:

> men's eyes are so curious, as be not all women equal with Venus for
> beauty, they cannot abide the sight of them; their stomachs so
> queasy, as do they taste but twice of one dish they straight surfeit,
> and needs must a new diet be provided for them.

(p. 178)

Viola's careful and caring instruction of the Duke as well as our
sympathy for her concealed love prepare us for the harmony of
their betrothal in the last scene of the play, but keep us from considering what their marriage will finally be like.

Jane Anger's treatise is unusual in its lack of interest in the subject
of matrimony, since most pamphlet-writers defending women during
this period praised them most highly for their capacity to be able
companions to men. Nicholas Breton in 'The Praise of Vertuous
Ladies' (1597) claims that a man should see a great part of a woman
in himself, since Eve was made out of Adám, and this proves that a
woman is 'no other substance but another himself'. For every excellent man, there is an excellent woman, who is 'everie waies his
match'. The treatise soon turns to the match it most prizes, that of
marriage, but here the equality of women stressed by the treatise
becomes a threat. The best companion to a wise man is a witty
woman, but 'it is wisdom for a man to take heed that a woman be
not wiser than himself'. Finally, the treatise states with a jesting tone,
but a serious purpose that the only worthy 'wit' of a maid is to

choose a husband well; of a married woman, to love none other; and of a widow, to provide for her children. This treatise suggests that the faculties which made women 'everie waies' a man's 'match' could only usefully be exercised within the institution of marriage, and that even in marriage these capacities had to be restrained.[20]

A woman's love was essential to a successful marriage, according to the manuals of the period, which prized marriage as a form of companionship rather than simply as a necessity for lawful pro-creation. For William Perkins, the creation of Eve proved that a woman should not rule her husband, since she did not come out of his head, nor be his slave, since she did not come out of his feet, but, since she came out of his side, 'man should take her as his mate'.[21] But the equality that this notion of companionship seems to promise is quickly qualified by the manuals, and the love of a wife for her husband begins to appear as another form of masculine control. Edmund Tilney's *Flower of Friendshippe* (1568) states:

> equalitie is principally to be considered in thys matrimoniall amitie, as well of yeares, as of the gifts of nature, and fortune. For equal-nesse herein, maketh friendliness ... In this long and troublesome journey of matrimonie, the wise man maye not be contented onely with his spouses virginitie, but by little and little must gently procure that he maye also steale away her private will, and appetite, so that of two bodies there may be made one onely hart, which she will soone doe, if love raigne in her, and without this agreeable concord matrimonie hath but small pleasure ... or none at all, and the man, that is not lyked, and loved of his mate, holdeth his lyfe in continuall perill, his goodes in great jeopardie, his good name in suspect, and his whole house in perdition.

John Dod and Richard Cleaver in *The Godly Form of a Household* (1598) use almost the same words as Tilney, but their sense of the relationship between love and possession has increased: 'The husband ought not to bee satisfied that, he hath robd his wife of her virginitie, but in that he hath possession and use of her will.' Dod and Cleaver recognise the tension between the requirements that men rule and that women love: 'For although the husband shall have power to his wife, to feare and obey him, yet he shall never have strength to force her to love him.'[22]

The marriage manuals emphasise the importance of personal choice and consent by the marriage partners, and such choice in-cludes women as well as men, but the equality of choice does not extend much farther than the original decision. The literature on marriage during this period as well as current historical studies suggest that individual desire did influence marriage negotiations much more than we previously believed: Keith Wrightson has shown that Lawrence Stone overemphasised the capacity of aristocratic parents to determine marriages for their children, and ignored the extent to which lower-class marriages were initiated by the partners. Marriage manuals consistently acknowledge the fact of individual choice in their very structure, at the same time that they insist on parental approval. These manuals include chapters on consent and on the contractual nature of marriage, in order to stress the extent to which the marriage must be a matter of free will. It may finally be the case that marriage manuals were written for the children of the gentry or the 'middling sort' rather than for the aristocracy, whose marriages were more consistently determined by issues of status and wealth rather than personal choice. It is clear that they were written more often for men than for women. The voluntary nature of the marriage vow, in which the promise 'must not come from the lippes alone, but from the wel-liking and consent of the heart', nevertheless preceded a relationship in which a woman's love had to be matched by submission and obedience to her husband's will. Many marriage manuals suggest, in fact, that the only real choice appropriate for a woman after marriage was to choose to love her husband. In Tilney's *The Flower of Friendshippe*, which celebrates 'perfite love' that 'knitteth loving heartes, in an insoluable knot of amitie', the female speaker, Lady Julia, urges women to apply themselves to their duty, not only to revere their husbands, but to love them:

> The first thing, therefore, which the married woman must labour to intende, the first thing which she must with all her force, applie her whole minde unto, and the first thing which she must hartily put in execution, is to lyke, and love well. For reason doth bind us to love them, with whom we must eate, and drinke.[23]

The fear of unloving wives in the marriage manuals is like the fear of female independence in *Twelfth Night*: in both cases, women refuse to authorise as mutually beneficial and as benevolent the form of social control inherent in the Renaissance institution of marriage. But this fear of the independent woman in *Twelfth Night* and the celebration of a romantic love that impels one to choose to be dependent on another mediates and controls the play's twin issue: the danger of self-interested rather than devoted servants. The play and its various literary and social sources testify to a society searching to articulate a new social bond between 'master' and 'servant', one which would acknowledge choice and ensure a new kind of 'dependability', based on contract rather than feudal obligation.[24]

In Act II, scene v, which directly follows the debate about love between Orsino and Viola, Malvolio imagines his new estate as 'Count Malvolio', and the play reveals that such self-interest has always motivated his government within the house. It is clear that Malvolio does not pursue Olivia with the poetic abandon of the other lovers in the play; he sees her as his ticket to a higher social position. His desire for Olivia as well as his ethical severity is a mask for a will-to-power:

> **Fabian** O, peace! Now he's deeply in. Look how imagination blows him.
> **Malvolio** Having been three months married to her, sitting in my state –
> **Toby** O for a stone bow, to hit him in the eye!
> **Malvolio** Calling my officers about me, in my branched velvet gown; having come from a day-bed, where I have left Olivia sleeping – ... And then to have the humour of state; and after a demure travel of regard, telling them I know my place, as I would they should do theirs, to ask for my kinsman Toby – ... Saying, 'Cousin Toby, my fortunes having cast me on your niece, give me this prerogative of speech.'
> **Toby** What, what?
> **Malvolio** 'You must amend your drunkenness'.
>
> (II.v.40–71)

Malvolio's fantasy reveals that his disciplinary zeal is impelled by a desire to dominate, unlike Viola's gracious deference. His imagined reproof, 'You must amend your drunkenness', is, like his branched velvet gown and his imperious looks, only another means by which he demonstrates his new position of power within the household. Malvolio's imagined reproof of Sir Toby is to be compared to the kindly correction of Orsino by Viola: their motives, according to the play, establish their difference. Malvolio's crime is not that he, as a gentleman, wants to marry a countess, or even that a steward wants to marry his mistress; it is that he will use his new position to disrupt traditional customs and rituals, and that such use of his 'prerogative' will be motivated by an ambition to establish his superiority and to impose his will on others. His sense of being virtuous is actually a desire for supremacy; for this reason, there will be no more cakes and ale, as Toby puts it (II.iii.116–17). We find during the play that Malvolio has brought Fabian 'out o' favour with my lady' Olivia for bearbaiting, and put Viola's benevolent captain into jail for some unidentified crime (II.v.6–7; V.i.275–6). Although Maria calls Malvolio only 'a kind of Puritan', Malvolio's fantasy of power constitutes the play's critique of London disciplinarians, those Puritan aldermen who were perhaps gentlemen but had originally been merchants, who condemned holiday revelry, bearbaiting and the theatre: such a concern for civil rule, according to the play, masks a self-interested desire to govern, an unwillingness to accept traditional social bonds, and a willingness to disrupt rather than harmonise the social order. London Puritans and Malvolio are like the 'politicians' and 'Brownists' that Sir Andrew fears (III.ii.30–1): each is a type of 'separatist', one who does not respect the bonds that tie the community together, bonds which may be flexible and fluid, but which must continue to hold if society is to survive.

In 'Pierce Pennilesse: His Supplication to the Divell' (1592), Thomas Nash, Gent., attacks those newly rich men who have no respect for the 'noble' virtue of liberality, which he feels is the main source of income for struggling writers. The contempt for tradition on the part of these 'new men' is the result of a frenetic upward movement of tradesmen and lawyers who dress 'as brave as any ... Nobleman'. He makes it clear that he does not oppose social mobility *per se*, but only that worthy men are left impoverished, whereas the undeserving obtain higher estates through 'delicious gold' or are unjustly promoted like 'some such obscure upstart gallants, as without desert or service are raised from the plough, to be checkmate with Princes'. Indeed, such social advancement would be appropriate if granted to writers whose talents make them superior to their patrons: 'This is the lamentable condition of our Times, that men of Arte must seeke almes of Cormorants, and those that deserve best, be kept under by Dunces.' Like *Twelfth Night*, Nash questions the traditional notion that social superiors are necessarily better than those they govern, but he also attacks merchants and tradesmen who have no respect for the traditional nobility and no respect for the theatre. 'Pierce' claims that the ethical severity of those citizens who condemn playgoing only masks a desire to usurp the place of the traditional nobility:

> I will defend [the theatre] against any Collier or clubfooted Usurer of them all, there is no immortalitie, can be given a man on earth like

unto Playes. What talke I to them of immortalitie, that are the only underminers of Honour, and doe envie any man that is not sprung up by base Brokerie like themselves. They care not if all the ancient houses were rooted out, so that like the Burgomasters of the Low-Countries they might share the government amongst them as States, and be quarter-maisters of our Monarchie ... [They respect] neither the right of Fame that is due to true Nobilitie deceased, nor what hopes of eternitie are to be proposed to adventurous mindes, to encourage them forward, but only their execrable luker, and filthie unquenchable avarice.

Social advancement is appropriate for 'adventurous mindes' and 'men of Arte', but not for those who seek to mount upward for the wrong reasons: a hunger for money and power over others. Such as these not only have no respect for the ancient houses of nobility, they want to cast society into a different form, so that, like the 'Burgomasters of the Low-Countries', they will be 'quarter-maisters of our Monarchie'. According to the treatise, this disruption of the social order is caused by the devil himself, '*Nicalao Malevolo* ... the great mister maister of hell'.[25]

In 'Pierce Pennilesse', Nash reacts against Puritan attacks on the theatres and against the influence of the London city government on the Privy Council. *Twelfth Night* (1602) was produced only a few years after the office of the Master of the Revels had affirmed its capacity to license theatrical companies and restrict the days of their performances, as well as the bearbaiting that occurred nearby. Such courtly and civic control over theatrical revelry mirrored the repression of holiday pastimes in the countryside in places like Shakespeare's Stratford. Local Puritan elites were prohibiting many village festivities, including the church ales, in the name of a more thorough 'civil rule' (II.iii.122).[26]

Nash's pamphlet illuminates one of the most important contexts for *Twelfth Night*: urban satire, including the Harvey–Nash quarrel, in which 'Pierce Pennilesse' figures, but also including the war of the theatres, occurring during this period and referring at times to this play. *What You Will* is one of John Marston's volleys in the war, and its connections to *Twelfth Night, or What You Will* clarify that, for these playwrights, the intersection between disguise and the problem of fluid social relations is commonplace. In a society where status categories are flexible, apparel becomes a 'god', and opinion, or 'what you will', according to Marston, determines all social value, including personal rank and identity. One of the central characters in Marston's play, Albano, is a merchant who for a time loses his wife, his property and his name because people assume that he is dead and the living person standing before them is an imposter. Whether *What You Will* appeared before or after *Twelfth Night*, the attributes they share suggest that *Twelfth Night* was not only about revelry or carnival, but about the difficulties of estimating the value of individuals when the externals of identity, including rank and gender, are so easily imitated. It is therefore relevant that Shakespeare's play and probably Marston's were put on before an Inns of Court audience, incipient lawyers, well versed in urban satire and preparing for the successes and dangers of social advancement in the city. 'What you will' for Marston refers to opinion, and for Shakespeare to desire, but both playwrights testify to a world in which individually initiated attitudes and acts have replaced a shared consensus about appropriate behaviour and the rules for evaluating it. Both plays fear such a world, in which every man and woman can be a phoenix; *Twelfth Night* offers us women and servants who exchange their independence for a willing desire for another and so preserve 'all relation'.[27]

Malvolio may be a kind of Puritan, but he is also the conventional butt of urban satire, the social climber who becomes obsessed with the externals of rank, 'the habit of some sir of note' (III.iv.77–8), without a sense of 'true' worth and its significance for the community. Viola's decision to trust the Captain at the beginning of the play takes on new importance in this context, because she, like all members of society, must learn to accept and analyse a difference between external appearance and internal value:

> There is a fair behaviour in thee, captain,
> And though that nature with a beauteous wall
> Doth oft close in pollution, yet of thee
> I will believe thou hast a mind that suits
> With this thy fair and outward character.
>
> (I.i.47–51)

Viola's trust in the Captain is a matter of judgement and of will, an opinion not a fact. The problems of disguise in *Twelfth Night* take the play into the world of Ben Jonson's exploration of character and the ambiguous relationship in his plays between inner worth and social rank.

For Jonson, the nobility are to be revered, but only if they

> Study the native frame of a true heart,
> An inward comeliness of bountie, knowledge,
> And spirit that may conforme them actually
> To *God's* high figures.[28]

In *Cynthia's Revels, Or the Fountayne of self-love* (1600), the Jonsonian surrogate Crites unmasks the narcissism that motivates decadent aristocrats as well as ambitious courtiers; the play uses terms that look forward to Shakespeare's presentation of the Duke and Malvolio. But unlike Shakespeare, Jonson proceeds to define a positive version of self-love, which transforms narcissism into an honourable method of establishing publicly one's inner value: 'allowable Self-love' quickens 'minds in the pursuit of honour', and impels individuals to reach a social position which will justly match 'that true measure of one's self' (V.vii.26–35). In the play, Cynthia the Queen singles out for promotion her playwright Crites, whom she describes as one 'whom learning, virtue, and our favour last / Exempteth from the gloomy multitude' (V.viii.32–3).

In *Twelfth Night*, Shakespeare pokes fun at a notion of 'allowable self-love' which results in the preferment of its author. He associates such self-love with the colour yellow theatrically attributed to it in *Cynthia's Revels*, and with an overly pretentious, censorious steward, who is convinced that his lady will thrust greatness upon him.[29] Malvolio's 'self-love' satirises Jonson's version of individual value not only as self-indulgent but as socially divisive, because it privileges censuring the faults of others and praising the self over the more difficult task of preserving the harmony of social relations. *Twelfth Night* suggests that Jonson's version of merit is just as 'separatist' as the Puritans he derides in his comedies. The 'railing' that Viola's social music tames is not only that of the Puritans but that of the satirists.

Shakespeare is as interested as Jonson in the relationship between the 'name' and 'nature' of nobility, but he explores the issue through 'Viola' rather than 'Crites'. The name of the Duke, Orsino (or 'the little bear'), indicates that the Duke as well as Malvolio is the subject of the play's bearbaiting. Marston's Duke in *What You Will* is blatantly frivolous and sensual; audiences must have understood that Orsino's attitude towards love and women was not presented uncritically by *Twelfth Night*. But such criticism never becomes biting satire in Shakespeare's play: 'there is no railing in a known discreet man, though he do nothing but reprove' (I.v.95–6).[30]

People can only move socially to

In *Twelfth Night*, Shakespeare celebrates the social arts, very like
his own, which can turn a servant into a master, a glove-maker's
son into a gentleman, a woman into a man, a man into a woman.
Nevertheless, he reproves those who would use this social fluidity
for their own benefit or as an opportunity to reorder the traditional
structure according to new ethical and political principles. Such
ethical and political blueprints, he suggests, are simply fantasies of
power, which exchange the community good for private profit.

The play links the issues of gender and status in order to make
marriage, with its inclusion of desire and its commitment to per-
manence, the model of all social bonds. The Priest's description of
Olivia's marriage betrothal to Sebastian represents the play's dream
of a perpetual community, in which each member willingly takes
his or her place:

> A contract of eternal bond of love
> Confirmed by mutual joinder of your hands,
> Attested by the holy close of lips,
> Strengthened by interchangment of your rings.
>   (V.i.156–9)

It is not a coincidence that in the last act, as the cases of mistaken
identity mount up, willing service is coordinated with the contract
of marriage, and the dangers of infidelity to such a contract are considered: Olivia's sense of her husband Cesario's betrayal is followed
by Antonio's sense of his master Sebastian's betrayal, and then by
Orsino's sense of his servant Cesario's betrayal. Antonio, of course,
is the model for the new servant imagined by the play, since his
service is based on desire rather than duty or reverence:

> I could not stay behind you. My desire
> (More sharp than filed steel) did spur me forth;
> ... My willing love ... Set forth in your pursuit.
>   (III.iii.4–5, 11–13)[31]

The marriage bonds that certify the socially acceptable 'willing
love' of man and woman are forged by the 'true' priest in the play,
who is opposed dramatically to the 'false' priest-fool, Sir Topas,
who baits Malvolio. This carnivalesque figure reproaches others in
society who have 'dissembled in such a gown' (IV.ii.5–6), but also
members of the aristocracy, who, like Chaucer's Sir Thopas,
provide only an empty image of aristocratic superiority. Such an
image becomes ridiculous when engendered by a non-aristocratic

author-fool, like the narrator of the *Canterbury Tales*, who cannot get a tale of nobility quite right, but also when manipulated by a Sir Toby, whose name is so close to the Sir Topas he concocts that he becomes implicated in his own critique. Such satirists as Sir Toby miss the point when they bait Malvolio: blood is not the issue, but rather some mysterious quality of inner nobility which Sir Toby himself does not possess.

Viola's 'courtesy' is evidence not only of this inner nobility, but of her willingness to use her performative talent for unselfish purposes, to spin out the modes of social behaviour that can preserve the ties that bind. Orsino and Olivia think nostalgically about 'the old age' or the 'merry world' before true love and loyal servants were replaced by 'these most brisk and giddy-paced times' (II.iv.6, 48; II.i.100–1). *Twelfth Night* is plagued by a fear that when the witty whirl that is its surface and its plot shuts down, no trustworthy social order will remain: 'with hey, ho, the wind and the rain' (V.i.391ff).

Perhaps this is one reason why the play so relentlessly excludes the figure of the merchant, although in the sources, the father of Viola and Sebastian is almost always a merchant, and frequently the father of Olivia is so as well.[32] In Marston's play, Albano the merchant most forcefully represents the fragility of an identity based on fortune or chance, since he has achieved his status in the community through the power of wealth rather than the tradition of family lineage. In *Twelfth Night*, a play that is filled with imagery of the sea, merchants are never mentioned, although the play does refer to a new map of the world which includes the West Indies, and which is used to describe the lines on Malvolio's smiling face as he pursues his hopes with Olivia (III.ii.76–8). The play evokes the sense of treasure that can be obtained from the sea, as well as the riches that can satisfy a desire which is as infinite as the sea. But the treasure from the ocean in this play is Viola and Sebastian; like aspirations for social ascent, commercial interests are turned into romantic appetites.

The play cannot afford the figure of the merchant because such a social role does not fit clearly enough into the traditional hierarchical order of servant and master. The relations of the commercial classes to the classes above them could not easily be described in terms of feudal norms – they are not mentioned in the homily on obedience – since they were constituted more by monetary exchange than by the traditional ideals of reverence and duty. Shakespeare has to consider Malvolio as 'a kind of Puritan'; a real Calvinist merchant would upset the delicate balance of a play which explores the issue of social mobility through the lens of willing servants rather than successful entrepreneurs.[33]

The play solves the problem of self-interested desire through Viola's harmonious social bonding, and so projects anxieties about status relations onto gender relations. The play's fear of independent women is implicated in its fear of independent servants, since Viola's dependence is constituted in opposition to Malvolio's self-interest. Therefore sexual-familial structures are linked rather explicitly to socio-economic structures, as Kelly puts it, in such a way as to suggest that Viola's attitude to her labour as a servant to the Duke is praiseworthy because it partakes of her attitude towards her beloved, Orsino. As such, loving male–female relations mediate master–servant relations: both partners may be quite equal in intelligence and moral capacity, or indeed the subordinate may be superior to his or her master; nevertheless, an appreciative love should tie both together. Such a formula redefines traditional hierarchical bonds as more flexible in themselves, but also turns anything but the most loving commitment to one's superiors into 'self-love'.

The play's superimposition of labour relations onto marital relations results in a model of 'willing service' formed in the image of the 'mutual consent' required in the marriage contract. The history of the various kinds of contract during this period demonstrates that Shakespeare's model of contract is a selective one, since such an agreement could act as either a conservative or a disruptive force. At the time that the play was produced, changes in the law were eroding traditional restraints on business contracts, and strengthening the individual's control over these transactions. Such agreements required voluntary and mutual consent at the cost of feudal models of obligation, since deference to status was replaced with an interest in the market and personal profit. But such 'freedom' was not extended to labouring individuals, whose tendency to move throughout the country in pursuit of work had resulted in the passing of the Statute of Artificers (1563), which prohibited the sudden termination of contracts between employer and employed, and made illegal a horizontal mobility of workers responsive to new commercial developments. Through its labour-contract clauses, the Statute sought to place labourers under the firm control of a 'master', and often within the structure of the employer's family and paternal authority. *Twelfth Night* also mediates between a status and a market society through marriage and the family: it dramatises voluntary consent and 'free' will as mitigating the rigidity of the master–servant relationship, but also as preserving this traditional bond at a time when market forces were wearing away its feudal foundations. Shakespeare may have taken his cue from the marriage manuals of the period, which employ the language of contractual 'freedom', but nevertheless hedge it about with a concern for status and authority: 'consent' includes parental agreement and 'equality' requires likeness in rank; both consent and equality fade quickly away before the customary necessities of male authority and female submission. Like the manuals and marital law during this period, Shakespeare attempts to negotiate between individual interests and those of traditional society. He follows Perkins by making marriage the model for 'the commonwealth'.[34]

Twelfth Night imagines a world in which one's social estate is a matter of desire or will rather than birth or title. Such desire is innocent and successful to the extent that it moves one to be bound unselfishly to another. Shakespeare divides and conquers in his play not only by praising Viola and condemning Malvolio, but also by obscuring what Viola and Malvolio share in the play's various literary and social sources: a connection with a commercial class whose access to money has the power to upset the traditional link between high birth, wealth and status. The ideal that is set before women, servants and merchants in the play is that of loving and willing service, a Viola who chooses her man, but who also chooses to correct gently rather than dethrone the tyrant who will rule over her in the future. We might imagine a play about Mal-Viola (or Jane Anger), who does not wish the Duke well and says so, and whose female desire cannot so easily be presented as 'good will'. Just as Jonson in *Cynthia's Revels* presents himself in Crites, Shakespeare in *Twelfth Night* presents himself in Viola, that figure so well versed in the 'arts' of social behaviour, far more intelligent than her superiors, who elects to preserve the social harmony rather than 'put down' her masters.

From *The Matter of Difference: Materialist Feminist Criticism of Shakespeare*, ed. Valerie Wayne (New York and London, 1991), pp. 29–57.

NOTES

[Cristina Malcolmson combines those approaches which foreground class and gender. She looks at historical attitudes towards women's social mobility, and sees them reflected to some extent in the fortunes of Viola in particular. She argues that 'the play represents as primarily a female achievement the advancement noted by (Shakespeare's) contemporaries'. Ed.]

1. I am grateful for the comments and suggestions made by the participants of the seminar 'Materialist feminist criticism of Shakespeare' held at the 1989 meeting of the Shakespeare Association of America. I would particularly like to thank Catherine Belsey, Barbara Bono, Mihoko Suzuki, Valerie Wayne and Marion Wynne-Davies. 'Perspectives' are discussed in Jurgis Baltrusaitis, *Anamorphic Act*, trans. W. L. Strachan (New York, 1977), pp. 11–18, 91–114. Orsino's comment on the perspective appears in *Twelfth Night*, V.i.215–16 in *The Complete Signet Classic Shakespeare*, ed. Sylvan Barnet (New York, 1972). Subsequent citations will refer to this edition and appear in the text of the essay.

2. Joan Kelly, 'The Doubled Vision of Feminist Theory', in Judith L. Newton, Mary P. Ryan and Judith R. Walkowitz (eds), *Sex and Class in Women's History* (London, 1983), pp. 264, 265, 266. The emphasis is Kelly's own.

3. 'An exhortation concerning good order, and obedience to rulers and magistrates', and 'An homilie of the state of matrimonie', in *Certaine Sermons or Homilies appointed by the Queenes Majestie, to be declared and read by all Parsons, Vicars, and Curates ...* (London, 1595), I3 and Gg7.

4. Of course, several Renaissance critics have already discussed quite successfully the relationship of gender and status in Renaissance Drama. Frank Whigham's 'Sexual and Social Mobility in *The Duchess of Malfi*' (PMLA, 100 [1985], 167–86) is the best of this sort, and I am indebted to his discussion of social mobility. Nevertheless, in his essay, the gender issues tend to collapse into the status issues: 'the duchess's enterprise is not primarily private and romantic: it is, rather, a socially adaptive action that extends to the zone of gender conflict a manoeuvre actively in play in the arena of class conflict' (p. 171). Whigham's quotation from Kenneth Burke on *Venus and Adonis* at the beginning of the essay clarifies this: 'The real subject is not primarily sexual lewdness at all, but "social lewdness" mythically expressed in sexual terms.' If feminist writers in the 1970s ignored problems of class (Paula Berggren, 'The Woman's Part: Female Sexuality as Power in Shakespeare's Plays', and Clara Claiborne Park, 'As We Like It: How a Girl can be Smart and still Popular', both in

Carolyn Lenz, Gayle Greene and Carol Neely [eds], *The Woman's Part: Feminist Criticism of Shakespeare* [Urbana, IL, 1980], pp. 17–34, 100–16), then new historicists and cultural materialists in the 1980s often reduced gender concerns into a symbolic means of articulating what is 'the real subject': status, or issues of power in general. See Leonard Tennenhouse, *Power on Display: The Politics of Shakespeare's Genres* (New York and London, 1986) [partially reprinted in this volume – Ed.] for a fascinating discussion of 'Staging Carnival', which attends to the role of women and Queen Elizabeth in the process of inheritance, but which finally defines the comedies and Petrarchan literature as 'presenting us with a political crisis which must be understood and resolved in sexual terms' (p. 19). This is the problem, I think, with focusing exclusively on Queen Elizabeth in discussing these issues: the sexual-familial questions can too easily disappear before the political or socio-economic concerns. Jean Howard avoids this difficulty in 'Crossdressing, the Theatre, and Gender Struggle in early modern England' (*SQ*, 39 [1988], 418–40), in which she discusses the 'various manifestations of crossdressing' as 'an interlocking grid through which we can read aspects of class and gender struggle in the period', and the particularity with which she does so is enlightening and refreshing. She interprets *Twelfth Night* quite differently from the way I do, however, because she sees Viola's crossdressing as 'in no way adopted to protest gender inequities' (p. 431).

5. In an essay in this collection [*The Matter of Difference*], 'The World Turned Upside Down: Inversion, Gender and the State', Peter Stallybrass argues that 'there is no *intrinsic* connection between inversions of class [and] gender ... Politics is precisely the work of *making* such connections.' I argue in this essay that *Twelfth Night* performs such work by coordinating the interests of women and servants, and by making female 'good will' the model for socially ambitious men.

6. It is not a coincidence that the centrality of 'will' to the play reproduces the role of 'will' in the sonnets, in which Shakespeare represents his own peculiar linking of love and the potential rewards of patronage. For a largely psychoanalytic account of will in the sonnets, see Joel Fineman, *Shakespeare's Perjured Eye* (Berkeley, CA, 1988). My analysis of tradition and emergent attitudes in the play is indebted to Raymond Williams' discussion of his terms 'dominant', 'emergent' and 'residual' in *Problems in Materialism and Culture* (London, 1980), pp. 31–49, and in *Marxism and Literature* (Oxford, 1977), pp. 121–8.

7. I disagree with those critics who diagnose and/or dismiss Viola's successes in this play as the result of her noble rank (Tennenhouse, *Power on Display*, p. 66; Elliot Krieger, *A Marxist Study of Shakespeare's Comedies* [London, 1979], pp. 105–30).

8. As with several other characters, the play confuses us about the status of Maria: she is represented by Sir Toby as 'my niece's chambermaid'

(I.iii.50), but is identified by Olivia as 'my gentlewoman' (I.v.162). But the play continually groups her with the 'lighter people', as Malvolio puts it (V.i.341). In her forged letter to Malvolio, Maria herself delineates the line she will eventually cross: 'Be opposite with a kinsman, surly with servants' (II.v.149–50).

9. William Harrison, 'A description of England' (1577), in F. J. Furnivall (ed.), *Elizabethan England* (London, 1902), pp. 7, 9; Thomas Smith, *De Republica Anglorum* (London, 1583), pp. 27–30; Thomas Wilson, *The State of England Anno-dom, 1600*, ed. F. J. Fisher (London, 1936), pp. 25, 38; Robert Sanderson, 'Ad populum; the fourth sermon ... London, Nov. 4, 1621' in *XXXVI Sermons* (London, 1986), p. 212.

10. Lawrence Stone, 'Social Mobility in England, 1500–1700', *Past and Present*, 33 (1966), 16, 23–4; see also David Cressy, 'Describing the Social Order of Elizabethan and Stuart England,' *Literature and History*, 3 (1976), 29–44.

11. Lawrence Stone, *An Open Elite? England 1540–1880* (Oxford, 1984), pp. 399–400; 405–6.

12. Keith Wrightson, *English Society 1580–1680* (London, 1982), pp. 26–30, 140.

13. Stone, 'Social Mobility', p. 38; Wrightson, *English Society*, p. 86, cites Vivien Brodsky Elliott, 'Mobility and Marriage in Pre-industrial England' (unpubl. PhD thesis, University of Cambridge, 1978), pt. 1, ch. 4; pt. 3, ch. 3. See also Elliott, 'Single Women in the London Marriage Market: Age, Status, Mobility, 1598–1619', in R. B. Outhwaite (ed.), *Marriage and Society: Studies in the Social History of Marriage* (London, 1981), pp. 81–100; and Stone, *The Family, Sex and Marriage in England, 1500–1800* (London, 1977), pp. 60–1, 491.

14. Cressy, 'Describing the Social Order', pp. 34–5.

15. Stone, 'Social Mobility', p. 38; Lawrence Manley, *London in the Age of Shakespeare: An Anthology* (London, 1986), pp. 77–8.

16. Krieger, *A Marxist Study*, pp. 100–1, and throughout [reprinted in this volume – Ed.].

17. See Whigham, 'Sexual and Social Mobility in *The Duchess of Malfi*'.

18. See Catherine Belsey's illuminating and convincing reading of this scene in 'Disrupting Sexual Difference: Meaning and Gender in the Comedies', in John Drakakis (ed.), *Alternative Shakespeares* (London, 1985), pp. 166–90. Belsey argues that Viola-as-Cesario calls 'into question that set of relations between terms which proposes as inevitable an antithesis between masculine and feminine, men and women' (p. 167). I am arguing that the differences between the categories of servant and master are also questioned by the play, and that Viola's success and 'good will' in disrupting these differences in scene

iv are compared to Malvolio's failure in scene v. Viola's noble rank, like her role as a wife, is affirmed at the end of the play, and, as Belsey says, closes off 'the glimpsed transgression ... But the plays are more than their endings' (pp. 187–8).

19. The full title of Anger's treatise is 'Jane Anger her Protection for Women. To defend them against the Scandalous Reportes of a late Surfeiting Lover, and all other like Venerians that complaine so to bee overcloyed with womens kindness' (London, 1589). See the abridged text in Katherine Henderson and Barbara McManus (eds), *Half Humankind: Contexts and Texts of the Controversy about Women in England, 1540–1640* (Urbana and Chicago, 1985). Page numbers from this edition will appear in the text of the essay. For commentary on the controversy about women and lists of texts, see Henderson and McManus, *Half Humankind*; Edmund Tilney, *'The Flower of Friendshippe': A Renaissance Dialogue Contesting Marriage*, ed. Valerie Wayne [Ithaca, NY, 1992]; Linda Woodhouse, *Women and the English Renaissance: Literature and the Nature of Womankind, 1540–1620* (Urbana, IL, 1984), pp. 139–51; and Louis B. Wright, *Middle-Class Culture in Elizabethan England* (Chapel Hill, NC, 1935), pp. 481–502. For a discussion of the intersection of the controversy and later drama, see Sandra Clark, 'Hic Mulier, Haec Vir and the Controversy over Masculine Women', *Studies in Philology*, 82 (1985), 157–83; and Mary Beth Rose, 'Women in Men's Clothing: Apparel and Social Stability in *The Roaring Girl'*, *English Literary Renaissance*, 14 (1984), 139–51.

20. Nicholas Breton, 'The Praise of Vertuous Ladies' in *The Wil of Wit, Wits Will, or Wils Wit, chuse you whether. Containing five discourses.* (London, 1597), pp. 65, 69, 70–1.

21. William Perkins, *Christian Oeconomy*, trans. T. Pickering (London, 1609), p. 125. The first occurrence of this representation of companionship is found in Bullinger, *Christen State of Matrimony* (1541), sig. A4v.

22. Tilney, 'A Brief and Pleasant Discourse of Duties in Marriage, called the Flower of Friendshippe' (London, 1568), B2, B6. John Dod and Richard Cleaver include passages from 'The Flower' in *A Godly Form of Householde Government* (London, 1598), pp. 167, 165.

23. For discussions on individual choice in marriage, see Stone, *The Family, Sex and Marriage in England, 1500–1800*, pp. 85–93, 117, 178–95, 270–95; Wrightson, *English Society 1580–1680*, pp. 70–88; Susan Dwyer Amussen, *An Ordered Society: Gender and Class in Early Modern England* (Oxford, 1988), pp. 70–6, 105–8; and William and Malleville Haller, 'The Puritan Art of Love', *Huntington Library Quarterly*, 5 (1941–2), 254–6, 265. Cleaver insists on the 'consent of the heart' (p. 115) and includes discussions of choice, consent, and

contract (pp. 96–129). Perkins includes chapters entitled 'Of the Contract', 'Of the Choice of Persons Fit for Marriage' and 'Of Consent in the Contract' (pp. 18, 23, 68). See Tilney, D4, for Lady Julia's advice on the choice of husbands and the practicality of love after the marriage has occurred.

24. Howard discusses the merging idea of contractual relations in 'Crossdressing', p. 428. Don Wayne applies it to Jonson's *Bartholomew Fair* in '*Drama and Society in the Age of Jonson*: An Alternative View', *Renaissance Drama*, N.S.13 (1982), 103–29. See Gordon Schochet, *Patriarchalism in Political Thought: The Authoritarian Family and Political Speculation and Attitudes* (Oxford 1975) for a consideration of the idea of contract in political relations, although not in socio-economic relations.

25. Thomas Nash, 'Pierce Penilesse: His Supplication to the Divell' (London, 1592), A2, C4, F3.

26. E. K. Chambers, *The Elizabethan Stage*, 4 vols (Oxford, 1923), vol. I, pp. 298–302; vol. II, pp. 355–6, 471; David Underdown, *Revel, Riot and Rebellion: Popular Politics and Culture in England, 1603–1660* (Oxford, 1987), pp. 56–7.

27. For the Nash–Harvey exchange, see Donald McGinn, *Thomas Nashe* (Boston, 1981), pp. 104–51; for the war of the theatres, see Roscoe Small, *The Stage Quarrel between Ben Jonson and the So-Called Poetasters* (Breslau, 1899), pp. 1010–14; and R. W. Ingram, *John Marston* (Boston, 1978), pp. 43–54. For the exploration of the fluidity of social relations in the drama of the period, see Jean-Christophe Agnew, *Worlds Apart: The Market and the Theatre in Anglo-American Thought, 1550–1750* (Cambridge, 1986), especially pp. 57–148; L. C. Knights, *Drama and Society in the Age of Jonson*: (London, 1937); Manley, *London in the Age of Shakespeare*, pp. 75–81, 285–90; and Wayne, '*Drama and Society in the Age of Jonson*: an Alternative View'. The date usually attributed to Marston's *What You Will* is 1601, one year before *Twelfth Night*, but this is just conjecture, as Philip Finkelpearl points out in *John Marston of the Middle Temple* (Cambridge, MA, 1969), pp. 162–3. Donne speaks of the disruption of traditional social bonds in 'An Anatomy of the World: The First Anniversary'.

28. *Cynthia's Revels, Or the Fountayne of self-love* in *Ben Jonson*, ed. C. H. Herford and Percy Simpson, 11 vols (Oxford, 1932), vol. 4, pp. 1–183, V, iv, 643–6. On Jonson's analysis of what constitutes 'nobility', see Don Wayne, *Penshurst: The Semiotics of Place and the Poetics of History* (Madison, WI, 1984), pp. 129–73.

29. I am not the first to entertain the notion that Malvolio may represent Jonson; John Hollander considers the possibility for reasons quite different from my own in his insightful and informative essay, '*Twelfth*

Night and the Morality of Indulgence', *The Sewanee Review*, 68 (1959), 220–38. Hollander dismisses the possibility, but reminds us that Marston's *What You Will* 'devotes much effort to lampooning Jonson' (p. 238). See V, vii, 26–35 in *Cynthia's Revels* for the yellow colour of 'allowable self-love', which later turns up as Malvolio's stockings.

30. As Hollander points out, the Duke's name and nature are affirmed as equally 'noble' (I.ii.25), but the name 'Orsino' suggests quite another character. Jean Howard offers a different interpretation of Shakespeare's treatment of Orsino in her article 'Crossdressing' (p. 432).

31. Antonio is also the character left without a clear social position at the end of the play, since Sebastian never explicitly claims him as his man, nor frees him from Orsino's indictment. The play's tentative sympathy for this homoerotic relationship cannot save it from an exclusion from the community produced at the end of the play and most literally from the social legitimacy of marital bonds. Like that of the other characters, the 'desire' of Antonio for Sebastian begins by flowing into the traditional bonds of master and servant; therefore accounts of its homoeroticism have to be historicised. Nevertheless, Antonio is left at the end of the play a 'masterless' man.

32. Emanuel Forde, *The Famous History of Parismus* (1578); *The Novels of Mateo Bandello*, trans. John Payne, 4 vols (London, 1890), vol. 4, pp. 121–61 (part II, no. 28); *Gl'Ingannati* (1537), ed. and abridged T. L. Peacock (London, 1862). See also the useful Morton Luce (ed.), *Rich's 'Apolonius and Silla', An Original of Shakespeare's Twelfth Night* (New York, 1912), which discusses all the sources.

33. Manley, *London in the Age of Shakespeare*, pp. 75–81; Ruth Mohl, *The Three Estates in Medieval and Renaissance Literature* (New York, 1962).

34. On changes in contract law, see David Little, *Religion, Order and Law* (New York, 1969), pp. 204–5. On the Statute of Artificers and its relation to market influences, see F. J. Fisher, 'Commercial Trends and Policy in the Sixteenth Century', *Economic History Review*, 10 (1940), 110–13; and Bernard Supple, *Commercial Crisis and Change in England, 1600–1642* (Cambridge, 1959), p. 251. Martin Ingram comments on the implicit use of the family as a 'little commonwealth' in the Statute in *Church Courts, Sex and Marriage in England, 1570–1640* (Cambridge, 1987), p. 126. Ingram also describes the mediation between individual and family interests in the courts (pp. 200–5). Consent was nothing new to the marriage contract; there were in fact some efforts made during this period to increase family control over individual decisions; see Ingram, pp. 135–6. On the contrast between a status and a market society, see C. B. Macpherson,

The Political Theory of Possessive Individualism, Hobbes to Locke (London, 1962), pp. 46–70. Perkins described marriage as a 'seminary to church and commonwealth' in *Christian Oeconomy*, ch. 6. Also interesting on this subject is David Zaret, *The Heavenly Contract: Ideology and Organization in Prerevolutionary Puritanism* (Chicago, 1985), who comments that 'by modifying Calvinism with ideas about a heavenly contract, Puritan clerics provided greater scope for individual initiative in religion, but they channelled this initiative in ways that maintained their authority' (p. 129).

8

Or What You Will

BARBARA EVERETT

Shakespeare's last romantic comedy poses in a nicely acute form a
problem inherent in all the earlier comedies: why do we take them
seriously? Or how, rather, best to explain the ways in which it is
hard *not* to take them seriously – the sense that at their best they
achieve a lightness as far as possible from triviality. This is probably
one of the most interesting problems in Shakespeare studies at
present, and it is not one that (for instance) discussion of thematic
meanings in such works has ever quite completely enough
answered. The fineness and depth of *Twelfth Night* is precisely of a
kind that makes most varieties of intellectual analysis, and in particular the thematic, seem imposed upon it, a system essentially
alien. Critically speaking, therefore, the play offers 'the fascination
of what's difficult'. And this 'fascination' seems to become almost
explicit in the provocation of a title which – like the immediate pre-
decessor, 'As You Like It' – appears, whether or not ironically, to
espouse unseriousness: 'Twelfth Night, or What You Will'. In
trying to define the true 'seriousness' of the best and last of
Shakespeare's comedies, I shall use its title as a guide-line in a pro-
cedure which may, in the nature of things, involve the circuitous; a
comedy such as this does not render itself up at once, or to the
abrupt question. The phrase of the title, 'Twelfth Night, or What
You Will', will however be throughout both a point of departure
and an end in view.

The title of *Twelfth Night* makes it seem appropriate to begin
with the play's date. Most critics are agreed that it was written not
long before that day in early February, 1602, when an Inns of
Court lawyer, John Manningham, made a reference in his diary to a

performance of the comedy. If *Twelfth Night* was written late in 1601, this would place it between the first performance of *Hamlet* and *Othello* – and with *All's Well* and *Measure for Measure*, in whichever order, to follow immediately. *Measure for Measure* has (at III.i) a brief narrative of Mariana's sad past, her brother's shipwreck and her lover's betrayal, which momentarily evokes the romance world of *Twelfth Night*. But everything in the later play that is harsh, urban and realistic makes this flashback to romance seem suddenly decades out of date: there's a sense of decisive pastness and discrepancy, one nailed by the unromantic re-iteration of the loss of Mariana's dowry.

To recall that nostalgic moment in *Measure for Measure* is a way of saying that the date of *Twelfth Night* matters. The play is very late for a romantic comedy, and this lateness is materially intrinsic to its character. Perhaps the finest comedy that Shakespeare ever wrote, it at the same time lacks any quality of poetic and dramatic 'urgency': which has, we might say, moved out into the emerging major tragedies and the nearly contemporary 'problem' or 'dark' comedies. *Twelfth Night* has a positive lack of urgency, a lack perhaps even teasingly realised in its two secluded small almost *ancien régime* courts or households, and in the whole sea-coasted yet as it were land-locked and clock-stopping kingdom of Illyria. When in the third act of the play the head of one of these households, Olivia, makes a declaration of love to Viola, and is turned down, something rather odd happens: a clock starts somewhere to strike or tick audibly, 'The clocke upbraids me with the waste of time'; and at that point, as Olivia grows decisive and even desperate, a corner is turned in the action, and the play has started to be over. Until then, there is no Time in Illyria, at least as far as the courts of Orsino and Olivia are concerned. Illyria is a name and a place that from the first maintains its own mocking half-echo of Elysium, a place of death as well as of immortality:

> And what should I do in Illyria?
> My brother he is in Elizium.
> Perchance he is not drowned: what thinke you saylors?
> – It is perchance that you your selfe were saved.[1]

'Illyria', 'Elizium', 'drown'd', 'saved', 'perchance' – the words chime in a harmony touched by irony, and 'chance' is in fact alluded to four times in as many lines; the ideal and the random make a kind of music together. You could put it another way and say that the whole comedy is played out within an area circumscribed by the 'If' with which Orsino begins, and the 'When' with which Feste ends the play, the two words both being spoken or sung with music behind them, that medium loved by nineteenth-century French Symbolism because alternative to the real.

This lateness and lack of urgency in *Twelfth Night* has a technical effect often remarked on. The comedy has the pure authenticity of the truly original work of art, and yet it is also probably Shakespeare's most derivative play in terms of plot: it takes its plot-materials, in themselves ancient romance materials, from almost all of the dramatist's earlier comedies. From *The Comedy of Errors* comes the shipwreck that brings about the final recognition, and the confusion of identity dependent on identical twins; from *The Two Gentlemen of Verona* the sad faithful girl who has to page the man she loves and to woo the woman he in turn loves; from *The Merchant of Venice* the loving and deserted friend, even down to the very name Antonio; from *Much Ado About Nothing* a love-gulling like Malvolio's; from *As You Like It*, a girl who falls in love with another girl; from *The Merry Wives of Windsor*, Falstaff and Slender, the prototypes of Sir Toby and Sir Andrew. The Renaissance regarded derivation as a virtue, a proof of quality like the provenance of a work of art. But there is perhaps something excessive, something special and ironic, in the equipment of *Twelfth Night*. The belief that the play induces is vitally dependent on certain forms of unbelief. Minor and unimportant as the point is, it is possible to find oneself reflecting that *two* pairs of identical twins in *The Comedy of Errors* is one thing, because all the babies involved are boys; *one* pair of identical twins in *Twelfth Night* is turning into something quite other than coincidence, because Elizabethans were probably very capable of having noticed that boy-and-girl *identical* twins just don't and can't happen.

Such impossibility fuses with the literary scepticism that so many plots so old and well-used can't help but generate. *Twelfth Night* is 'late', that is, in a sense matched by metaphors like 'way out'. Its action, which is never tedious, careless or meaningless, is nonetheless everywhere distant, detached, as if deeply meditated and then become ironic. The play has a quality of removal, which doesn't however stop it from being genuinely moving (as well as intensely funny): indeed it is the terms of this removal which actually help to make this Shakespeare's most feeling and felt comedy. This can be perceived through a moment's reflection on the last scene of

Twelfth Night. We might have expected the action to move towards the happy uniting, the grand reunion as it were, of the two pairs of lovers, Orsino and Viola and Olivia and Sebastian. They might all the more seem to need this seal of action, so much are they in a way still strangers to one another – Olivia and Sebastian much in love while hardly having met, Orsino and Viola long familiar yet unknown in their true persons. But this finale is set aside in the oblique movement of the play. An important part of the last scene is taken up by two of the play's solitaries, the vengeful Malvolio and the desperately generous Antonio (not to mention the cool Feste). And when it does come, this intensely holding and touching discovery brings together, not lover and lover but brother and sister – a meeting that in its slight air of avoidance of expectation, its reticent but deeply purposive substitution, explains something of the fusion of joy and sadness which the play comes to communicate.

This curious and impressive lack of urgency in *Twelfth Night* is crystallised in the two tableaux I mentioned earlier. Everyone remembers how *Twelfth Night* begins and ends (and there probably aren't many plays of Shakespeare that you can say just that about): Orsino, sitting alone listening to music and thinking about a hopeless love, and Feste, singing on an empty stage about the way life passes and leaves us with the consequences of our actions. These two moments are so alike that it's hard not to feel that they were intended to 'rhyme', as it were, holding the rest of the play's line between them. It's surely their representative quality that makes them so memorable: they reflect a certain solitariness or detachment that rules each character in the comedy, but they reflect too what it is that has flowed into the work as recompense for this loneliness and lack of urgency. This is a quality of musicality. There is of course a good deal of actual music in *Twelfth Night*, though in fact less than in for instance *As You Like It*. If we speak of the musicality of the later play, we mean that as compared to the sparkling prose-governed pastoral comedy, the songs in *Twelfth Night* are more of a piece, they as it were count for more. They relate more to, even seem to perfect a *cantabile* quality not only in *Twelfth Night's* everywhere ravishing verse, but intrinsic to the romantic comedy as a whole. The power of the famous scene of night-revelry at II.iii, and its transposition into something more than mere prosaic clowning (Auden described this scene as being 'in inverted commas') has to do with the music at the centre that Malvolio can never quite silence: Sir Toby and Feste evade the Steward by floating into and out of song. Everyone who reads or sees the scene responds to a certain magical self-enclosure which the music gives to the occasion – it's to the point that one of the songs is a 'catch' or canon or round, that could have gone on for ever. This fine fantasy of self-perpetuation is underlined by the 'framing' given to the scene by Sir Toby: who opens it by proclaiming that 'not to be a bedde after midnight, is to be up betimes', and closes it satisfiedly with the conclusion, 'Tis too late to go to bedde now'. Any reader or audience recognises the illogic, just as we know to what degree the 'time-server' Malvolio is in the right. But it is true, too, that 'We did keep time, sir, in our Catches': that the scene is, like its music, both 'in tune', harmonising with our needs, and 'out of time', timeless.

The musicality of *Twelfth Night* goes much further than the local presence of music in it. It is a matter of internal harmonies, both technical or formal and substantial. Consider a small fact not (I think) noticed by editors or commentators: even the listed *Dramatis Personae* is a song. The play's names are so exquisitely harmonised to each other that some are near-anagrams: Viola, Olivia, Malvolio; others are finely attuned to these – Orsino, Valentine, Fabian, Feste. It is surely easy to sympathise with Orsino's belief that Olivia must marry him, because of the simple fact that her name begins with the same letter as his; even at the end of the play there is a faint sense of things gone amiss, of the two having been 'made for each other'. The exceptions to this literal patterning are of course Belch and Aguecheek, who however only disturb the harmony as an anti-masque does a masque. We also know them as Sir Toby and Sir Andrew, softer names.

This character of the *Dramatis Personae* prefigures the play itself. *Twelfth Night* is like *Antony and Cleopatra* or *The Tempest*, later, in its extraordinarily fine and sustained stylistic character. Compared to the other two later works in their high originality, what is heard here is an equable music that controls and sweetens everywhere:

> all this to season
> A brothers dead love, which she would keep fresh
> And lasting, in her sad remembrance.
>
> Why then methinkes 'tis time to smile agen:
> O worlde, how apt the poor are to be proud?

Of charity, what kinne are you to me?
What Countreyman? What name? What Parentage?

A foolish thing was but a toy,
   for the rain it raineth every day.

It is vital to listen to the style of a poetic drama, and *Twelfth Night* is peculiar in its dignity and felicity of utterance. And this fact is more notable in not being confined to verse or to the more aristocratic among the characters. Sir Andrew quoting the Fool can produce a mannerist grace that would surely surprise in any other comedy:

> Insooth thou wast in very gracious fooling last night, when thou spok'st of *Pigrogromitus*, of the *Vapians* passing the Equinoctial of *Queubus*; 'twas very good yfaith: I sent thee sixe pence for thy Lemon, hadst it? – I did impeticos thy gratillity: for *Malvolio*'s nose is no whip stocke. My lady has a white hand, and the Mermidons are no bottle-ale houses.

Feste is not, in fact, alone in leaving the play strewn with enigmas like the '*Vapians*' – Sir Toby's 'My Lady's a *Catayan*', and Malvolio's 'the Lady of the *Strachy*' remain unsolved to this day; but the Fool seems to me to provide the clue worth following. Commentators have had little to say about this present exchange other than to remark, perhaps, a derivation from Rabelais. What is more interesting, though, is the effect of Feste's having discarded the pervasive obscenity of Rabelais. Without that element of obfuscation or disguise, what is left oddly resembles nothing so much as an early, Edward Lear-ish nonsense poetry: a romantic language whose law is a sardonic and charming evasion of the restraints of social reality.

I have used the word 'evasion' of Feste's verbal style. It happens to be curiously relevant too to his behaviour in the play. The fact that he has a habit of not being where or when he is wanted is made plain on his first entrance and at important points later. This is a topic I want to return to. For the moment it's enough to note that there is something in the Fool's verbal fantasy that both links it with the linguistic grace of his betters, and in its quality of evasion or withdrawal suggests something striking about the behaviour patterns of the characters of the comedy. *Twelfth Night* is itself an elusive work, which – perhaps because of this quality of 'musicality' or aesthetic self-consistency, an expressive reticence, – seems to resist critics' attempts to explain or define or even describe the work as a whole, to say how or why it succeeds and why we value and admire it so. These attributes reappear as modes of behaviour in its characters. Every person in Illyria is, one might say, both an evader and something of a 'musician', in a sense that meshes with the play's musicality. Music is an art of passing time, as the scene of night-revelry makes clear. Like all the arts, but to a specialised degree, music defends itself against the destructive chaos of existence by imposing on to that chaos its own perfected if abstract and rigorously exclusive forms of control. It thus converts the Time which is the destructive medium of our lives into the more perpetual and beautiful medium, the time of music. All the persons of Illyria are 'Musicians' in this sense, a sense not too far from the well-known phrase coined by Mallarmé to describe the poet, 'Musician of silence'. Their lives strive to bring – and the words are this time Donald Davie's – all art 'into the terms of art'. Love is the most dignified and intense of these paradoxical pastimes, which 'keep time' as a way of forgetting the passing of time, but the same is true of all the other characteristic behaviours of the comedy: singing, observing, remembering, walking in the sun, drinking late into the night.

It is in this respect that Shakespeare has brought his 'high' characters or romantics, Orsino and Olivia, interestingly close to his low characters or clowns. All are subject to the magisterial folly of 'playing' at life, like actors or violinists, of trying to control and master what is in this case beyond their mastery: existence itself. Even Sir Toby and Sir Andrew are a kind of connoisseur ('What is thy excellence in a galliard, knight?') – not wholly ignorant in civilised pastimes and habits, even if they refuse to confine themselves 'within the modest limits of order'. The artistry these free spirits cultivate, a matter largely of singing and drinking, has its simple dark realistic proof in the fact that neither, at least, does anything *else* for a living – Sir Toby is living off Sir Andrew's money, which will, as Maria points out, 'have but a yeare in all these ducates'. Their licentiousness is as elegantly delimited as is the lovesickness of Malvolio, which comes down to a fantasy about 'my some rich jewell'.

For even Malvolio, the able, ambitious and vulgar middle-class Steward, is in his way as much of a 'musician' as his enemies the knights and the Fool. In the scene of night-revelry (II.iii) the three of them, until interrupted by the Steward, set about transforming the rules of time into their own harmonies – 'Tis too late to go to bedde now'. But in the play's most hilarious passage, the letter scene (II.v), the Steward himself surprises us by similarly unleashing his imagination and setting it to work on the stuff of his own mundane existence. And (an important difference between Shakespeare's treatment and the many cruel gulling scenes in the drama of the time) Malvolio is revealed as rapt in imagination well before he lights on the gulling letter, which merely serves to bring out into the daylight his own delicious preconceptions. He maddens Sir Toby with his lustful aspirations to Olivia; but the fact is that he is more ambitious than lecherous, and more day-dreamily, touchingly and absurdly vain than he is ambitious. His wild promise of revenge 'on the whole pack of you' at the end of the play is another vain fantasy, a darker and more disturbing one. Here there is an almost innocent love of grandeur in the beautifully orchestrated ballet of power Malvolio organises in his head:

> Calling my Officers about me, in my branch'd Velvet gowne ...
> Seaven of my people with an obedient start make out for him: I
> frowne the while, and perchance winde up my watch, or play with
> my some rich jewell.

There is a peculiar charm in the fact that the Steward is cast by Shakespeare as a kind of playwright, and also actor, director, and stage manager in one; but Malvolio's comedy of love stars only himself, and it never actually leaves his head. Yet even the rigid, solitary, almost neurotic Malvolio does 'play', even if only with a jewel, and that jewel imagined. His capacity to do so sets him alongside his betters, Orsino and Olivia (and Orsino similarly starts the play like a dramatist, ordering 'Play on'). These romantics are often treated as figures of satire, and Orsino spoken of as a man in love with love. He is that, certainly. But to phrase it so is to dissociate him from everything in the comedy that makes his love-dream haunting if finite – it is to take away its 'music', which makes it re-echo in our own consciousness:

> O, when mine eyes did see *Olivia* first,
> Me thought she purg'd the ayre of pestilence.

The Olivia whom we see is a direct, peremptory young woman, and not Orsino's huntress-goddess inscribed on a votive tablet hung up against the plague. But the Duke's intense, restless and exquisite idealism is not meaningless, either: it is a permanent human emotion pitched against the 'pestilence' or plague of life. There is the same quality of intense if self-enclosed imagination in the image with which Valentine describes Olivia as she in wish sees herself, in a willed, high perpetuation of grief for her loved dead brother. The description has a timeless and fine security, like a Renaissance medallion of a moon-goddess:

> like a Cloystresse she will vailed walke,
> And water once a day her Chamber round
> With eye offending brine.

These are high dreams, not low dreams, even if both are possessed of a certain aristocratic cruelty and sterility; and even if both fade under the exposure to daylight. The negation in both images is noble too; they force us to admit that love is not merely foolish in not requiring the possession of an object, or in not merely preferring any living person to any dead. There is in the end of the play a kind of sadness, as well as content, in Olivia's helplessness before the fact that something in her honestly prefers living people to dead, and especially to a rapidly fading memory of the dead; and there is a kind of shame in Orsino's acceptance of his knowledge that he has needed the ordinary listening actual company of his page more than any image of the Lady Olivia. That helplessness and that shame or indignity are factors of the comic reality. If Viola and Sebastian resolve the play's various *impasses*, they do so by their shipwrecked quality. They have no ideals and no illusions because they have nothing. They know nothing of the fine exclusiveness of the 'musical' world they enter; they know only helplessness and indignity ('it is perchance that you your selfe were saved'), and in these qualities they are experts, almost maestros. Aware of their essential human limitation, the twins manage in themselves and despite themselves to open a gate for the others out of 'dream' or 'play' into reality. But the happy ending of their doing so leaves some Illyrians still solitary, perhaps more deeply so; and even for those whom it makes happy it is also the end of the 'music'. Hence the deep and felt relevance, which everyone feels as sadness, of the theme of Feste's last song, which says 'The party's over now'.

This last romantic comedy of Shakespeare's catches up into itself a great complex of human reactions to all our lighter, but still serious, attempts to shape time, to control our lives. A useful image of that light attempt is the human giving of parties, the keeping of festivities. And the greatest 'party' of the Christian world of the Renaissance took place on Twelfth Night (January 6th), the last evening of the ten-day Christmas period in which Elizabethans exchanged gifts and made merry to celebrate the 'showing' or Epiphany of the new-born Christ-child to the gift-bringing Kings and shepherds. Something of this Elizabethan Saturnalian night, ruled over by Festus the Lord of Misrule, is reflected in Shakespeare's comedy: in its stress on ordinary human content and good-fellowship, 'Cakes and Ale' as Sir Toby puts it; in its commendation of generosity of spirit, as in Olivia's 'To be generous, guiltless and of free disposition'; and in its sense of the wintriness of ordinary human existence, the 'winde and the raine' that impel us to do what the Fool calls 'make a good voyage out of nothing'. But the comedy is perhaps a 'Twelfth Night' play most, one could say, in its 'musicianship', the impassive complex of irony and approbation, of sympathy and ridicule, with which it regards all Illyria's intense, beautiful and expensive time-evasions, systems of stopping the clock.

But many critical approaches of the last half-century have gone much farther than this, and have seen *Twelfth Night* as a work filled with revel and festive debauchery. Perhaps our anxiously scholarly would-be historicism needs to give way more often to a simpler sense of what the play is actually like. Samuel Pepys, seeing it only sixty years after it was written, when Twelfth Night ceremonies were better remembered or preserved, found it 'but a silly play, *and not relating at all to the name or day*' (my italics). It may be that we let the title distort our expectations of the comedy because we don't get the title right in the first place. The diary-entry I mentioned earlier, John Manningham's in 1602, runs 'At our feast we had a play called "Twelfth Night, or What you Will" '. Twenty years later, the play's only authentic original text, the First Folio, would use this same form not only in its list of contents but in its page-headings too: 'Twelfth Night, or What You Will'. We now regard this as the play's title, followed by its sub-title. But it needs to be said, that if this is a sub-title, then no other play by Shakespeare has one (*Henry VIII* was given in practice an alternative title, rather than a sub-title).

What both Manningham and the Folio seem to make clear is that Shakespeare's final title was *Twelfth Night, or What You Will*, in which the 'sub-title' is really no sub-title, but a generic, perhaps primary, and certainly important part of the title.[2] The title read as a whole doesn't name a festival, it coins a phrase, and a phrase which is in itself an entire social and psychological atmosphere. It could almost be said to define the play it introduces. For to concede that so fine a master-work is (of course) no more than a sport, a 'Christmas gambold' – 'Twelfth Night, or What You Will' – is an example of that specifically courtly style of throwaway lightness which the age itself called *sprezzatura*. No comedy whose aristocrats are as full of folly as Orsino and Olivia, and as subjected to humiliation and loss of dignity as they are, can be said to view the courtly ideal without irony. But irony may be transformative without being destructive. One of the elements which *Twelfth Night* does carry over from the Epiphany rituals is the reversal, while the Feast lasts, of all worldly dignities and hierarchies; yet, reversed or not, there is still a King of the Feast. In the same way we may speak of a stable centre for the comedy in its questioning and achievement of whatever we mean by human dignity. Its mood is thus a matter neither of the boisterously festive, which past criticism has so often implied, nor of that elegiac wistfulness which recent productions so often create, but of something that rises above and masters both: as we might say that the chief stylistic capacity of the play resembles the curious poise of its most famous image, 'Patience on a Monument, / Smiling at greefe'.

The play's courtly quality may be focused by a small bibliographical problem which the text happens to pose. In general the manuscripts of Shakespeare's comedies allude in speech-headings to such older men as are rulers, as 'Duke', and to such younger men as are lovers, as 'Count'. (It may tell us something of the nature of *Measure for Measure* that its chief male role is a *Duke*, and that we always think of him by this title, and not by his personal name.) *Twelfth Night* has perplexed editors by using both words for Orsino. But the fusing, in Orsino and more largely in Illyria, of love and government is surely material to the play. It is love that tests and proves the true dignity, just as it threatens and undermines the false.[3] To read the play in this way is of course to argue for a certain philosophical habit of mind within all its lightness. But the world of *Twelfth Night* is given precisely to such debates and discriminations. It was the Italian Courts of the Renaissance which produced the most intellectually distinguished 'definitions of love' of Shakespeare's time, the *Dialoghi d'amore*, with discussions which we see reflected, for instance, in the grave yet gracious debates of Castiglione's *The Courtier*. Orsino's is just such a court, or is so in wish at least. (It is to the point that his chief gentleman, with whom he enters the play, is called 'Curio', a name which means 'the Courtier'.)

But the Illyrian habit of mind goes beyond the Duke's restless questioning. Very early in the action the sea-captain describes Sebastian as surviving shipwreck

> like *Orion* on the Dolphines back,
> I saw him hold acquaintance with the waves,
> So long as I could see.

Arion was a great Greek mythical musician, saved from attempted murder at sea by the kindness of a passing dolphin appreciative of his art. This delightful image has rather little to do with the simple well-mannered well-born young Englishman who is Viola's twin, but it has all the same a good deal to do with the play. 'Hold acquaintance with the waves' means to carry on a poised social relationship with them, to be *'nice'* to them; and the connoisseur dolphin and the talked-to waves are somewhere near the heart of the comedy. In *Twelfth Night*, managing to survive comes from the courtly civilised habit of 'riding' experience, scrutinising it, thinking about it. The Fool looks back to 'When that I was and a little tiny boy' as a place a long way away, and it is true that Illyria is some-where far from certain primal or natural states, from infancy or great age. Instead, the play's action has a large admixture of what one might call sheer adult social consideration, of people's steady and reflective judgement of each other. It has a surprising amount of connoisseurs' praise, of compliments and civilities, some meant and some not; there is an incessant exchange of courtesies, a con-tinual sharp evaluation of others' skill – and indeed of one's own. Not wholly unlike the world of Restoration comedy, this clear social awareness can be satirised through fops: Sir Andrew thinks his leg 'does indifferent well in a lemon colour'd stocke', Malvolio reflects with excitement that 'she did commend my yellow stockings of late, she did praise my legge being crosse garter'd'.[4] But it is a fact too that Viola's eloquence is rarely passed over without notice, and even Viola herself remarks ambiguously that her praise of Olivia is 'excellently well pend'. Meeting Olivia face to face, Viola asks to see her more clearly, watches the curtain drawn and the picture unveiled, and gives her honest regretful impressed verdict:

> I see you what you are, you are too proud:
> But if you were the divell, you are faire.

Olivia listens to Viola performing rhetorically – and it is an example of that indirection in the comedy that I mentioned earlier, that this is an hypothetical wooing, a conditional performance, a question of what Viola could or would do as a suitor – and then she too gives her considered judgement, 'You might do much'. The Duke listens to Feste singing and expresses his appreciation, 'There's for thy paines'; it is characteristic of this play that Feste looks hard back at him, and says what he sees: 'Thy minde is a very Opall'. And this art-image of an exquisite changing jewel summarises a real element in the play, just as does Viola's funerary monument that seems from its height to come alive as it smiles at grief.

Feste's image of a jewel is characteristic of the play in its beauty. But it is suggestive in another way too. An Elizabethan love-sonnet, that intensely courtly mode, will use jewel imagery in a way that reminds us that the woman is beautiful *and* that the love involved is, as it were, expensive, estimable, an index of the lover's standing and power. *Twelfth Night* is sometimes interestingly reminiscent of this world of court-love, and of what Shakespeare makes of it in *his* sonnets. The court-lover there is the man who 'bore the canopy', who renders service to and even partly creates the royalty of his subject.[5] When Feste looks at the Duke and sees a changeable jewel, he says something about the way in which all the play's connoisseurship delicately tends towards real processes of judgement and estimation. I described earlier a kind of 'musicianship' in the characters, and the manner in which this is precisely delimited: as when Maria cuts off Sir Toby's bland summary of Sir Andrew's riches with 'I, but hee'l have but a yeare in all these ducates: He's a very foole, and a prodigall'. Such comments sustain through the play the ruthless morality of Feste's song, which 'shuts the gate' against follies and dreams. For the Fool is the play's chief 'shutter of gates' in person, the dangerous underminer of worldly estimates: 'As the old hermit of *Prage* that never saw pen and inke, very wittily said to a Neece of King *Gorbodacke*, that that is, is.'

Feste is in the play to make insecure all ordinary sense of hierarchy: to clear the field for re-definitions of dignity. He is himself clearly the lowest person in the comedy, the Duke's anti-type. But Bradley was right when he remarked 'We never laugh at Feste', even if wrong in his conclusion – that the Fool is a tragical personage. We don't laugh at the Fool because he makes sure we don't. He achieves through the play something akin to that lordliness which is nominally the Duke's: his own hard poise, an unbending presence of mind. Nor is this violated by the song Shakespeare added a verse to so that the Fool could end the entertainment with it:

> A great while ago the worlde began,
>   with hey, ho, the winde and the raine:
> But that's all one, our play is done,
>   and wee'l strive to please you every day.

This song has earned itself a legend of unbearable poignancy. But its power to touch a nerve does not involve its sadness but its un-sadness, its absence of mood, its self-containment. It's not what Feste says but what, with greater detachment, he leaves unsaid that speaks in his 'hey, ho' (a kind of yawn). The theme of the song is, after all, simply growing up, accepting the principle that nights before have mornings after; that life consists in passing time, and in *knowing it*.

This last song only climaxes everything in Feste's role that throughout the play exhibits the same achievement of mastery, even of standing. I've already mentioned the way his rhetoric replaces the Fool's usual bawdy punning and quibbling with a specialised and fastidious prose poetry. In addition to this Feste is always 'going free' in ways that have got themselves interpreted as tech-nical accidents of performance and publication, but which seem to me far too self-consistent for this. We never do find out the answer to Maria's 'Tell me where thou hast been' which greets his first entry, an effect underlined by his unexplained absence from the gulling of Malvolio. Feste is noticeably not at hand, but wandering around a house not his, when Orsino wants him to sing to him (II.iv); and when Feste does arrive, he exercises that alternative to absence, exclusion, by upstaging the Duke, first by silencing him, then after the song by ripostes of offended aesthetic dignity:

> There's for thy paines.
> No paines sir, I take pleasure in singing sir.
> Ile pay thy pleasure then.
> Truly sir, and pleasure will be paide one time, or another.

– a passage that irritates the Duke into giving the Fool an ironic and reversed-status order to leave, 'Give me now leave, to leave thee'. Again, at V.i Orsino's use of what was to an Elizabethan ear the politely placing or condescending 'my good fellow' starts Feste off on some subversive rejection of the Duke's good fellowship. In the same way, he has at II.i told Cesario, the gentleman whom his aristocratic mistress loves, 'In my conscience sir, I do not care for you', – not, as Bradley supposed, out of romantic jealousy, but out of antipathy for the rival status granted by love to its adored object.

Feste, in fact, earns himself a certain kind of inviolable standing in the play ('We never laugh at Feste') precisely because love never comes near him. His untouchable Fool's nature leaves him free to enjoy whatever it is that he is enjoying on the empty stage at the end. The absolute and conclusive quality of his solitude is perhaps opposed to that of Antonio, whom love has isolated, not wholly unlike the 'enslaved' poet of the Sonnets, because he pursues a service that asks for nothing whatever. The third of the solitaries, Malvolio, is presented with a fine difference again. Throughout the play Shakespeare handles the involvement of love and power in the Steward with extraordinary light pitilessness; even the brilliant farce of the letter scene has its own seriousness. Maria introduces Malvolio with a darkly glittering image, 'He has been yonder i' the sunne practising behaviour to his own shadow this halfe houre: observe him for the love of Mockerie ...' We do observe; and Malvolio in love is discovered to be only the more completely what we already knew him as, 'the best persuaded of himselfe ... it is his ground of faith that all who look on him love him'. The darkness of the cell in which Malvolio is confined is really the darkness of 'his own shadow'; he loses his dignity because he loves it so much. There is a fine consonancy in the fact that in the end he can in no way leave behind the illusorily crowded court world that means so much to him, but his 'love' has turned to nothing but the threat of revenge 'on the whole packe of you'.

Helena in *All's Well* alludes enigmatically to what she calls 'ambitious love'. When they are shipwrecked on the coast of Illyria, Viola and Sebastian come as strangers to this court-world of 'ambitious love'. Viola knows nothing of the power-games which the Fool, for instance, plays and wins. She could have chosen to serve Orsino as soon as the Captain described him as a 'noble Duke'. But she doesn't; she thinks first and instinctively of taking refuge with Olivia, 'A vertuous maid', and one abjuring the world in grief for her brother. Only the fact that Olivia will never admit her forces her into the Duke's household, at the price of the humiliation of appearing as an 'Eunuch'. In a sense the role has no other purpose than that of humiliation, for Viola never sings; but the humiliation goes on. Without status or even gender, without all that she herself implies by her dense phrase 'my estate', her part in the play is to transform being a heroine into being merely useful, merely enduring not dishonourably nor entirely hopelessly. The shadows in her relation with a largely unnoticing Orsino are matched in a reversed form, and expressed more articulately, by the shadow her twin carries with him in the pain of Antonio: an Antonio who in the end receives nothing but 'thankes, and thankes' as Sebastian allows himself delightedly to be carried off by Olivia. Viola bears, as Cesario, the reproach that Antonio can never voice to Sebastian himself. All this is, I think, implied by our first image of the twins as shipwrecked, an embodiment of a love acquainted with indignity, like Arion 'holding acquaintance with the waves'.

Yet it is the depth of this humiliated tenderness which, as it were, steadies Viola through the action, and gives her, by the end, what we can feel to be a greater human dignity than anyone. It emerges, despite her fineness of rhetoric, as a kind of reticence. The play's best-known love-speech involves a fictive sister who 'never told her love'. Viola embodies, on her own and her brother's behalf, a love without ambition, without 'estate' and as near as a comedy can decently come to being without fulfilment too. I have touched more than once on the play's obliquities and indirections. It is a striking fact that when (in V.i) brother and sister meet again at last even this coming together is oblique and conditional:

> Were you a woman, as the rest goes even,
> I should my teares let fall upon your cheeke,
> And say, thrice welcome drowned Viola.

Because we never do see Viola again in her woman's garments, there is a sense that as long as the play lasts she remains unembraced, the action never absolutely confirmed, its consummation only the image of tears of joy falling on to another face.

To make this point is not to demand some kind of open end for the comedy, and still less to try to categorise it as tragi-comedy. The meeting of the brother and sister is quickly succeeded by a bustle of conclusive action, and the pairs of lovers scarcely leave behind them any sense of desolation. And yet the moment of re-union has a peculiar and intense quality of its own, which holds within itself the expressive possibilities of *Twelfth Night* as I have hoped to describe them here. All that is suggestive in the play's simplicities allows the twins to embody in themselves, by the end of the action, a whole shimmer of alternatives and of relationships, all multiplied by the conventions of the Elizabethan stage (e.g., boys playing girls disguised as boys). Uncomplicated as the plot is, when the twins come together there also come together what one might list as Orsino's love for Olivia, Olivia's for Cesario, Olivia's for Sebastian, Olivia's for Viola, Viola's for Orsino, Orsino's for Cesario, Orsino's for Viola, Sebastian's for Viola, Sebastian's for Antonio, Antonio's for Sebastian, Antonio's for Cesario, Antonio's for Viola. The Court setting, as well as the conventions I have mentioned, permit all these relationships – adumbrated in shadowy or fragmentary form through the twins' difference and through their identical likeness to each other – to seem like formulations of that great question asked alike by the Court *Dialogues* I mentioned earlier, and by many lyrics of Shakespeare's time: the question, 'What is love?'. Shakespeare himself asks it in a Sonnet, in a form that also includes the sense of fragmentation precluding any simple answer:

> What is your substance, whereof are you made,
> That millions of strange shadows on you tend?

Though not 'millions', *Twelfth Night* possesses its own 'strange shadows' of love: at the most obvious, there is one in the hastiness of the matching of Olivia and Sebastian, and the belatedness of the mutual recognition of Orsino and Viola. If the coming together of the parted brother and sister has a peculiar intensity in the play, it is because it offers that simplicity, that sense of the absolute in love, elsewhere lacking. When Sebastian appears at V.i the whole scene, in a sense the whole play moves into a stillness like a roundabout slowing down. Everyone is joined in the comedy's supreme act of 'observation'. The language delicately but signally takes on what can only be called metaphysical dimensions, a style different from any other moment in the action, speaking of 'Deity', 'charity', 'spirits', and asking questions almost too profound and philosophical for a romantic comedy: 'Sebastian are you?' and 'Do I stand there?' and (most movingly) 'Of charity, what kinne are you to me?'. If we return to the musical image I used earlier, we can say that the moment of the discovery brings with it a sense of transposition, a sense of momentary change of key into an area, both more exalted and more inward than anything else in the comedy.

We could perhaps say that this moment becomes less 'discovery' than 'epiphany', an insight into absolutes. The term would of course be consonant with the whole Twelfth Night *topos* of the play. Yet it seems to me to be in its specificity slightly misleading. Rather, the moment affords us an awareness that even a work as light as this 'Twelfth Night, or What You Will' is not without affiliations with the great and complex learned body of Christian-classical materials that in the Renaissance sought to define human love in terms of the spiritual life. The most distinguished of the wide and mixed sources of this quest for definition was of course that work, in itself commemorating a love-feast, which in a half-comic form made Aristophanes evoke the soul's possession of 'some other longing which it cannot express, but can only surmise and obscurely hint at ... Love is simply the name for the desire and pursuit of the whole'.[6] I am not arguing that when Shakespeare set out (as he seems to have done) to write a comedy called 'What You Will' he had in mind Plato's great evocation of 'some other longing which [the soul] cannot express'. But there is enough in his handling of the twinship of brother and sister, in itself a romantic myth, an impossibility in nature, to make us see it as perhaps the play's image of the pursuit of a kind of wholeness beyond expression and perhaps even beyond possibility: 'thrice welcome, drowned Viola'. It is in honour of this achievement that we should sometimes do deference to the play's full title.

From *Essays in Criticism*, 35 (1985), 294–314.

NOTES

[Barbara Everett can be seen as issuing a challenge to some of the other writers represented in this volume, when she says 'Perhaps our anxiously scholarly would-be historicism needs to give way more often to a simpler sense of what the play is actually like.' She reads the play primarily as 'poetic drama', as the interplay between characters' emotional states, in the nature of a complex musical piece where motifs interrelate. Her intention in this is to regain a sense of the play as a text rather than as ideology. Ed.]

1. In this essay I quote throughout from the play's only authentic original text, the First Folio, in its New Variorum edition. This may occasionally produce an unfamiliar reading (as in 'my some rich jewel' for the now more current 'my ... some rich jewel') but this in itself can help a reader to see a somewhat over-familiar text more freshly and from new angles.

2. Marston's *What You Will*, though not published till 1607, was almost certainly written and first performed not long before the first performance of Shakespeare's comedy. This suggests that its choice of title

necessitated a change in Shakespeare's – though of course Marston himself can hardly have been unaffected by Shakespeare's titling of *As You Like It*. But this in turn suggests that Shakespeare's first choice of title must have been not 'Twelfth Night' but 'What You Will'. All in all, the best index to what the dramatist seems to have judged the mood and style of his new comedy is the final complete title given by both Manningham and the First Folio.

3. Shakespeare's intention is suggested by the fact that the impurity in Orsino's love, its taint of power that leads him wildly to threaten to murder Cesario, doesn't affect us as making him dangerous; what it does do is to impair his dignity.

4. In an article in *RES* (May 1986), 'Two Damned Cruces: *Othello* and *Twelfth Night*', I suggest that these two comments should be seen as connected with each other and that the Folio crux at I.iii. 127, 'dam'd colour'd stocke', should be emended to 'limond colour'd (i.e., lemon-coloured) stocke'.

5. Sonnet 125.

6. The grave and almost ritualistic language with which this meeting of brother and sister is handled may be explained by a context worth mentioning here, though it hardly affects directly our experience of the play. In Sonnet 20 Shakespeare invents (or mentions) what he calls 'the Master Mistris of my passion'; in *Twelfth Night* V.i. 341 Orsino calls Viola, still dressed as Cesario, 'Your Masters Mistris'. The invention of the 'Fair Young Man / Dark Lady' pair may, I believe, be connected with his conception of the boy–girl identical twins. Each pair may represent a different form of Shakespeare's awareness of a myth now perhaps most familiar to literary students through the cancelled stanzas which portray lovers as a species of 'Hermaphroditus' at the end of the 1590 Book III of the *Faerie Queene*. All three of these images – Master Mistris, twins, and lovers making love – could be said to have some common relationship with an ancient and widespread tradition that expressed spiritual wholeness in love through the symbol of the hermaphrodite or androgyne: an inheritance still pervasive in Shakespeare's time. Its best-known source probably was and still is Plato's account in the *Symposium* of the creation of primeval human creatures in the form of spheres holding in one body twinned males (who after Jove's punitive severing would become homosexual men), twinned females (homosexual women), and androgynes or hermaphrodites (who become heterosexual men and women). But this love-myth was also supported by *Genesis* and its succeeding mystical commentators: 'Male and female created he them' – an utterance tenable of ambiguity. The best brief account of the history and significance of the Hermaphrodite – which includes reference, as it happens, to the Renaissance *Dialoghi d'amore* – is Mircea Eliade's *The Two and the One* (1965), *passim* but see e.g. p. 107:

In Plato's metaphysical speculations, as in the theology of Alexandria, in the neo-Platonic and neo-Pythagorean theosophists as in the hermetic school who quote the authority of Hermes Trismegistus or Poimandres, and in a number of Christian Gnostics, *human perfection is imagined as an unbroken unity* ... 'God has both sexes'.

Edgar Wind's *Pagan Mysteries in the Renaissance* (1967) has some account of the myth in ch. XIII, 'Pan and Proteus'.

Further Reading

Generally speaking, not so much criticism in the last decade has been focused on an individual comedy like *Twelfth Night* as on each tragedy, or the late play *The Tempest*. Therefore, a lot of the reading suggested below is in the form of general books and essays on Shakespeare's comedies, each of which may have a section on *Twelfth Night*, or at least suggest ideas for interpreting the play from a 'contemporary critical' point of view. The listings are arranged by date in each section.

HISTORY, POLITICS AND CARNIVAL

The list begins with books by Barber, Frye and Bakhtin, because, although they belong to an earlier generation of critics, yet their approaches can be seen as pioneering, direct predecessors of 'carnivalesque' approaches.

C.-L. Barber, *Shakespeare's Festive Comedy: A Study of Dramatic Form and its Relation to Social Custom* (Princeton, NJ: Princeton University Press, 1959). Has a long and still illuminating chapter on *Twelfth Night*.

Northrop Frye, *A Natural Perspective: The Development of Shakespearian Comedy and Romance* (New York: Columbia University Press, 1965).

Mikhail Bakhtin, *Rabelais and his World*, trans. Helene Iswolsky (Cambridge, MA: MIT Press, 1968). This translation of a work published and banned in Russia became very influential in the West because it complements Barber and Frye.

Robert B. Heilman, *The Ways of the World: Comedy and Society* (Seattle: University of Washington Press, 1978). Marxist.

Terry Eagleton, *William Shakespeare* (Oxford: Blackwell, 1986).

Robin Headlam Wells, *Shakespeare, Politics and the State* (London: Macmillan, 1986).

Leah Marcus, *Puzzling Shakespeare* (Berkeley, Los Angeles and London: University of California Press, 1988).

Kiernan Ryan, *Shakespeare: Harvester New Readings* (Hemel Hempstead: Harvester Wheatsheaf, 1989).

Laurie E. Osborne, 'The Texts of Twelfth Night', *English Literary History*, 57 (1990), 39–61.

Graham Holderness, Nick Potter and John Turner, 'Twelfth Night: the Court in Transition', *Shakespeare Out of Court: Dramatizations of*

Court Society. (London: Macmillan, 1990), pp. 105–25. Draws on 'psychoanalysis and social anthropology', seeing the play as a critique of Elizabeth's court in a tense and watchful period.

François Laroque, *Shakespeare's Festive World* (Cambridge: Cambridge University Press, 1991; first published in French in 1988).

Howard Felperin, *The Uses of the Canon: Elizabethan Literature and Contemporary Theory* (Oxford: Clarendon Press, 1990).

Hugh Grady, *The Modernist Shakespeare: Critical Texts in a Material World* (Oxford: Clarendon Press, 1991).

FEMINISM, ANDROGYNY, SEX AND GENDER

Juliet Dusinberre, *Shakespeare and the Nature of Women* (London: Macmillan, 1975).

Michel Foucault, *The History of Sexuality*, vol. 1, trans. Robert Hurley (London: Allen Lane, 1979). Although not remotely concerned with Shakespeare, Foucault has had widespread influence over newer Shakespeare criticism.

Carolyn Ruth Swift Lenz, Gayle Greene and Carol Thomas Neely (eds), *The Woman's Part: Feminist Criticism of Shakespeare* (Urbana: University of Illinois Press, 1980).

Coppélia Kahn, *Man's Estate: Masculine Identity in Shakespeare* (Berkeley: University of California Press, 1981).

William W. E. Slights, 'Maid and Man in *Twelfth Night*', *Journal of English and Germanic Philology*, 80 (1981), 327–48. On androgyny.

Linda Bamber, *Comic Women, Tragic Men: A Study of Gender and Genre in Shakespeare* (Stanford: Stanford University Press, 1982).

Marilyn French, *Shakespeare's Division of Experience* (London: Cape, 1982).

A. Bray, *Homosexuality in Renaissance England* (2nd edn, London: Gay Men's Press, 1988).

Lisa Jardine, *Still Harping on Daughters* (Brighton: Harvester, 2nd edn 1989).

Marianne Novy, *Love's Argument: Gender Relations in Shakespeare* (Chapel Hill: University of North Carolina Press, 1984).

Linda Woodbridge, *Women and the English Renaissance: Literature and the Nature of Womankind. 1540–1620* (Urbana: University of Illinois Press, 1984).

Catherine Belsey, 'Disrupting Sexual Difference: Meaning and Gender in the Comedies', in *Alternative Shakespeares*, ed. John Drakakis (London: Methuen, 1985), pp. 166–90.

W. Thomas MacCary, *Friends and Lovers: The Phenomenology of Desire in Shakespearean Comedy* (New York: Columbia University Press, 1985). Homoerotic approach.

Peter Erickson, *Patriarchal Structures in Shakespeare's Drama* (Berkeley and London: University of California Press, 1985).

Marilyn Williamson, *The Patriarchy of Shakespeare's Comedies* (Detroit, MI: Wayne State University Press, 1986).

Jean Howard, 'Crossdressing, the Theatre and the Gender Struggle in early modern England', *Shakespeare Quarterly*, 39 (1988), 418–40.

Ann Thompson, ' "The Warrant of Womanhood": Shakespeare and Feminist Criticism', in *The Shakespeare Myth*, ed. Graham Holderness (Manchester: Manchester University Press, 1988), pp. 74–88.

S. Amussen, *An Ordered Society: Gender and Class in Early Modern England* (Oxford: Clarendon Press, 1988).

Claire MacEachern, 'Fathering Herself: A Source Study of Shakespeare's Feminism', *Shakespeare Quarterly*, 39 (1988), 269–90.

Philip C. Kolin, *Shakespeare and Feminist Criticism: An Annotated Bibliography and Commentary* (New York and London: Garland Press, 1991).

Lisa Jardine, 'Twins and Travesties: Gender Dependency and Sexual Availability in *Twelfth Night*', in *Erotic Politics: Desire on the Renaissance Stage*, ed. Susan Zimmerman (New York and London: Routledge, 1992), pp. 27–38.

STRUCTURALISM, DECONSTRUCTION AND TEXTUALITY

Keir Elam, *Shakespeare's Universe of Discourse: Language Games in the Comedies* (Cambridge: Cambridge University Press, 1984).

Malcolm Evans, 'Deconstructing Shakespeare's Comedies', in *Alternative Shakespeares*, ed. John Drakakis (London: Methuen, 1985), pp. 67–94.

Stephen Orgel, 'The Authentic Shakespeare', *Representations*, 21 (1988), 1–25.

G. Douglas Atkins and David M. Bergeron (eds), *Shakespeare and Deconstruction* (New York, Bern, Frankfurt and Paris: Peter Lang, 1988).

TWELFTH NIGHT IN PERFORMANCE

Lois Potter, *Twelfth Night* (Text and Performance Series, London: Macmillan, 1983).

Karen Greif, 'A Star is Born: Feste on the Modern Stage', *Shakespeare Quarterly*, 39 (1988), 61–78.

Mark Hamburger, 'A Spate of *Twelfth Nights*: Illyria Rediscovered?' in *Images of Shakespeare: Proceedings of the Third Congress of the International Shakespeare Association*, 1986, ed. Werner Habicht (London: Associated University Presses, 1988), pp. 236–44.

Notes on Contributors

Michael D. Bristol is Professor of English at McGill University, Montreal, Quebec, Canada. He is the author of *Carnival and Theater: Plebian Culture and the Structure of Authority in Renaissance England* (Methuen, 1986) and of *Shakespeare's America/America's Shakespeare* (Routledge, 1990).

Dympna Callaghan has written several essays on topics ranging from Renaissance literature to contemporary poetry. She is also author of *Woman and Gender in Renaissance Tragedy* (Harvester, 1994) and co-author, with Lorraine Helms and Jyotsna Singh of *The Weyward Sisters: Shakespeare and Feminist Politics*. She is currently writing a book entitled *Shakespeare without Women*.

Barbara Everett has held Fellowships in both Oxford and Cambridge and is now Senior Research Fellow at Somerville College, Oxford. Her publications include *Poets in Their Time: Essays in English Poetry from Donne to Larkin* (Faber, 1986; OUP, 1991) and *Young Hamlet: Essays on Shakespeare's Tragedies* (OUP, 1989, 1990).

Stephen J. Greenblatt is the Class of 1932 Professor of English at the University of California at Berkeley. He is the author of *Renaissance Self-fashioning: From More to Shakespeare* (1980), *Shakespearean Negotiations: The Circulation of Social Energy in Renaissance England* (1988) and *Learning to Curse: Essays in Early Modern Culture* (1990).

Geoffrey Hartman is Sterling Professor of English and Comparative Literature, Yale University and Advisor and Project Director of the Fortunoff Video Archive for Holocaust Testimonies. He is the author of *Minor Prophecies: The Literary Essay in the Culture Wars* (1991) and editor of *Holocaust Remembrance: The Shapes of Memory* (1994).

Elliot Krieger is the editor of *The Rhode Islander Magazine*, the Sunday magazine of the Providence (R.I.) *Journal-Bulletin*.

Cristina Malcolmson is Associate Professor of English at Bates College. Her published articles on gender and society include 'As Tame as the Ladies': Politics and Gender in *The Changeling*', and 'The Garden Enclosed/The

Woman Enclosed: Marvell and the Cavalier Poets'. She is currently completing a book on George Herbert and vocation.

Leonard Tennenhouse teaches in the Department of Comparative Literature, English, and Modern Culture and Media at Brown University. He is the author of *Power on Display: The Politics of Shakespeare's Genres* (London and New York, 1986) and, with Nancy Armstrong, *The Imaginary Puritan: Literature, Intellectual Labor, and the Origins of Personal Life* (Berkeley, 1992).

Index

219